THE **HUTCHINSON**

Dictionary *of*

BUSINESS
QUOTATIONS

THE HUTCHINSON

Dictionary *of*

BUSINESS
QUOTATIONS

Helicon

First published 1996

Copyright © Helicon Publishing 1996

Helicon Publishing Ltd
42 Hythe Bridge Street
Oxford OX1 2EP

Printed and bound in Great Britain by
The Bath Press Ltd, Avon, Bath

ISBN 1-85986-044-3

British Cataloguing in Publication Data

A catalogue record of this book is available from the British Library

Managing Editor
Hilary McGlynn

Compilers
Julia Cresswell
Anna Leinster

Project Editor
Clare Ramos

Screen Editor
Sue Donaldson

Index
Frances Coogan

Production
Tony Ballsdon

Typesetting
TechType

When putting together a collection of quotations it is tempting to concentrate on the witty ones, and to ignore the more serious material. However, while this may be more fun, it is not the most useful sort of collection to produce. We hope that we have provided a good balance between the light and serious; the neat expression of an obvious truth and the thought provoking; quotations for and against a wide range of views. We hope that the resulting collection will prove useful for an equally wide range of occasions, from the light after-dinner speech to the heavy report. The quotations have been grouped under themes which are presented in alphabetical order and which are listed at the front of the book. Obviously, themes will overlap, and it may be worth your while looking under a number of headings to find just the right quotation. In addition, there is an index of authors at the back of the book.

No dictionary of quotations appears without a lot of background support. We have special thanks to give to two people in particular. To Fred McDonald, who with her usual expertise and generosity, provided us with a number of excellent quotations; and above all to Professor Robin Stuart-Kotze, without whose expert advice on what to read and generous loan of books this book could never have been compiled.

Julia Cresswell
Anna Leinster

LIST OF THEMES

Accountability and Blame
Accountancy and Financial
  Management
Administration
Advertising and Product Promotion
Advice
AGMs
Agreement and Conflict
Ambition
Appraisal and Performance
  Evaluation
Assets
Bankers and Financiers
Bankrupts and Bankruptcy
Board and Boardroom
Bonuses and Gifts
Borrowing and Lending
Bosses
Brainstorming
Budgets
Bureaucrats and Bureaucracy
Business Is ...
Buying and Selling Goods
Capital
Capitalism
Careers
Cash Flow
Chairmen, Chairwomen, and CEOs
City, the
Committees
Communication
Commuters, Commuting, and Travel
Competence
Competition and Competitiveness
Competitors
Compromise
Computers and Computing
Conferences
Consultants and Experts
Consumers and Consumerism
Contracts
Costs
Credit and Creditors
Crime and Corruption
Criticism

Customers and Customer Relations
Deals
Debt and Debtors
Decisions and Decision-Making
Delegation
Design
Developing Countries
Diplomacy and Tact
Easy Money
Economists, Economics, and the
  Economy
Education and Training
Efficiency
Employers and Employees
Employment
Entrepreneurs and Enterprise
Equality and Discrimination
Ethics
Expedience
Exploitation
Failure
Forecasting and Planning
Fraud
Free Market Economy
Friends and Enemies
Future
Gambling and Lotteries
God and Mammon
'Going for It'
Government
Greed and Self-Interest
Green Consumerism
Growth and Expansion
Health
Hiring and Firing
Home and Family Life
Honesty
Ideas and the Creative Process
Image and Self-Image
Incentive and Motivation
Income
Industrial Relations
Industry and Manufacturing
Inflation
Information and Informing

Information Technology
Initiative and Independence
Innovation
Insurance
Interviews and Job Hunting
Inventors and Invention
Investors and Investment
Jargon versus Plain English
Justice and Injustice
Lawyers, Law, and Litigation
Leaders and Leadership
Leisure
Loyalty
Luck
Machinery
Management and Managers
Marketing and Market Research
Market Forces and Supply and
  Demand
Mavericks
Media Coverage
Meetings
Memorable Lines
Mistakes
Money
Monopoly
Nationalization versus Privatization
Negotiations
Non-Executive Directors
Office Life
Opportunity
Organizations
Organizing
Pay
People and People Management
Point of Sale
Politics and Politicians
Poverty
Power
Pressure and Stress
Prices and Value
Priorities
Problems
Productivity
Profit and Loss

Profit Sharing
Progress and Change
Promotion
Property
Prosperity
Public Office
Public Relations
Public Speaking
Publicity
Quality
Redundancy and Resignation
Reorganizing and Restructuring
Reputation
Research and Development
Retirement and Old Age
Risk and Risk Avoidance
Sales Executives
Saving and Economy
Secretaries and Personal Assistants
Self-Employment
Social Responsibilities of Business
Statistics
Stocks and Shares
Stockbrokers and Stockbroking
Stock Markets
Strikes
Success
Takeovers and Mergers
Taxation and Tax Avoidance
Technology
Telecommunications
Teleworking
Theft and Piracy
Theory versus Practice
Time
Top Executives
Trade
Unemployment
Vision
Wealth
Work
Worker Participation

Final Statement

ACCOUNTABILITY AND BLAME

Accountability breeds *response-ability*.
STEPHEN R COVEY
Founder of the Institute of Principle-
Centred Leadership
Principle-Centred Leadership

Good men prefer to be accountable.
MICHAEL EDWARDES
South African-born British industrialist
Quoted in Ray Wilde, *How to Manage*

Peak performers concentrate on solving problems rather than placing blame for them.
CHARLES GARFIELD
President of Performance Science Corp.
Peak Performers

Entrepreneurs are risk takers, willing to roll the dice with their money or reputations on the line in support of an idea or enterprise. They willingly assume responsibility for the success or failure of a venture and are answerable for all its facets. The buck not only stops at their desks, it starts there too.
VICTOR KIAM
CEO of Remington
Going for It!

It's not whether you win or lose, but how you place the blame.
JOHN PEERS
President of Logical Machine Corp.
1,001 Logical Laws

When you're right you take the bows, and when you're wrong you make the apologies.
BENJAMIN WARD
Police commissioner in New York City
New York Times 1988

ACCOUNTANCY AND FINANCIAL MANAGEMENT

It sounds extraordinary but it's a fact that balance sheets can make fascinating reading.
MARY ARCHER
British scientist and business executive
Independent 1989

What is high finance? It's knowing the difference between one and ten, multiplying, subtracting and adding. You just add noughts. It's no more than that.
JOHN BENTLEY
British director of Wordnet plc
Sunday Mirror 1973

Finance The art or science of managing revenues and resources for the best advantage of the manager.
AMBROSE BIERCE 1842–c. 1914
US writer
The Devil's Dictionary

I wake up every morning and thank God I'm not a chartered accountant any longer, but involved with property.
GODFREY BRADMAN
British property executive and chairman and
joint chief executive of Rosehaugh plc
Independent 1989

It is time that financial types developed a greater tolerance for imprecision, because that's the way the world is.
JOHN C BURTON
US writer
Time 1977

He was a CPA [certified public accountant] and looked it every inch. He even had ink on his fingers and there were four pencils in the pocket of his open vest.
RAYMOND CHANDLER 1888–1959
US novelist
The Lady in the Lake

You need to have enough immediate profits that you can finance the long-range growth without diluting the stock.

PAUL COOK
CEO of Raychem Corp.
Forbes 1987

Of course I'm doing something about my overdraft: I'm seeing my accountant.

BARRY FANTONI
British cartoonist, writer, and broadcaster
The Times 1985

The system of book-keeping by double entry is, perhaps, the most beautiful one in the wide domain of literature or science. Were it less common, it would be the admiration of the learned world.

EDWIN T FREEDLEY 1827–1904
British business writer
Practical Treatise on Business

The truth is that the drudgery of the numbers will make you free.

HAROLD GENEEN
Business consultant and chairman of ITT
Managing

The pen is mightier than the sword, but no match for the accountant.

JONATHAN GLANCEY
British journalist
Independent 1995

Whenever decisions are made strictly on the basis of bottom-line arithmetic, human beings get crunched along with the numbers.

THOMAS R HORTON
President of American Management Association
Management Review 1987

Accounting and control – that is *mainly* what is needed for the smooth working, for the proper functioning, of the *first phase* of communist society.

VLADIMIR ILLYCH LENIN 1870–1924
Russian communist leader
The State and Revolution

Few have heard of Fra Luca Parioli, the inventor of double-entry bookkeeping; but he has probably had more influence on human life than has Dante or Michelangelo.

HERBERT J MULLER
US economist and historian
The Uses of the Past

Most of the troubles accountants have in ... judging soundness of accounting practices are caused by an inevitable conflict in the need for figures which are both realistic and objectively measurable.

G EDWARD PHILLIPS
Professor at the University of California
Accounting Review 1963

A financier is a pawnbroker with imagination.

ARTHUR WING PINERO 1855–1934
English dramatist
The Second Mrs Tanqueray

Financial accounting helps the manager to 'keep score' for the firm. It watches the flow of resources and lets those who have an interest in them know where they stand. Managerial accounting calls attention to problems and the need for action. It also aids in planning and decision making. It is aimed more at *control* and less at *valuation* than financial accounting.

JOHN A REINECKE AND WILLIAM F SCHOELL
US academics
Introduction to Business

Creativity is great – but not in accounting.

CHARLES SCOTT
US CEO of Intermark
Inc. Magazine's Guide to Small Business Success

My constant insistence on seeing only the big numbers is the subject of interminable jokes at the company.

The finance people say they only arrive at the big numbers by adding up all the little ones. Therefore, they go on, a budget with only the big numbers actually requires more effort to understand than one with every little detail. This is an expensive fallacy, but one that is difficult to eradicate.

RICARDO SEMLER
Brazilian CEO of Semco
Maverick

Learning to read a balance sheet does not take a great deal more intelligence than learning to read racing form, and is more consistently rewarding.

TREVOR SYKES
Business writer
Two Centuries of Panic

Accountants can be smarter than anybody else or more ambitious or both, but essentially they are bean counters – their job is to serve the operation. They can't run the ship.

ROBERT TOWNSEND
CEO of Avis
Further Up the Organization

Men with accountancy training occupy positions in business from book-keeper to chairman. All of them will be referred to, often in a derogatory sense, as accountants.

R IAN TRICKER
Professor of finance and accounting
The Accountant in Management

Nowadays, you hear a lot about fancy accounting methods, like LIFO and FIFO, but back then we were using the ESP method, which really sped things along when it came time to close those books. It's a pretty basic method: if you can't make your books balance, you take however much they're off by and enter it under the heading ESP, which stands for Error Some Place.

SAM WALTON 1918–1992
Founder of Wal-Mart Stores
Sam Walton: Made in America

With creative accountancy, who needs cheating?

KATHARINE WHITEHORN
British journalist
Observer 1987

ADMINISTRATION

For at least the first ten years, I handled the presidency of ITT alone because I had a horror, based on past experience, of administrative assistants. With no authority of their own, they somehow presumed or were presumed to speak for the chief executive. I'd seen administrative assistants issue orders, subtly or not, without the knowledge of the men they were assisting. I preferred to have my communications come directly from me.

HAROLD GENEEN
Business consultant and chairman of ITT
Managing

The difference between management and administration (which is what the bureaucrats used to do exclusively) is the difference between choice and rigidity.

ROBERT HELLER
US business writer and editor of *Management Today*
The Supermanagers

What has always frustrated me about staff is that the people you want solving problems end up administering.

CHARLES KNIGHT
Chairman of Emerson Electric
Quoted in Robert M Tomasko, *Downsizing*

Bad administration, to be sure, can destroy good policy; but good administration can never save bad policy.

ADLAI STEVENSON 1900–1968
US politician
Speech, Los Angeles, 1952

Most people in big companies are administered, not led. They are treated as personnel, not as people.

ROBERT TOWNSEND
CEO of Avis
Further Up the Organization

ADVERTISING AND PRODUCT PROMOTION

The essence of good advertising is not to inspire hope, but to create greed.

CHARLES ADAMS
Advertising and real-estate executive
Common Sense in Advertising

Telling lies does not work in advertising.

TIM BELL
British publicity expert
Sunday Times 1985

Any fool can write a bad ad – but it takes a real genius to keep his hands off a good one.

LEO BURNETT
US advertising executive
Quoted in Milton M Mandell, *Advertising*

Advertising is the most fun you can have with your clothes on.

JERRY DELLA FEMINA
US advertising executive
From Those Wonderful Folks that Gave You Pearl Harbor

You can tell the ideals of a nation by its advertisements.

NORMAN DOUGLAS 1868–1952
Scottish novelist and essayist
South Wind

'Be comfortable with who you are', reads the headline on the *Hush Puppies* poster. Are they mad? If people were comfortable with who they were, they'd never buy any products except the ones they needed, and then where would the advertising industry be?

MARK EDWARDS
British journalist
Guardian 1995

I thought everlastingly damned was about as in trouble as you could possibly get without actually working in advertising.

TOM HOLT
British novelist
Faust Among Equals

It is far easier to write ten passably effective sonnets, good enough to take in the not too inquiring critic, than one effective advertisement that will take in a few thousand of the uncritical buying public.

ALDOUS HUXLEY 1894–1963
British novelist and writer
Quoted in Milton M Mandell, *Advertising*

Advertising may be described as the science of arresting human intelligence long enough to get money from it.

STEPHEN LEACOCK 1869–1944
Canadian political scientist,
historian, and humorist
Garden of Folly

Half the money I spend on advertising is wasted, and the trouble is I don't know which half.

LORD LEVERHULME 1851–1925
British industrialist and founder of Lever Bros.
Quoted in David Ogilvy,
Confessions of an Advertising Man

You can fool all the people all of the time if the advertising is right and the budget is big enough.

JOSEPH E LEVINE 1905–1987
US film producer
Joseph E Levine Presents

I've always had a passionate belief that advertising should be a force for good and that it should enrich the environment and not impoverish it. People aren't stupid and I don't worry about them buying things they don't want.

FRANK LOWE
British advertising executive
Interview, *Daily Express* 1987

Everyday someone's trying to sell me something/ Through coloured images flashing on my TV screen/ My mind is stripped there's no reaction/ I don't get what they're saying to me no more.

EDDIE MACDONALD AND MIKE PETERS/THE ALARM
Welsh rock musicians
From the song *Prison without Prison Bars*

Undoubtedly some advertisements lead to fantasies. Life would be pretty intolerable without fantasies.

LORD MCGREGOR
Scottish academic and chairman of the Advertising
Standards Authority
Observer 1986

Advertising is the greatest art form of the twentieth century.

MARSHAL MCLUHAN 1911–1980
Canadian communications theorist
Advertising Age 1976

When you have nothing to say, sing it.

DAVID OGILVY
Advertising guru and founder
of Ogilvy and Mather
Ogilvy on Advertising

You cannot bore people into buying your product.

DAVID OGILVY
Advertising guru and founder
of Ogilvy and Mather
Ogilvy on Advertising

Living in an age of advertisement, we are perpetually disillusioned.

J B PRIESTLY 1894–1984
British novelist and playwright
Attributed

Rules, though unavoidable, always have weaknesses. Particularly so in advertising, where originality is part of its primary force, and where violation of 'what others do' is often a way of success.

RAYMOND RUBICAM
US founder of Young & Rubicam Advertising
Quoted in Milton M Mandell, *Advertising*

Don't Tell My Mother I Work in an Advertising Agency – She Thinks I Play Piano in a Whorehouse.

JACQUES SÉGUÉLA
US advertising executive
Title of his memoirs

Two ads a day keep the sack away.

JEREMY SINCLAIR
Chief creative director at Saatchi & Saatchi
Sunday Times 1988

Corporate sponsors only deliver large cheques in return for even larger name-checks.

THOMAS SUTCLIFFE
British journalist
Independent 1995

Advertising reacts to and reflects society and cannot hope to change it.

RODERIC WHITE
British advertising executive
Advertising – What It Is and How To Do It

ADVICE

Don't over-react to the trouble makers.

WARREN G BENNIS
Business academic and president of the University
of Cincinnati
University of Maryland symposium, 1988

Advice is judged by results, not by intentions.

MARCUS TULLIUS CICERO 106–43 BC
Roman writer, lawyer, orator, and politician
Letters to Atticus

When in doubt, don't.

SAUL W GELLERMAN
US academic
Harvard Business Review 1986

Whatever you do, the most important thing is to keep your eye on it. You don't want to be ruined when you are off doing something else.

HAROLD GENEEN
Business consultant and chairman of ITT
Managing

Always be nice to bankers. Always be nice to pension fund managers. Always be nice to the media. In that order.

LORD HANSON
Business executive and chairman of Hanson plc
Financial Weekly 1990

The time to be toughest is when things are going best.

DONALD KEOGH
President of Coca-Cola Company
Working Woman 1988

Never tell people how to do things. Tell them *what* to do and they will surprise you with their ingenuity.

GEORGE PATTON 1885–1945
US general
War As I Knew It

Always assume your opponent to be smarter than you.

WALTHER RATHENAU 1867–1922
German CEO of AEG
Reflexionen

If you do things well, do them better. Be daring, be first, be different, be just.

ANITA RODDICK
British entrepreneur and
founder of The Body Shop
Observer Magazine 1989

If you want something said, ask a man. If you want something done, ask a woman.

MARGARET THATCHER
British prime minister
Favourite saying

I always pass on good advice. It is the only thing to do with it. It is never any use to oneself.

OSCAR WILDE 1856–1900
Irish poet, dramatist, and wit
An Ideal Husband

AGMs

The City's reluctance to take a stand on an issue like the British Gas pay row makes a mockery of corporate governance and shareholders' ability to influence annual general meetings. Institutions should be obliged to make public how they vote at such events. They should be obliged to provide customers with a record of how they vote on every kind of issue.

PATRICK DONOVAN
British financial journalist
Guardian 1995

It is surprising, in the welter of questions that one gets at [AGMs], how few actually relate to the performance of the company, or the decisions taken by the board in particular areas.

JOHN HARVEY-JONES
Business writer and chairman of ICI
Making It Happen

It is for the board to decide how it wishes to respond to any resolution which is submitted by shareholders to the company's annual general meeting. It is not for the Government to determine the stance which either the directors or the shareholders should adopt.

JOHN MAJOR
British prime minister
Written answer, House of Commons, 1995

There is a statutory requirement to have an annual meeting, and yet it is hard to find anyone who thinks it achieves much.

PAUL MYNERS
Chairman of Gartmore
Daily Telegraph 1995

AGREEMENT AND CONFLICT

I'm not one to waste energy and time having arguments.

RICHARD BRANSON
Entrepreneur and founder of Virgin Group
Inc. Magazine 1987

Agree, for the law is costly.

WILLIAM CAMDEN 1551–1623
British antiquary
Remains

The only way to get the best of an argument is to avoid it.

DALE CARNEGIE 1888–1955
US writer and teacher of public speaking
How to Win Friends and Influence People

You can get assent to almost any proposition as long as you are not going to do anything about it.

JOHN JAY CHAPMAN 1862–1933
US author
Practical Agitation

When your argument has little or no substance, abuse your opponent.

MARCUS TULLIUS CICERO 106–43 BC
Roman lawyer, writer, orator, and politician
Rhetorica

I cannot divine how it happens that the man who knows the least is the most argumentative.

GIOVANI DELLA CASA 1503–1556
Papal secretary of state
Galateo

I'm not a combative person. My long experience has taught me to resolve conflict by raising the issues before I or others burn their boats.

ALISTAIR GRANT
Chairman of Argyll Group
Observer 1987

The best way I know of to win an argument is to start by being in the right.

LORD HAILSHAM
British lord chancellor, lawyer,
and politician
New York Times 1960

Nobody ever forgets where he buried the hatchet.

**FRANK McKINNEY ('KIN')
HUBBARD** 1868–1930
US writer
Indianapolis News 1925

Anybuddy'll agree with you if you've been eatin' onions.

**FRANK McKINNEY ('KIN')
HUBBARD** 1868–1930
US writer
New Sayings by Abe Martin

Organizations ought to thrive on most personal and professional differences, because in the long run they account for the dynamics of organizational growth.

STEPHEN S KAAGAN
US management consultant
Personnel Journal 1978

The achievement of excellence can occur only if the organization promotes a culture of creative dissatisfaction.

LAWRENCE MILLER
US business consultant
American Spirit

The easiest, the most tempting, and the least creative response to conflict within an organization is to pretend that it does not exist.

LYLE E SCHALLER
US academic
The Change Agent

If you're the boss and your people fight you openly when they think you're wrong, that's healthy. If your people fight each other openly in your presence for what they believe in, that's healthy. But keep all conflict eyeball to eyeball.

ROBERT TOWNSEND
CEO of Avis
Further Up the Organization

When angry, count to four; when very angry, swear.

MARK TWAIN 1835–1910
US author
Pudd'nhead Wilson's Calendar

It is much easier to avoid disagreement than to remove discontent.

GEORGE WASHINGTON 1732–1799
1st president of the USA
Letter to John Sullivan, 1781

Managers in business and government in the United States appear to have insulated themselves from views that differ from their own. Harmony and amiability are so highly valued that many organizations operate with ineffectual policies because managers are reluctant to risk unpleasantness by speaking up.

DALE E ZAND
US academic
Information, Organization and Power

If two men on the same job agree all the time, then one is useless. If they disagree all the time, then both are useless.

DARRYL F ZANUCK 1902–1979
US film producer
Quoted in *Observer* 1949

AMBITION

Very few people are ambitious in the sense of having a specific image of what they want to achieve. Most people's sights are only toward the next run, the next increment of money.

JUDITH M BARDWICK
US academic
The Plateauing Trap

When we are blinded by ambition, we seek first to be understood and to get glory, position, power, and promotion rather than looking at time, talents, and possessions as a stewardship for which we must account.

STEPHEN R COVEY
Founder of the Institute of Principle-
Centred Leadership
Principle-Centred Leadership

I want to work with the top people, because only they have the courage and the confidence and the risk-seeking profile that you need.

LAUREL CUTLER
US vice-chairman of FCB/Leber Katz Partners
Inc. Magazine 1987

If you can dream it, you can do it.

WALT DISNEY 1901–1966
Film maker, animator, and pioneer
of family entertainment
Quoted in Warren Bennis and Burt Nanus,
Leaders: The Strategies for Taking Charge

Goals should be specific, realistic, and measurable.

WILLIAM G DYER
US academic
Strategies for Managing Change

For me coming second is the same as coming last.

LORD GRADE
British film and television magnate
You Magazine 1987

I've got a great ambition to die of exhaustion rather than boredom.

ANGUS GROSSART
Managing director of Noble Grossart Ltd
Sunday Telegraph Magazine 1984

Big results require big ambitions.

MICHAEL HAMMER AND JAMES CHAMPY
US international management
consultants and business authors
Reengineering the Corporation

Though ambition itself is a vice, yet it is often the parent of virtues.

**MARCUS FABIUS (QUINTILIANUS)
QUINTILIAN** C. AD 35–95
Roman writer and teacher of rhetoric
Institutio Oratoria

What ambitious people want is to get ahead, which means they would do their best even at jobs they loathed.

ROBERT J SCHOENBERG
US business author
The Art of Being a Boss

APPRAISAL AND PERFORMANCE EVALUATION

People need the protection of promotion and evaluation procedures that diminish the importance of internal politics.

JUDITH M BARDWICK
US academic
The Plateauing Trap

Evaluate what you want – because what gets measured, gets produced.

JAMES A BELASCO
US academic and management consultant
Teaching the Elephant to Dance

Make sure you have someone in your life from whom you can get reflective feedback.

WARREN G BENNIS
Academic and president of the
University of Cincinnati
University of Maryland Symposium, 1988

Achieving good performance is a journey, not a destination.

**KENNETH H BLANCHARD
AND ROBERT LORBER**
US business executives
Putting the One Minute Manager to Work

Understanding should precede judging.

LOUIS DEMBITZ BRANDEIS 1856–1941
US Supreme Court justice
Burns Bakery Co. v. Bryan 1923

When your work speaks for itself, get out of the way.

THOMAS 'WAYNE' BRAZELL
US Army materiel command
Training session, McLean, Virginia, 1988

Appraisals are where you get together with your team leader and agree what an outstanding member of the team you are, how much your contribution has been valued, what massive potential you have and, in recognition of all this, would you mind having you salary halved.

GUY BROWNING
British humorist
Guardian 1995

It is much more ennobling to let people judge themselves than to judge them ... In many cases people know in their hearts how things are going much better than the records show. Discernment is often far more accurate than either observation or measurement.

STEPHEN R COVEY
Founder of the Institute of Principle-
Centred Leadership
The Seven Habits of Highly Effective People

How you measure the performance of your managers directly affects the way they act.

JOHN DEARDEN
US academic
Harvard Business Review 1987

We judge others according to results; how else? – not knowing the process by which results are arrived at.

GEORGE ELIOT (MARY ANN EVANS) 1819–1880
English novelist
The Mill on the Floss

I think it is an immutable law in business that words are words, explanations are explanations, promises are promises – but only performance is reality.

HAROLD GENEEN
Business consultant and chairman of ITT
Managing

I'm still waiting for an employee to complain that he or she has received too much feedback from his supervisor.

GARY F JONAS
Chairman of University Research Corp.
Staff meeting, 1984

It is common ... to see supervisors trying to give all their employees high ratings so that they can buy employee cooperation and 'look good' as managers.

ROSABETH MOSS KANTOR
US academic
Personnel 1987

Keep it simple. The purpose of performance evaluation should be to draw a line between above and below average performers.

JOE KELLY
Canadian academic
How Managers Manage

Don't let the performance appraisal be a one-sided lecture. Give your employee a chance to talk.

MARGIE MARKHAM
US contributing editor of *Meeting News*
Meeting News

ASSETS

Most people ... find a disorientating mismatch between the long-term nature of their liabilities and the increasingly short-term nature of their assets.

HOWARD DAVIES
Deputy governor of the Bank of England
Evening Standard 1995

No one has a greater asset for his business than a man's pride in his work.

MARY PARKER FOLLETT 1868–1933
US author
Freedom and Co-ordination

The meek shall inherit the earth, but not the mineral rights.

J PAUL GETTY 1892–1976
US millionaire oil executive
Quoted in Robert Lenzer, *The Great Getty Crown*

Take my assets – but leave me my organization, and in five years I'll have it all back.

ALFRED SLOAN 1875–1966
CEO of General Motors
Quoted in Mary Kay Ash,
Mary Kay on People Management

Forget return on assets. What is most important is how a company is leveraging its scarcest resource, its management.

PAUL STRASSMANN
Vice-president of Xerox
Inc. Magazine 1988

BANKERS AND FINANCIERS

Every banker knows that if he has to *prove* that he is worthy of credit, however good may be his arguments, in fact his credit is gone.

WALTER BAGEHOT 1826–1877
English writer and economist
Lombard Street

Any careful person who is experienced in figures, and has real sound sense, may easily make himself a good banker.

WALTER BAGEHOT 1826–1877
English writer and economist
Lombard Street

What's breaking into a bank compared with founding a bank?

BERTOLT BRECHT 1898–1956
German dramatist and poet
Threepenny Opera

Because bankers measure their self-worth in money, and pay themselves a lot of it, they think they're fine fellows and don't need to explain themselves.

JAMES BUCHAN
British journalist
Independent on Sunday 1995

Central banks don't have divine wisdom. They try to do the best analysis they can and must be prepared to stand or fall by the quality of that analysis.

EDDIE GEORGE
Governor of the Bank of England
Guardian 1995

I hate banks. They do nothing positive for anybody except take care of themselves. They're first in with their fees and first out when there's trouble.

HARVEY GOLDSMITH
British rock-concert promoter
The Times 1989

Good bankers, like good tea, can only be appreciated when they are in hot water.

JAFFAR HUSSEIN
Governor of the Malaysian Central Bank
Financial Times 1989

A sound banker, alas! is not one who foresees danger and avoids it, but one who, when he is ruined, is ruined in a conventional and orthodox way along with his fellows, so that no one can really blame him.

JOHN MAYNARD KEYNES 1883–1946
English economist
Essays in Persuasion

If you owe your bank a hundred pound, you have a problem, but if you owe it a million it has.

JOHN MAYNARD KEYNES 1883–1946
English economist
Attributed

We persist in the cosy fiction that our bankers are steady, conservative types who'd never dabble in short-term, dodgy fiscal adventures. But they compete in a global banking market which is greatly enlarged and, therefore, increasingly stuffed with crooks and chancers.

PETER McKAY
British journalist
Evening Standard 1995

I doubt there is any occupation that is more consistently and unfairly demeaned, degraded, denounced and deplored than banking.

WILLIAM PROXMIRE
US senator
Fortune 1983

It seems to me that [derivatives trader] Mr Leeson pulled the trigger. But the bank gave him the ammunition, and when he wanted more ammunition they gave him as much as they could give him until they ran out, and then the bank was bust.

CHRISTOPHER SHARPLES
Financier and chairman of the Securities
and Futures Authority
On the collapse of Baring Brothers and the debate
on whether, and how, one employee could be
blamed for such a colossal banking disaster,
Panorama BBC television broadcast, 1995

BANKRUPTS AND BANKRUPTCY

Capitalism without bankruptcy is like Christianity without hell.

FRANK BORMAN
US astronaut and business executive
Observer 1986

Insolvency practitioners make their living out of other people's misery and I've always regarded myself as a parasite.

MICHAEL JORDAN
Senior partner in Cork Gully
Independent 1990

It has long been my deliberate judgement that all bankrupts, of whatsoever denomination, civil or religious, ought to be hanged.

CHARLES LAMB 1775–1834
English essayist
Letter to Bernard Barton, 1829

A cynic has observed that if you go bust for £700 you are probably a fool, if you go bust for £7,000 you are probably in the dock, and if you go bust for £7 million you are probably rescued by the Bank of England.

LORD MESTON
English lawyer
House of Lords, 1985

Bankruptcy is not for bankrupts. If you want to use chapter 11 to reorganize a business, you have to have a war chest. You've got to have some money available to you immediately.

HARVEY MILLER
US bankruptcy lawyer
On the Federal Bankruptcy Act's chapter 11,
formulated to offer companies a reprieve, or
eventual rescue, from liquidation, *Harper's* 1992

Insolvency is not a very thrilling or amusing subject.

LORD MISHCON
English solicitor
Speech, House of Lords, 1985

I had assumed that the financial elements like the banks and major bondholders would have a very strong desire to save the company. In fact, they often wished to be rid of the problem and wanted to move toward liquidation. Once they are secured they don't care.

RYAL R POPPA
CEO of Storage Technology
New York Times 1992

BOARD AND BOARDROOM
(*SEE ALSO* NON-EXECUTIVE DIRECTORS)

Get me inside any boardroom and I'll get any decision I want.

ALAN BOND
Australian entrepreneur
Daily Telegraph 1989

I don't see how you can run a company with a board of directors. I have only one experience of it and I hated it.

RICHARD BRANSON
Entrepreneur and founder of Virgin Group
The Times 1984

You don't want to get the same kind of advice from everyone on your board.

RUBEN CARDENAS
US lawyer and business executive
Hispanic Business 1987

Women do not win formula one races, because they simply are not strong enough to resist the G-forces. In the boardroom, it is different.

I believe that women are better able to marshal their thoughts than men and because they are less egotistical they make fewer assumptions.

NICOLA FOULSTON
Managing director of Brands Hatch
motor-racing track
Interview, *Independent* 1995

Is the company doing well? Fine and good. It is doing well because of the chief executive and his management team. You don't need a board of directors at all. It is a rubber stamp. But if the company is not doing well, or as well as it could, then what? What can the board of directors do about it? How do they know the company is not living up to its potential? All they can learn is what they are taught from that selfsame management team; all they can get is what they are given.

HAROLD GENEEN
Business consultant and chairman of ITT
Managing

The more the formalities of boards can be loosened up the better, and it is worth experimenting, and varying the layout until you find the one which works best for your particular team.

JOHN HARVEY-JONES
Business writer and chairman of ICI
Making It Happen

We have a peculiarity in Britain, inasmuch as the clear responsibility for the company rests with each member of the board in a collegiate sense. No one can remove that personal responsibility from you, and if you do not discharge it ... you should not have accepted the job in the first place. It is a sad commentary that in many cases and places, board members have failed to observe their responsibilities, and powerful chief executives have, to a large extent, hijacked their boards.

JOHN HARVEY-JONES
Business writer and chairman of ICI
Making It Happen

What goes on in the boardroom is a travesty. And the chairman doesn't want someone under him who is a threat, so he picks someone a little less capable. It's like an anti-Darwinian theory – the survival of the unfittest and it's getting worse.

CARL ICAHN
US corporate raider
Fortune 1985

We are going to see directors of public companies being forced to remember that they are acting as custodians of shareholders' money: that – whether they are executives or non-executives – when acting as a director they have a fiduciary duty to shareholders that is paramount.

HAMISH McRAE
Scottish journalist
Independent 1995

Lesson for stockholders and directors: If the chief executive doesn't retire gracefully after five or six years – throw the rascal out.

ROBERT TOWNSEND
CEO of Avis
Further Up the Organization

When an academic decries business for being so boring, you know he's never seen the thrills and spills of a boardroom.

KATHERINE WHITEHORN
British journalist
Observer 1987

BONUSES AND GIFTS

(*SEE ALSO* INCENTIVE AND MOTIVATION)

I sincerely believe that a forty-cent gift given with one hundred dollars worth of recognition is a thousand times more effective that a $100 gift in a dollar box given with forty cents' worth of recognition.

MARY KAY ASH
US entrepreneur and founder
of Mary Kay cosmetics
On motivating her staff, *Mary Kay
on People Management*

A wage hike is very hard to take away, but bonuses and profit-sharing can disappear very quickly in hard times ... More people are realizing that bonuses look like raises, but really aren't.

AL BAUMAN
Economist with the US Bureau of Labor Statistics
New York Times 1988

The idea of thanking staff should mean giving them something that they would never buy for themselves.

JAYNE CROOK
Director of·sales at Virgin Vouchers
Marketing Week 1995

A reward cannot be valued if it is not understood.

PHILLIP C GRANT
US academic
Personnel Journal 1988

Benefits please like flowers when they are fresh.

GEORGE HERBERT 1593–1633
English clergyman and writer
Jacula Prudentum

Most Americans say they want more money. Yet non-cash awards appear to be more effective motivators.

JERRY MCADAMS
Vice-president of Maritz Information Resources
Management 1987

Beyond salaries, plenty of companies offer special bonuses or achievement awards. The people who receive such awards generally have an excellent manager pulling for them.

PHILIP W METZGER
US computer analyst and management writer
Managing Programming People

There are no real free gifts in this world, only deferred payments.

WARREN TUTE
Writer
The Golden Greek

Do not trust the horse, Trojans. Whatever it is, I fear the Greeks, even when they are bringing gifts.

VIRGIL 70–19 BC
Roman poet
Aeneid

BORROWING AND LENDING

(*SEE ALSO* CREDIT AND CREDITORS;
DEBT AND DEBTORS)

In our modern economy it seems unlikely that the middle-class morality will be able to survive. I, for example, was brought up never to buy anything until I had the cash to pay for it. If everyone did the same, i.e. bought nothing on credit, our economy would go smash.

W H AUDEN 1907–1973
English-born US poet
A Certain World

The borrower is the servant to the lender.

BIBLE
Proverbs 22:7

Of all the icy blasts that blow on love, a request for money is the most chilling and havoc-wreaking.

GUSTAVE FLAUBERT 1821–1880
French novelist
Madame Bovary

Would you know what money is, go borrow some.

GEORGE HERBERT 1593–1633
English cleric and writer
Outlandish Proverbs

We at Chrysler borrow money the old-fashioned way. We pay it back.

LEE IACOCCA
CEO of Chrysler Corporation
Iacocca: An Autobiography

How can you have production unless you borrow the money to produce? I do not believe in the theory that you must first produce and then borrow the money. That is not what my grandfather did. He borrowed the money and then produced.

HAROLD MACMILLAN 1894–1986
British prime minister
Speech, House of Lords, 1985

Moneylenders have seldom been figures of popular acclaim.

HAMISH MCRAE
Scottish journalist
Independent on Sunday 1995

BOSSES
(SEE ALSO MANAGEMENT AND MANAGERS; POWER)

Most bosses know instinctively that their power depends more on employee's compliance than on threats or sanctions.

FERNANDO BARTOLME AND ANDRÉ LAURENT
French business academics
at INSEAD, Fontainebleau
Harvard Business Review 1986

The difference between a boss and a high street bank is that a bank sometimes gives you credit. Bosses give you things to do and then blame you for doing them.

GUY BROWNING
British humorist
Guardian 1995

By working faithfully eight hours a day you may eventually get to be a boss and work twelve hours a day.

ROBERT FROST 1874–1963
US poet
Quoted in Rowes, *The Book of Quotes*

Being the boss anywhere is lonely. Being a female boss in a world of mostly men is especially so.

ALISON GOMME
British prison governor
Radio Times 1995

I would be a billionaire if I was looking to be a selfish boss. That's not me.

JOHN GOTTI
US Mafia boss
New York Times 1991

If you think your boss is stupid, remember: you wouldn't have a job if he was any smarter.

ALBERT A GRANT
President of the American
Society of Civil Engineers
Speech, Washington DC, 1988

Bosses can be misinformed or mistaken: people aren't automatically right just because they're being paid twice or even ten times as much as you are.

ROS MILES
British publishing editor
Cosmopolitan 1995

That's what's wrong with bosses, I thought to myself. So many of them are better prepared to find error and to criticize than to add to effort. To be the boss is what counts to most bosses. They confuse authority with authoritarianism. They don't trust their subordinates.

RICARDO SEMLER
Brazilian CEO of Semco
Maverick

BRAINSTORMING
(SEE ALSO IDEAS AND THE CREATIVE PROCESS)

The ideas that come out of most brainstorming sessions are usually superficial, trivial, and not very original. They are rarely useful. The process, however, seems to make uncreative people feel that they are making innovative contributions and that others are listening to them.

A HARVEY BLOCK
CEO of Bokenon Systems Inc.
American Psychological Association annual
meeting, 1973

Clearly no group can as an entity create ideas. Only individuals can do this. A group of individuals may, however, stimulate one another in the creation of ideas.

ESTILL I GREEN
Vice-president of Bell Telephone Laboratories
Effective Administration of Research Programs

In his experience, anything really important never got written down, because by then people were too busy shouting.

TERRY PRATCHETT
British writer
Soul Music

In a typical freewheeling discussion in most companies, everybody throws out a certain number of thoughts and suggestions. A good boss will keep track of which idea came from which person, and then in his summary he'll compliment the various workers who made significant contributions.

DONALD SEIBERT
US business writer and CEO of J C Penney Co.
The Ethical Executive

BUDGETS

Budgets are for cutting, that's why you set them.

DR LAURENCE BUCKMAN
British GP
On his reasons for refusing to be a fundholding
GP, quoted in *Independent* 1995

The budget evolved from a management tool into an obstacle to management.

FRANK C CARLUCCI
US secretary of defence
Frank Carlucci on Management in Government

We didn't actually overspend our budget. The health Commission allocation simply fell short of our expenditure.

KEITH DAVIS
Chairman of Wollongong Hospital, Sydney
Sydney Morning Herald 1981

At any given moment, there is always a line representing what your boss will believe. If you step over it, you will not get your budget. Go as close to that line as you can.

GRACE MURRAY HOPPER
Retired US Navy rear admiral
Speech, Washington DC, 1987

Any jackass can draw up a balanced budget on paper.

LANE KIRKLAND
US president of AFL-CIO
US News & World Report 1980

Under budgetary pressure (arbitrary or not) it is truly remarkable how many options one discovers one can do without.

JAMES R SCHLESINGER
US secretary of defence
Memorandum to the Senate Committee on
Government Operations, 1968

Budgets should always be based on rethinking the company; most of the time, though, they're not much more than last year's numbers projected forward and are about as good as warmed-up coffee at two in the morning.

RICARDO SEMLER
Brazilian CEO of Semco
Maverick

The largest determining factor of the size and content of this year's budget is last year's budget.

AARON WILDAVSKY
US political scientist
The Politics of the Budgetary Process

BUREAUCRATS AND BUREAUCRACY

The perfect bureaucrat everywhere is the man who manages to make no decisions and escape all responsibility.

BROOKS ATKINSON 1894–1984
US drama critic and writer
Once Around the Sun

A memorandum is written not to inform the reader but to protect the writer.

DEAN ACHESON 1893–1971
US politician
Quoted in *Wall Street Journal* 1977

In the US we find the label requirements are crazy. It is almost as if we had to label a bookcase with the warning 'do not eat this bookcase – it can be harmful to your health'.

BJORN BAYLEY
President of IKEA, USA Inc.
International Management 1988

If the copying machines that came along later had been here during the war, I'm not sure the allies would have won. We'd all have drowned in paper.

ALAN DICKEY
World War II Pentagon architect
Quoted in Brinkley, *Washington Goes to War*

The inventor of the Xerox machine will, I am sure, find a special place reserved for him on one of the inner circles of Dante's Inferno.

NICHOLAS GOODISON
Business executive and chairman
of the London Stock Exchange
Quoted in Ray Wilde, *How to Manage*

Companies that earnestly set out to 'bust' bureaucracies are holding the wrong end of the stick. Bureaucracy is not the problem. On the contrary, bureaucracy has been the solution for the last two hundred years. If you dislike bureaucracy in your company, try getting by without it. Chaos will result.

MICHAEL HAMMER AND JAMES CHAMPY
US international management
consultants and business authors
Reengineering the Corporation

Endless meetings, sloppy communications and red tape steal the entrepreneur's time.

JAMES L HAYES
President of the American Management Association
Memos for Management: Leadership

There is never that feeling, which I have experienced a lot in business, of excitement, of brainstorming. They [bureaucrats] never get in that mood.

JOHN HOSKYNS
Chairman of Burton Group
Daily Telegraph 1982

I can't stand this proliferation of paperwork. It's useless to fight the forms. You've got to kill the people producing them.

VLADIMIR KABAIDZE
Russian director of Ivanovo Machine
Building Works
Fortune 1988

Sometimes I think the Civil Service suffers from a terrible disease. I call it N.I.H. meaning 'not invented here' – anything they don't think up they don't like.

FREDDIE LAKER
Entrepreneur and founder of Laker Airlines
Daily Express 1972

Bureaucracy, the rule of no one, has become the modern form of despotism.

MARY MCCARTHY 1912–1989
US novelist and critic
New Yorker 1958

I find it mind-boggling. We do not shoot paper at the enemy.

JOSEPH METCALF
US admiral
On the glut of paper and filing cabinets
to be found on modern frigates, quoted in
Newsweek 1987

Our customer's paperwork is profit. Our own paperwork is loss.

JOHN PEERS
President of Logical Machine Corp.
1,001 Logical Laws

Gradually, studies began to show that bureaucratic organizations could change faster than nonbureaucratic ones, and that morale could be higher where there was clear evidence of bureaucracy.

CHARLES PERROW
US industrial sociologist
Organizational Dynamics 1973

You won't reduce the paperwork in a lasting fashion until you remove the underlying cause for it – mistrust and adversarial relations.

TOM PETERS
US international management consultant
and bestselling business author
Thriving on Chaos

Bureaucracy is the layer, or layers, of management that lie between the person who has decision-making authority on a project and the highest level person who is working on it full time.

HERBERT REES
President of Eastman Technology Inc.
Inc. Magazine 1987

If you're going to sin, sin against God, not the bureaucracy. God will forgive you but the bureaucracy won't.

HYMAN RICKOVER 1900–1986
US admiral
On the deferment by a Senate committee of his
appointment to the directorship of the Selective
Service System, quoted in *New York Times* 1986

Within a complicated bureaucratic structure distortions inevitably creep into the process of acquiring and organizing evidence.

JAMES R SCHLESINGER
US secretary of defence
Memorandum to the Senate Committee
on Government Operations, 1968

We decided to stop the company for half a day and hold the First Biannual Semco File Inspection and Clean-Out ... Our instructions were simple: we told everyone to look inside every file and folder and purge every nonessential piece of paper. They were to ask themselves a question attributed to Alfred Sloan of General Motors: 'What is the worst thing that can happen if I throw this out?'.

RICARDO SEMLER
Brazilian CEO of Semco
Maverick

He was beginning to grow annoyed at the glib civil servants of Galactic Centre. They had an answer for everything; but the fact was, they simply didn't do their jobs very well, and they blamed their failures on cosmic conditions.

ROBERT SHECKLEY
US science-fiction writer
Dimension of Miracles

Most managers were trained to be the thing they most despise – bureaucrats.

ALVIN TOFFLER
US writer
Newsweek 1988

Britain has invented a new missile. It's called the civil servant – it doesn't work and it can't be fired.

WALTER WALKER
British general
Observer 1982

It isn't necessary to imagine the world ending in fire or ice – there are two other possibilities: one is paperwork, and the other is nostalgia.

FRANK ZAPPA 1940–1993
US rock musician, bandleader, and composer
Real Frank Zappa Book

BUSINESS IS ...

Business is more exciting that any game.

LORD BEAVERBROOK 1879–1964
Financier, newspaper proprietor, and politician
Attributed

Business is a fluid, ever-changing, living thing, sometimes building to great peaks, sometimes falling to crumbled lumps.

HAROLD GENEEN
Business consultant and chairman of ITT
Managing

The soul of business is a curious alchemy of needs, desires, greed, and gratifications mixed together with selflessness, sacrifices, and personal contributions far beyond material rewards.

HAROLD GENEEN
Business consultant and chairman of ITT
Managing

Big business is only small business with an extra nought on the end.

ROBERT HOLMES À COURT 1937–1990
Australian business executive
Sydney Morning Herald 1985

Business is Darwinism: only the fittest survive.

ROBERT HOLMES À COURT 1937–1990
Australian business executive
Observer Magazine 1986

Business is business, and must not be made a pleasure of.

ANTHONY TROLLOPE 1815–1882
English novelist
Last Chronicle of Barset

BUYING AND SELLING GOODS
(*SEE ALSO* SALES EXECUTIVES)

Every crowd has a silver lining.

PHINEAS T BARNUM 1810–1891
US showman
Favourite saying

Buying is a profound pleasure.

SIMONE DE BEAUVOIR 1908–1986
French author
The Second Sex

What good is the moon if you cannot buy it or sell it?

IVAN BOESKY
US financier
Reply to his wife after she remarked on the beauty of the moon, *The Times* 1986.

What is a man if he is not a thief who openly charges as much as he can for the goods he sells?

MAHATMA GANDHI 1869–1948
Indian nationalist leader
Non-Violence is Peace and War

The smell of profit is clean/ And sweet, whatever the source.

JUVENAL c. AD 60–140
Roman poet
Satires

Any one who had the trade of buying and selling is easily recognized: he has a vigilant eye and a tense face, he fears fraud or considers it, and he is on guard like a cat at dusk. It is a trade that tends to destroy the immortal soul; there have been courtier philosophers, lens-grinding philosophers, and even engineer and strategist philosophers; but no philosopher, as far as I know, was a wholesaler or shopkeeper.

> **PRIMO LEVI** 1919–1987
> Italian novelist
> *The Periodic Table*, English translation
> by Raymond Rosenthal

More money tends to buy more of the same.

> **LYLE E SCHALLER**
> US academic
> *The Change Agent*

Everyone lives by selling something, whatever be his right to it.

> **ROBERT LOUIS STEVENSON** 1850–1894
> Scottish novelist and poet
> 'Beggars' in *Across the Plains*

There are few faster ways of going broke than by buying goods and then passing them on to customers who cannot pay for them.

> **TREVOR SYKES**
> Business writer
> *Two Centuries of Panic*

CAPITAL

Capital as such is not evil; it is its wrong use that is evil. Capital in some form or other will always be needed.

> **MAHATMA GANDHI** 1869–1948
> Indian nationalist leader
> *Harijan* 1940

Capital is a result of labor, and is used by labor to assist it in further production. Labor is the active and initial force, and labor is therefore the employer of capital.

> **HENRY GEORGE** 1839–1897
> US economist
> *Progress and Poverty*

Raising venture capital is a full time job.

> **BETTY KADIS**
> Co-founder of Wakefield Software Systems, Inc.
> *Working Woman* 1988

Parsimony, and not industry, is the immediate cause of the increase of capital. Industry, indeed, provides the subject which parsimony accumulates. But whatever industry might acquire, if parsimony did not save and store up, the capital would never be the greater.

> **ADAM SMITH** 1723–1790
> Scottish economist and philosopher
> *The Wealth of Nations*

CAPITALISM

Making capitalism out of socialism is like making eggs out of an omelette.

> **VADIM BAKATIN**
> Candidate in first Russian presidential election
> Speech, 1991

History suggests that capitalism is a necessary condition for political freedom. Clearly it is not a sufficient condition.

> **MILTON FRIEDMAN**
> US economist
> *Capitalism and Freedom*

It [Lonrho] is the unpleasant and unacceptable face of capitalism.

> **EDWARD HEATH**
> British prime minister
> On Lonrho's business dealings,
> House of Commons, 1973

I think that Capitalism, wisely managed, can probably be made more efficient for attaining economic ends than any alternative system yet in sight, but that in itself it is in many ways extremely objectionable.

JOHN MAYNARD KEYNES 1883–1946
English economist
End of Laissez-Faire

99% of what we say is about values. I firmly believe that ethical capitalism is the best way of changing society for the better.

ANITA RODDICK
British entrepreneur and
founder of The Body Shop
Today 1990

Of course being called the acceptable face of capitalism would be equally insulting.

TINY ROWLAND
Entrepreneur and CEO of Lonrho
Response to Edward Heath's comment
on Lonrho, cited above, quoted in Jeffrey
Robinson,
The Risk Takers

CAREERS
(*SEE ALSO* EDUCATION AND TRAINING; THEORY VERSUS PRACTICE)

Use the dual career ladder to retain competent technical people and reflect your vision of technical excellence. Many high-tech firms use dual career ladders to encourage their technical employees to remain in their technical fields. It is not uncommon for scientists and engineers ... to earn as much as or more than managers.

JAMES A BELASCO
US academic and management consultant
Teaching the Elephant to Dance

Few people do business well who do nothing else.

LORD CHESTERFIELD 1694–1773
British politician and writer
Letter to his son, 1749

Whom the gods wish to destroy they first call promising.

CYRIL CONNOLLY 1903–1974
English critic and author
Enemies of Promise

Your business is to put me out of business.

DWIGHT ('IKE') EISENHOWER 1890–1969
34th president of the USA
Address to a graduating class at a university

For a career in the City one needs to be honourable and trustworthy, but for a career in industry one needs a more determined will to win.

JAMES GOLDSMITH
British financier
Quoted in Geoffrey Wansell, *Sir James Goldsmith*

There's no time for dreams when commerce calls.

PAUL WELLER/THE JAM
British rock musician
From the song *Burning Sky*

Think of the sequence. You create something. You grow it. You look for a competitive advantage. Then you really tie it down tight, making it as efficient as possible. Those are very different jobs.

ALAN ZAKON
US computer scientist and entrepreneur
Quoted in Craig R Hickman
and Michael A Silva, *Creating Excellence*

CASH FLOW

Concentrate on cash flows and cash-based return. That's the way to create value for shareholders and employees. The value of a business is the value of its future cash flow after it's discounted by its cost of capital.

JAMES A BELASCO
US academic and management consultant
Teaching the Elephant to Dance

Ah, take the Cash, and let the Credit go,/ Nor heed the rumble of a distant Drum!

EDWARD FITZGERALD 1809–1883
English poet
The Rubaiyat of Omar Khayyam

We all know how the size of sums of money appears to vary in a remarkable way according as they are being paid in or paid out.

JULIAN HUXLEY 1887–1975
British scientist
Essays of a Biologist

Let us all be happy, and live within our means, even if we have to borrow the money to do it with.

ARTEMUS WARD 1834–1867
US humorist and writer
Science and Natural History

CHAIRMEN, CHAIRWOMEN, AND CEOS
(SEE ALSO NON-EXECUTIVE DIRECTORS; TOP EXECUTIVES)

Managing directors are not paid to be busy, they are paid to think.

KENNETH CORK
Senior partner at Cork Gully
You Magazine 1983

The authority vested in the chief executive of a large company is so great, so complete, and the demands made upon his time are so consuming, that most chief executives slip into authoritarian roles without realizing that the process is going on. In the vast majority of large American companies, the chief executive lives in a world of his own.

HAROLD GENEEN
Business consultant and chairman of ITT
Managing

Most CEOs got their jobs because their predecessors and the directors liked them. They slapped the right backs and laughed at the right jokes. It's reverse Darwinism: Once a backslapper gets the top job, he sure as hell isn't going to have somebody better than him as his heir apparent. So management gets worse and worse.

CARL C ICAHN
CEO of TWA
Fortune 1988

In the industrial age, the CEO sat on the top of the hierarchy and didn't really have to listen to anybody ... In the information age, you have to listen to the ideas of people regardless of where they are in the organization.

JOHN SCULLY
CEO of Apple Computer Co.
Quoted during *Nation's Business Today*, television broadcast, 1987

I can't bear being called Chair. Whatever I am, I am not a piece of furniture.

BEATRICE SEEAR
British academic and personnel expert
Observer 1988

Among the CEOs I know, the most successful ones have a very positive outlook. Every CEO has to be a cheerleader. At times you feel that you can list a series of disaster scenarios for your company ... Still, you have to be a cheerleader at least part of the time.

RICHARD A ZIMMERMAN
CEO of Hershey Foods
Chief Executive

THE CITY
(SEE ALSO STOCKBROKERS AND STOCKBROKING; STOCK MARKETS)

The City attaches an exaggerated importance to the healing power of lunch.

CHRISTOPHER FIELDES
British financial journalist
International Management 1986

You've got to twittle on for the City.

GEOFFREY HOWE
British chancellor of the Exchequer
Explanation of why the Budget speech is
so long, *Daily Express* 1982

The basic rule of the City was that if you are incompetent you have to be honest, and if you're crooked you have to be clever. The reasoning is that, if you are honest, the chaps will rally round if you make a pig's breakfast out of your business dealings. Conversely, if you are crooked, no one will ask questions so long as you are making substantial profits.

JONATHAN LYNN AND ANTHONY JAY
British writers
From the *Yes, Minister* television series

Allowing the City to fund it's own regulatory body is like asking a potential burglar to pay for the police service.

LEIF MILLS
British general secretary of BIFU
Speech, TUC annual conference, 1987

I always thought the City was a game. I happened to be good at it and I made a great deal of money, but it was always a game.

JIM SLATER
Founder of Slater Walker Securities
Observer 1977

COMMITTEES
(SEE ALSO CONFERENCES; MEETINGS)

A committee is a cul-de-sac down which ideas are lured and then quietly strangled.

BARNETT COCKS 1907–1989
British scientist
New Scientist 1973

What is a committee? A group of the unwilling, picked from the unfit, to do the unnecessary.

RICHARD HARKNESS
US journalist
New York Herald Tribune 1960

No committee could ever come up with anything as revolutionary as a camel – anything as practical and as perfectly designed to perform effectively under such difficult conditions.

LAURENCE J PETER 1910–1990
Canadian writer, educationalist, and
self-proclaimed researcher of
remedies for incompetence
Peter's Quotations

The ideal committee is a committee of one.

LORD STOKES
Chairman of British Leyland
Interview, *Daily Express* 1969

A committee is something that keeps minutes but wastes hours.

Traditional saying

A committee should consist of three men, two of whom are absent.

HERBERT BEERBOHM TREE 1853–1917
British actor-manager
Quoted in H Pearson, *Beerbohm Tree*

COMMUNICATION

(*SEE ALSO* INFORMATION AND INFORMING;
TELECOMMUNICATIONS)

You people are telling me what you think I want to know. I want to know what is actually happening.

CREIGHTON ABRAMS
US commander of forces in Vietnam
To his subordinates, quoted in *Time* 1971

You can learn something from a ranting complainer, but you learn nothing from a stiff upper lip.

Anonymous comment, *Marketing* 1995

All through school we're taught to read, write, and speak – we're never taught to listen. But while listening may be the most undervalued of all the communication skills, good people managers are likely to listen more than they speak.

MARY KAY ASH
US entrepreneur and founder
of Mary Kay Cosmetics
Mary Kay on People Management

I've not got a first in philosophy without being able to muddy things pretty satisfactorily.

JOHN BANHAM
Director general of the
Confederation of British Industry
On his interview technique, *Guardian* 1986

Communication creates meaning or people. Or should. It's the only way any group, small or large, can become aligned behind the overarching goals of an organization.

WARREN BENNIS AND BURT NANUS
US business academic and president of
the University of Cincinnati; US business
academic and writer
Leaders: The Strategies for Taking Charge

This report, by its very length, defends itself against the risk of being read.

WINSTON CHURCHILL 1874–1965
British statesman and prime minister
Remark at a Cabinet meeting

Listen. Don't explain or justify.

WILLIAM G DYER
US academic
Strategies for Managing Change

Communication in Britain is often about what people don't say, rather than what they do. Uniquely in our country, a manager can interpret his subordinate's silence as assent, while they see it as their ultimate protest.

JOHN HARVEY-JONES
Business writer and chairman of ICI
Managing to Survive

Managers lost the art of talking to each other and exchanging ideas because they are fed too much information before they get a chance to meet.

JOHN LAWLESS
British journalist
Sunday Times

The danger lies in becoming a feedback fanatic ... constantly trying to get in even better touch through more focus groups, more surveys. Not only can that distract you from the real work at hand, but it may also cause you to create new offerings that are safe and bland.

JUSTIN MARTIN
US journalist
Fortune

If you want people to understand, you've got to explain.

JOE J MCKAY
US CEO of Blackfeet Indian Writing Co.
Success 1988

There is no quicker way for two executives to get out of touch with each other than to retire to the seclusion of their offices and write each other notes.

R ALEC MACKENZIE
US management consultant
The Time Trap

Communication is everyone's panacea for everything.

TOM PETERS
US international management consultant
and bestselling business author
Thriving on Chaos

The longer the message, the greater the chance of misinterpretation.

RICARDO SEMLER
Brazilian CEO of Semco
Maverick

If you really want someone to evaluate a project's chances, give them but a single page to do it – and make them write a headline that gets to the point, as in a newspaper. There's no mistaking the conclusion of a memo that begins: 'New Toaster Will Sell 20,000 Units for $2 Million Profit'.

RICARDO SEMLER
Brazilian CEO of Semco
Maverick

You don't hear things that are bad about your company unless you ask. It is easy to hear good tidings, but you have to scratch to get the bad news.

THOMAS J WATSON JR
US ambassador to the former
Soviet Union and CEO of IBM
Fortune 1987

COMMUTERS, COMMUTING, AND TRAVEL

As an airline boss I can travel first class and free on other airlines, but frankly, I don't think I have the courage to ring them up and ask.

RICHARD BRANSON
Entrepreneur and founder of Virgin Group
The Times 1984

If God had meant us to travel in the rush hour, He would have made us smaller.

Graffiti on the London Underground
Reported in *Financial Times* 1989

The use of travelling is to regulate imagination by reality, and instead of thinking how things may be, to see them as they are.

SAMUEL JOHNSON 'DR JOHNSON' 1709–1784
English man of letters and lexicographer
Johnsoniana

The front of the plane arrives at the same time as the rear.

VICTOR KIAM
CEO of Remington
On why he abolished first-class travel for
company executives, *United Magazine* 1984

The car has become the carapace, the protective and aggressive shell, of urban and suburban man.

MARSHALL McLUHAN 1911–1980
Canadian communications theorist
Understanding Media

There are some lines where it would be cheaper to give every one a Bentley and ask them to drive to work.

LORD MARSH
Chairman of British Rail
On the costs of running a railway,
Liverpool Daily Post 1971

A commuter is one who never knows/ how a show comes out because he has to leave early to catch a train to get him back to the country in time to catch a train to bring him back to the city.

OGDEN NASH 1902–1971
US poet
'The Banker's Special' in *Versus*

You have your own company, your own temperature control, your own music – and don't have to put up with dreadful human beings sitting alongside you.

STEVEN NORRIS
British minister responsible
for public transport in London
In defence of the use of cars by commuters
before the House of Commons Environment
Select Committee, 1995

Commuter – one who spends his life/ In riding too and from his wife;/ A man who shaves and takes a train/ And then rides back to shave again.

E B WHITE 1899–1985
US writer
The Commuter

COMPETENCE
(*SEE ALSO* EDUCATION AND TRAINING;
THEORY VERSUS PRACTICE)

God didn't have time to make a nobody: we all have the capacity for greatness.

MARY KAY ASH
US entrepreneur and founder
of Mary Kay Cosmetics
Mary Kay on People Management

No letters after your name are ever going to be a total guarantee of competence any more than they are a guarantee against fraud. Improving competence involves continuing

professional development ... That is the really crucial thing, not just passing an examination.

COLETTE BOWE
Chief executive of Personal Investment Authority
Interview, *Independent* 1995

It is not enough to have a good mind: the main thing is to use it well.

RENÉ DESCARTES 1596–1650
French philosopher and mathematician
Discourse on Method

The test of a first-rate intelligence is the ability to hold two opposed ideas in mind at the same time and still retain the ability to function.

F SCOTT FITZGERALD 1896–1940
US novelist and writer
The Crack-Up

There is more money in not being dumb than in being smart.

MICHAEL HAMMER AND JAMES CHAMPY
US international management consultants
and business authors
Reengineering the Corporation

Some men are born mediocre, some men achieve mediocrity, and some men have mediocrity thrust upon them. With Major Major it had been all three.

JOSEPH HELLER
US novelist
Catch-22

People differ not only in their ability to do but also in their 'will to do'.

**PAUL HERSEY AND
KENNETH H BLANCHARD**
US academics
Management of Organizational Behaviour

It is a fine thing to have ability, but the ability to discover ability in others is the true test.

ELBERT HUBBARD 1856–1915
US writer and printer
The Philosophy of Elbert Hubbard

It is a great ability to be able to conceal one's ability.

> FRANÇOIS LA ROCHEFOUCAULD 1613–1680
> French moralist and writer
> *Maxims*

Only a mediocre person is always at his best.

> LAURENCE J PETER 1910–1990
> Canadian writer, educationalist, and self-proclaimed
> 'researcher of remedies for incompetence'
> *The Peter Principle*

High achievers are magnets for work.

> LEAH ROSCH
> US associate editor of *Working Woman*
> *Working Woman* 1988

Mastery might suggest gaining dominance over people or things. But mastery can also mean a special level of proficiency ... People with a high level of personal mastery are able to consistently realize the results that matter most deeply to them – in effect, they approach their life as an artist would approach a work of art.

> PETER M SENGE
> Academic and director of the organizational
> learning programme at MIT
> *The Fifth Discipline: The Art and Practice of
> the Learning Organization*

Martyrdom is the only way in which a man can become famous without ability.

> GEORGE BERNARD SHAW 1856–1950
> Irish dramatist and critic
> *Essays in Fabian Socialism*

Ability is the art of getting credit for all the home runs someone else hits.

> CASEY STENGEL 1889–1975
> US baseball player and manager
> Quoted in Ira Berkow and Jim Kaplan,
> *The Gospel According to Casey*

Against stupidity the very gods themselves struggle in vain.

> JOHANN VON SCHILLER 1759–1805
> German poet and playwright
> *The Maid of Orleans*

Does he have seventeen years of experience or one year of experience seventeen times?

> PAUL R WIESENFELD
> US attorney
> Maryland Bar Association meeting, 1987

COMPETITION AND COMPETITIVENESS

World trade means competition from anywhere; advancing technology encourages cross-industry competition. Consequently, strategic planning must consider who our *future* competitors will be, not only who is here today.

> MARY ANN AND ERIC ALLISON
> US business executive; US financial writer
> *Managing Up, Managing Down*

Thou shalt not covet; but tradition/ Approves all forms of competition.

> ARTHUR HUGH CLOUGH 1819–1861
> English poet
> *The Latest Decalogue*

The ability to learn faster than your competitors may be the only sustainable competitive advantage.

> ARIE DE GEUS
> Business strategist and head of
> planning at Royal Dutch/Shell
> Quoted in Peter M Senge, *The Fifth Discipline: The
> Art and Practice of the Learning Organization*

Military competition is generally won by the biggest battalions. But business competition is not. Economies of scale are a minor source of competitive advantage, and competitive success goes to the smart and skilful, not the large. Ask Britain's former industrial giants.

> JOHN KAY
> British economics journalist
> *Daily Telegraph* 1995

I love the competitive environment.
Money becomes part of the scorecard.

DONALD P KELLY
US chairman of Beatrice Co.
Business Week 1988

Contrary to what you may think,
your company will be a lot more
productive if you refuse to tolerate
competition among your employees.

ALFIE KOHN
US management lecturer and author
No Contest: The Case Against Competition

The meek shall inherit the earth but
they'll never increase market share.

WILLIAM McGOWAN
Chairman of MCI Communications
Fortune 1982

[I've] always realized that if I'm
doing well at business I'm cutting
some other bastard's throat.

KERRY PACKER
Australian chairman of Consolidated
Press Holdings
Daily Mail 1988

The heart and soul of competing is
knowing how to appeal to your
customers.

DON PETERSON
Chairman of Ford Motor Co.
Speech, San Francisco, 1987

Cutting prices is usually insanity if
the competition can go as low as you
can.

MICHAEL PORTER
US academic
Newsweek 1988

I don't meet competition; I crush it.

CHARLES REVSON 1906–1975
Entrepreneur and founder of Revlon Inc.
Time 1958

Competition brings out the best in
products and the worst in people.

DAVID SARNOFF 1891–1971
Founder of RCA Corporation
R Barron and J Fisk, *Great Business Quotations*

We have found what we believe
to be the distilled essence of
competitiveness. It is the reservoir of
talent and creativity and energy that
can be found in each of our people.
That essence is liberated when we
make people believe that what they
think and do is important – and then
get out of their way while they do it.

JOHN WELCH
CEO of General Electric
Quoted in James A Belasco,
Teaching the Elephant to Dance

I have never heard of circumstances
in which competition did not mean
lower prices.

LORD YOUNG
British business executive and politician
Independent 1989

COMPETITORS

Frankly, I don't want to see a rapid
upturn. I want it to hold until
some of these idiotic competitors go
bust.

JOE BAMFORD
Chairman of J C Bamford Excavators Ltd
The Times 1971

If they were drowning to death, I'd
put a hose in their mouth.

RAY KROC 1902–1984
Founder of McDonald's
On his competitors, quoted in
International Management 1988

The whole point of a dog race is that
the runners chase the bunny but
never catch it. Microsoft is sitting in
the cart, riding the bunny – so there's
no more race.

SCOTT McNEALY
President and chief executive of Sun Microsystems
Quoted in *BusinessAge* 1995

Without competitors there would be no need for strategy.

KENICHI OHMAE
Japanese management consultant and
business author
The Mind of the Strategist

In business we cut each others throats, but now and then we sit around the same table and behave – for the sake of the ladies.

ARISTOTLE ONASSIS 1906–1975
Greek shipping tycoon
Commenting on his rivalry with Stavros Niarchos,
quoted in *Sunday Times* 1969

Treating a competitor's brand as if it didn't exist doesn't mean your customers will do the same.

MARGIE SMITH
US senior vice-president of Mark Ponton Ltd
Working Woman 1987

Gentlemen: You have undertaken to cheat me. I will not sue you, for the law takes too long. I will ruin you.

CORNELIUS VANDERBILT 1798–1877
US financier
Letter to competitors, 1854, quoted in Robert
M Sharp, *The Lore and Legends of Wall Street*

COMPROMISE

We know what happens to people who stay in the middle of the road. They get run down.

ANEURIN ('NYE') BEVAN 1897–1960
British politician
Observer 1953

A compromise is the art of dividing a cake in such a way that everyone believes that he has got the biggest piece.

LUDWIG ERHARD 1897–1977
West German politician
Quoted in *Observer* 1958

The 'morality of compromise' sounds contradictory. Compromise is usually a sign of weakness, or an admission of defeat. Strong men don't compromise, it is said, and principles should never be compromised. I shall argue that strong men, conversely, know when to compromise and that all principles can be compromised to serve a greater principle.

CHARLES HANDY
Business executive and writer, and
professor at the London Business School
The Empty Raincoat

Like all weak men he laid an exaggerated stress on not changing one's mind.

W SOMERSET MAUGHAM 1874–1965
English novelist
Of Human Bondage

COMPUTERS AND COMPUTING
(*SEE ALSO* INFORMATION TECHNOLOGY; TECHNOLOGY)

Control over computing belongs with users.

BRANDT ALLEN
US academic
Harvard Business Review 1987

To err is human, but to really foul things up you need a computer.

Computer-age adaptation of a traditional saying,
often pronounced using stronger language

Few companies that installed computers to reduce the employment of clerks have realized their expectations ... they now need more, and more expensive, clerks even though they call them 'operators' or 'programmers'.

PETER F DRUCKER
US management expert
Management in Turbulent Times

A computer won't clean up the errors in your manual of procedures.

SHEILA M EBY
US business writer
Inc. Magazine's Guide to Small Business Success

The workers and professionals of the world will soon be divided into two distinct groups. Those who will control computers and those who will be controlled by computers. It would be best for you to be in the former group.

LEWIS D EIGEN
Executive vice-president of
University Research Corp.
Lecture, Colombia University, 1961

A computer will not make a good manager of a bad manager. It makes a good manager better faster and a bad manager worse faster.

EDWARD M ESBER
US CEO of Ashton-Tate
Fortune 1987

I really don't care that I don't have what's current because whatever is at the moment, it will be infinitely better in a few months and even better months later.

WILLIAM FINK
Superintendent with US Park Service
On the latest computer technology,
Personal Computing 1987

Software reengineering often produces nothing more than sophisticated computerized systems that automate obsolete processes.

MICHAEL HAMMER AND JAMES CHAMPY
US international management
consultants and business authors
Reengineering the Corporation

It is said that if the automobile industry had developed as rapidly as the processing capacity of the computer we would now be able to buy a 400 mile-per-gallon Rolls-Royce for £1.

CHARLES HANDY
Business executive and writer, and
professor at the London Business School
The Age of Unreason

Man is still the most extraordinary computer of all.

JOHN F KENNEDY 1917–1963
35th president of the USA
Speech, 1963

Training is probably the most important aspect of buying a computer system.

BARRY KNOWLES
US owner of Valcom Computer Center
Inc. Magazine 1987

'Our computer's down.' This is another great lie. Unfortunately, it is true so often that you seldom can attack it head on.

CHARLES W KYD
US financial consultant and author
Inc. Magazine 1987

I am a firm believer that it is far easier to teach the creative business person something about computers than it is to teach the programmer something about business.

PETER LAWSON
CEO of Brenton Management Corp.
Quoted in McNitt, *The Art of Computer Management*

The real definition of a supercomputer is a machine that is just one generation behind the problems it is asked to solve.

NEIL LINCOLN
US computer architect
Time 1988

The technology of the computer allows us to have a distinct and individually tailored arrangement with each of thousands of employees.

JOHN NAISBITT
US chairman of Naisbitt Group
Megatrends

Computer technology has, quite simply, not delivered its long awaited productivity payback.

STEPHEN S ROACH
US economist
PC Week 1987

Computer advertising hit £200 million last year yet eight out of ten computer advertisements became wallpaper through relentlessly pushing technology itself over the benefits of the technology to the individual.

KINGSLEY REED
Advertising executive
Marketing Week 1995

Always remember what you originally wanted the system to accomplish. Having the latest, greatest system and a flashy data center to boot is not what data processing is supposed to be all about. It is supposed to help the bottom line, not hinder it.

RICHARD S RUBIN
Telecommunications manager of Citibank
Harvard Business Review 1986

[Computer professionals] ... leveraged their special knowledge into a sort of priesthood, inventing enchanted words and sacred hymns, throwing hardware and software at people more comfortable with 'Tupperware', and making most of us feel like dimwits.

RICARDO SEMLER
Brazilian CEO of Semco
Maverick

Most managers don't even understand what they don't know about [computer] security.

BOB SEMPLE
Computer employee of Price Waterhouse
On computer viruses, *Daily Telegraph* 1995

The hardware and the software are only a small part – certainly less than half – of the true costs of bringing PCs into the organization.

JIM SEYMOUR
US syndicated computer columnist
PC Week 1987

The largest computer in our section can landscape an entire planet; but it cannot fry an egg or carry a tune, and it knows less about ethics than a newborn wolf cub. Would you want something like *that* to run your life?

ROBERT SHECKLEY
US science-fiction novelist
Dimension of Miracles

There is a world market for about five computers.

THOMAS J WATSON 1874–1956
US founder and first president of IBM
Quoted in Cerf and Navasky, *The Experts Speak*

CONFERENCES
(*SEE ALSO* COMMITTEES; MEETINGS)

A conference is a gathering of important people who singly can do nothing, but together can decide that nothing can be done.

FRED ALLEN 1894–1956
US comedian
Letter, 1940

No grand idea was ever born in a conference, but a lot of foolish ideas have died there.

F SCOTT FITZGERALD 1896–1940
US writer
Quoted in Prochnow, *The Toastmaster's Treasure Chest*

The shape and size of a conference table will be crucial to the behaviour of the group that will sit around it.

C NORTHCOTE PARKINSON
British historian, writer, and formulator of Parkinson's law
Parkinson's Law and Other Studies in Administration

There is no better place in the world to find out the shortcomings of each other than a conference.

WILL ROGERS 1879–1935
US cowboy and humorist
Quoted in Richard M Ketchum,
Will Rogers, His Life and Times

Never dump a good idea on a conference table. It will belong to the conference.

JANE TRAHEY
US writer
New York Times 1977

CONSULTANTS AND EXPERTS

An expert is someone who knows some of the worst mistakes that can be made in his subject and how to avoid them.

WERNER CARL HEISENBERG 1901–1976
German physicist
Part and the Whole

The truly well-rounded consultant, and generally the most successful one, functions well in many professional capacities: Consultant, lecturer, writer, teacher, leader, and mentor. Consulting itself is only the beginning.

HERMAN HOLTZ
US government operations consultant
How to Succeed as an Independent Consultant

Consulting is a business as well as a profession, and you must never lose sight of that. If being businesslike ever costs you a client or a sale, it is almost certain that the client or sale would not have been worth having.

HERMAN HOLTZ
US government operations consultant
How to Succeed as an Independent Consultant

To be a consultant is the ideal work, the sort from which you derive prestige and money without dirtying your hands, or breaking your backbone, or running the risk of ending up roasted or poisoned: all you have to do is take off your smock, put on your tie, listen in attentive silence to the problem, and then you'll feel like the Delphic oracle. You must then weigh your reply very carefully and formulate it in convoluted, vague language so that the customer also considers you an oracle, worthy of his faith and the rates set by the Chemists' Society.

PRIMO LEVI 1919–1987
Italian novelist
The Periodic Table, English translation
by Raymond Rosenthal

We have not overthrown the divine right of kings to fall down for the divine right of experts.

HAROLD MACMILLAN 1894–1986
British prime minister
Speech, Strasbourg, 1950

We could have come up with some of the ideas they [the consultants] suggested, but we aren't very creative.

JOHN MADDEN
Chairman of First National
Bank of Lagrange, Illinois
Forbes 1987

A specialist is someone who does everything else worse.

RUGGIERO RICCI
US violinist
Daily Telegraph 1990

For young MBAs, being a consultant means big money. In middle age it means you're unemployed. At our age, it means you're retired.

JOHN SHAD
Chairman of Drexel Burnham
Speech at the 40th reunion of the Harvard
Business School's class of 1949

An expert is a man who has stopped thinking. Why should he think? He is an expert.

FRANK LLOYD WRIGHT 1869–1959
US architect
Quoted in *Daily Express* 1959

CONSUMERS AND CONSUMERISM

(*SEE ALSO* ADVERTISING AND PRODUCT PROMOTION; GREEN CONSUMERISM)

When articles rise the consumer is the first that suffers, and when they fall, he is the last that gains.

CHARLES CALEB COLTON *c.* 1780–1832
British cleric, sportsman, and wine merchant
Lacon

In the affluent society no useful distinction can be made between luxuries and necessaries.

J K GALBRAITH
US diplomat, economist, and writer
The Affluent Society

In a consumer society there are inevitably two kinds of slaves: the prisoners of addiction and the prisoners of envy.

IVAN ILLICH
US radical philosopher and activist
Tools for Conviviality

The consumer today is the victim of the manufacturer who launches on him a regiment of products for which he must make room in his soul.

MARY MCCARTHY 1912–1989
US novelist and critic
On the Contrary

Give us the luxuries of life, and we will dispense with its necessities.

JOHN LOTHROP MOTLEY 1814–1877
US historian and diplomat
Attributed

You in the West think of products as consumer *durables*, things which last. For you consumption is an act which you undertake in bursts, periodically. Japanese consumption is a continuous cycle of new products replacing old products, everything is in a process of change, nothing endures. We do not seek permanence.

MASATOSHI NAITO
Chief of design at Matsushita Electric
Financial Times 1991

The consumer isn't a moron: she is your wife. You insult her intelligence if you assume that a mere slogan and a few vapid adjectives will persuade her to buy anything.

DAVID OGILVY
Advertising guru and founder
of Ogilvy and Mather
Confessions of an Advertising Man

Nearly all consumer businesses are bent on getting people to buy things which they do not need. The record industry pulled off the extraordinary coup of getting people to buy something they didn't need which they already had.

GILES SMITH
British journalist
On the rapid switch from vinyl records
to compact discs, *Independent* 1995

Conspicuous consumption of valuable goods is a means of reputability to the gentleman of leisure.

THORSTEIN VEBLEN 1857–1929
US social critic
Theory of the Leisure Class

CONTRACTS

(*SEE ALSO* DEALS)

I work in a strange business, and trust is a word that's not even in the vocabulary.

KIM BASINGER
US actress
On film contracts, *Cosmopolitan* 1995

The old idea of a good contract is a transaction which is good for both parties to it.

> **LOUIS DEMBITZ BRANDEIS** 1856–1941
> US Supreme Court justice
> *Business – A Profession*

What usually comes first is the contract.

> **IRA GERSHWIN** 1869–1983
> US songwriter
> Riposte when asked 'Which comes first,
> the words or the music?', reported in
> Gershwin's obituary in *Guardian* 1983

His verbal contract is worth more than the paper it's written on.

> **SAMUEL GOLDWYN** 1882–1974
> Film producer and founder of Goldwyn
> Pictures Corporation (later Metro-Goldwyn-Mayer),
> famed for his off-beat sayings ('goldwynisms')
> Of Joseph M Schenk, quoted in Carol Easton,
> *Search for Goldwyn*

Corporation An ingenious device for obtaining individual profit without individual responsibility.

> **AMBROSE BIERCE** 1842–c. 1914
> US writer
> *The Devil's Dictionary*

The act of becoming a member is something more than a contract, it is entering into a complex and abiding relation.

> **OLIVER WENDELL HOLMES JR** 1841–1935
> US Supreme Court justice
> *Modern Woodman* v. *Mixer* 1924

A corporation is an artificial being, invisible, intangible, and existing only in contemplation of the law.

> **JOHN MARSHALL** 1755–1835
> US supreme justice of the Supreme Court
> *Trustees of Dartmouth College* v. *Woodward* 1819

Trying to control corporate power and abuse by American corporate law has proven about as effective as drinking coffee with a fork.

> **RALPH NADER**
> US lawyer and consumer campaigner
> *The Times* 1976

A criminal is a person with predatory instincts who has not sufficient capital to form a corporation.

> **HOWARD SCOTT**
> US economist
> *New Dictionary of Thoughts*

Corporations have neither bodies to be punished, nor souls to be condemned, they therefore do as they like.

> **LORD THURLOW** 1731–1806
> English lawyer
> Quoted in Poynder, *Literary Extracts*

COSTS

Watch the costs and the profits will take care of themselves.

> **ANDREW CARNEGIE** 1835–1919
> Industrialist and philanthropist
> Quoted in *Wall Street Journal* centennial edition 1989

Cutting costs without improvements in quality is futile.

> **W EDWARDS DEMING**
> US management consultant
> *Forbes* 1988

Because its purpose is to create a customer, the business enterprise has two – and only two – basic functions: marketing and innovation. Marketing and innovation produce results; all the rest are 'costs'.

> **PETER F DRUCKER** 1909
> US management expert
> *People and Performance*

Everyone is always in favour of general economy and particular expenditure.

> **ANTHONY EDEN** 1897–1977
> British prime minister
> *Observer* 1956

The three most important things ... are costs, costs, costs. And costs can

be summed up in one word:
productivity.

> ANN KNIGHT
> US financial analyst
> *New York Times* 1987

Expenditure rises to meet income ...
Individual expenditure not only rises
to meet income but tends to surpass
it ... what is true of individuals is
also true of governments.

> C NORTHCOTE PARKINSON
> British historian, writer, and formulator
> of Parkinson's law
> *The Law and the Profits*

CREDIT AND CREDITORS
(*SEE ALSO* BORROWING AND LENDING; DEBT AND DEBTORS)

Creditors have no real affection for
their debtors, but only a desire that
they may be preserved that they may
repay.

> ARISTOTLE 384–322 BC
> Greek philosopher
> *Nicomachean Ethics*

Not since Lincoln had there been
such an artful manipulator of the
good, the bad and the bewildered
in between. I believe he [Franklin
D Roosevelt] saved the capitalist
system by deliberately forgetting to
balance the books, by transferring
the gorgeous resources of credit
from the bankers to the
government.

> ALISTAIR COOKE
> Writer and broadcaster
> Of Franklin D Roosevelt and
> the New Deal, *America*

Creditors have better memories than
debtors.

> JAMES HOWELL c. 1594–1666
> Welsh diplomat and writer
> *Proverbs*

Using [charge] cards on a daily basis
has become cash management for
many people.

> GEORGE RATAJCZAK
> US academic
> *Evening Standard* 1995

Money is used to pay bills and credit
is used to delay paying them.

> ALAN WALTERS
> British economist
> Quoted in *Observer* 1989

CRIME AND CORRUPTION
(*SEE ALSO* FRAUD; HONESTY; THEFT AND PIRACY)

Financial crime is not defined from
ethical considerations: it is just
conduct that costs money ... Similarly,
incompetence is action or inaction
that loses money. All judgements are
by hindsight.

> JAMES BUCHAN
> British writer
> *Independent on Sunday* 1995

Never underestimate the effectiveness
of a straight cash bribe.

> CLAUD COCKBURN 1904–1981
> Irish writer
> *In Time of Trouble*

The louder he talked of his honour,
the faster we counted our spoons.

> RALPH WALDO EMERSON 1803–1882
> US philosopher and poet
> 'Worship' in *Conduct of Life*

Corruption, the most infallible
symptom of constitutional liberty.

> EDWARD GIBBON 1737–1794
> English historian
> *The History of the Decline and Fall
> of the Roman Empire*

Financial misbehaviour, in particular,
matters to us all, because it strikes at
the very heart of that confidence

which people must have in ministers and the motive behind their decision.

LORD NOLAN
British law lord
Report from the Nolan Committee
on Standards in Public Life, 1995

He's a businessman ... I'll make him an offer he can't refuse.

MARIO PUZO
US novelist
The Godfather

Crime is a logical extension of the sort of behaviour that is often considered perfectly respectable in legitimate business.

ROBERT RICE
US criminologist
The Business of Crime

Organized crime inevitably gravitates to cash.

DANIEL SELIGMAN
US business reporter
Fortune 1987

The faults of the burglar are the qualities of the financier.

GEORGE BERNARD SHAW 1856–1950
Irish dramatist and critic
Major Barbara

They [the Mafia] compete with other businesses, but if they feel they are losing out they will revert to breaking legs. True American corporate competition does not include breaking legs.

THOMAS L SHEER
FBI agent
On the Mafia, *Fortune* 1987

A crowded police court docket is the surest of all signs that trade is brisk and money plenty.

MARK TWAIN 1835–1910
US writer
Roughing It

CRITICISM

Never giving criticism *without* praise is a strict rule for me. No matter what you are criticizing, you must find something good to say – both *before* and *after*. This is what's known as the 'sandwich technique'.

MARY KAY ASH
US entrepreneur and founder
of Mary Kay Cosmetics
Mary Kay on People Management

Criticism is a frequent by-product of significant actions. Receptivity to criticism is as necessary as it is loathsome. It tests the foundations of positive self-regard as does nothing else. And the more valid the criticism, the more difficult is it to receive.

WARREN BENNIS AND BURT NANUS
Business academic and president of the
University of Cincinnati; business
academic and writer
Leaders: The Strategies for Taking Charge

It is much easier to be critical than to be correct.

BENJAMIN DISRAELI 1805–1881
British prime minister and novelist
Speech, Houses of Parliament, 1860

The test of a true businessman is that he always wants to do better, but it's all too easy to believe your own propaganda and let your organization become full of echo chambers, people looking to the boss for a nod and a wink. It takes guts and self-confidence to lay yourself open to criticism.

JOHN HARVEY-JONES
Business writer and chairman of ICI
Interview, *Radio Times* 1995

Management that is destructively critical when mistakes are made kills initiative and it's essential that we have many people with initiative if we're to continue to grow.

LEWIS LEHR
US president of 3M
Quoted in Douglas McGregor,
The Human Side of Enterprise

Compliment before you correct. Try to find something on which to compliment a man before you correct him. He will be more receptive of your correction.

JAMES C MILLER
Personnel development manager
at Standard Brands Inc.
Leadership in the Office

Two and two continue to make four, in spite of the whine of the amateur for three, or the cry of the critic for five.

JAMES MCNEILL WHISTLER 1834–1903
US artist
The Gentle Art of Making Enemies

All cruel people describe themselves as paragons of frankness.

TENESSEE WILLIAMS 1914–1983
US writer
The Milk Train Doesn't Stop Here Anymore

CUSTOMERS AND CUSTOMER RELATIONS

We don't want to push our ideas on to customers, we simply want to make what *they* want.

LAURA ASHLEY 1925–1985
Welsh fabric and clothes designer
Sunday Times 1985

Make a customer, not a sale.

KATHERINE BARCHETTI
US clothing retailer
Independent on Sunday 1995

The 1990s customer expects service to be characterized by fast and efficient computer-based systems.

STEVE CUTHBERT
British director general of the
Chartered Institute of Marketing
Nottingham Evening Post 1995

If you love your customer to death, you can't go wrong.

GRAHAM DAY
Chairman and CEO of The Rover Group plc
and director of Cadbury Schweppes plc
Daily Express 1987

The absolute fundamental aim is to make money out of satisfying customers.

JOHN EGAN
Chairman of Jaguar plc
Quoted in Berry Ritchie and Walter
Goldsmith, *The New Elite*

Industry must manage to keep wages high and prices low ... One's own employees should be one's best customers.

HENRY FORD 1863–1947
Pioneering industrialist and car manufacturer
Quoted in Clifton Fadiman,
The American Treasury 1455–1955

There's a saying in the United States that the customer is king. But in Japan the customer is God.

TAK KIMOTO
Sumitronics Inc.
International Management 1986

One cannot employ just anyone to do the work of Customers' Service. It is a delicate and complex job, not much different from that of diplomats: to perform it with success you must infuse faith in the customers and therefore it is indispensable to have faith in yourself and in the products you sell.

PRIMO LEVI 1919–1987
Italian novelist
The Periodic Table, English translation
by Raymond Rosenthal

Better service for the customer is for the good of the public, and this is the true purpose of enterprise.

KONOSUKE MATSUSHITA
Entrepreneur and founder of Matsushita Electric
Quest for Prosperity

Consumers are statistics. Customers are people.

STANLEY MARCUS
Chairman emeritus of Neiman-Marcus
Quoted in Tom Peters and Nancy
Austin, *A Passion for Excellence*

Do something for his [the customer's] kids. It always means far more to a customer than doing anything for him.

MARK MCCORMACK
Founder of the International Management Group
*What They Don't Teach You
at Harvard Business School*

Treat the customer as an appreciating asset.

TOM PETERS
US international management consultant
and bestselling business author
Thriving on Chaos

We should never be allowed to forget that it is the customer who, in the end, determines how many people are employed and what sort of wages companies can afford to pay.

LORD ROBENS
Chairman of National Coal Board
Observer 1977

The customer is always right.

H GORDON SELFRIDGE 1857–1947
US entrepreneur and founder of Selfridges, London
Saying adopted as Selfridges company motto

The customer is not always right and we let them know it from time to time.

ALAN SUGAR
Entrepreneur and founder of Amstrad plc
Speech, City University Business School, 1987

Marks & Spencer loves you. Securicor cares, IBM say the customer is king. At Amstrad we want your money.

ALAN SUGAR
Entrepreneur and founder of Amstrad plc
Speech, City University Business School, 1987

Customers are people! They appreciate being made to feel special and they like being treated as they expect and love it when their expectations are exceeded. It is like the golden rule. 'Do as you would be done by (and then do it better and more quickly)'.

DAVID WEST
British business executive and director of
Behavioural Science Systems
Real Customer Service

DEALS
(*SEE ALSO* CONTRACTS; NEGOTIATIONS)

He that resolves to deal with none but honest men must leave of dealing.

THOMAS FULLER 1608–1661
English writer
Gnomologia

I had grown up on a culture which believed that a good negotiation was one in which only one of us, myself, came away smiling, but concealed that smile lest the other guess that one had got the better of him or her. Negotiation was about winning at the expense of the other party. You then had to enforce your side of the deal using the law or the threat of the law. I had met a culture where negotiation was about finding the best way forward for both parties. No wonder we needed so many more lawyers in our culture.

CHARLES HANDY
Business executive and writer, and
professor at the London Business School
On his first experience of the Chinese
contract, *The Empty Overcoat*

A business deal should not be a win/lose contest but rather should be an effort to seek an arrangement which has something in it for everyone. Without that, the deal will not endure. Business is not about one-off deals, it is about building relationships.

JOHN HARVEY-JONES
Business writer and chairman of ICI
Quoted in *BusinessAge* 1995

Deals aren't usually blown by principals; they're blown by lawyers and accountants trying to prove how valuable they are.

ROBERT TOWNSEND
CEO of Avis
Further Up the Organization

Deals are my art form.

DONALD TRUMP
Real-estate executive
Sunday Times Magazine 1988

When money is at stake, never be the first to mention sums.

SHEIK AHMED YAMANI
Saudi Arabian oil minister
Quoted in Jeffrey Robinson, *Yamani*

DEBT AND DEBTORS
(*SEE ALSO* BORROWING AND LENDING; CREDIT AND CREDITORS)

It is better to pay a creditor than to give to a friend.

ARISTOTLE 384–322 BC
Greek philosopher
Nicomachean Ethics

Debt rolls a man over and over, binding him hand and foot, and letting him hang upon the fatal mesh until the long-legged interest devours him.

HENRY WARD BEECHER 1813–1887
US preacher
Proverbs from Plymouth Pulpit

Debt is a prolific mother of folly and of crime.

BENJAMIN DISRAELI 1804–1881
British prime minister and novelist
Henrietta Temple

If there's anyone listening to whom I owe money, I'm prepared to forget it if you are.

ERROL FLYNN 1909–1959
Actor
Quoted in Leslie Halliwell,
Filmgoers Book of Quotes

The 1980s are to debt what the 1960s were to sex. The 1960s left a hangover. So will the 1980s.

JAMES GRANT
US international business consultant
Business Review Weekly 1989

It is incumbent on every generation to pay its own debts as it goes – a principle which, if acted on, would save one-half the wars of the world.

THOMAS JEFFERSON 1743–1826
3rd President of the USA
Letter to Destutt Tracy, 1820

It is unanimously and without qualification assumed that when anyone gets into debt, the fault is entirely and always that of the lender, and not the borrower.

BERNARD LEVIN
British journalist
The Times 1986

A nation is not in danger of financial disaster merely because it owes itself money.

ANDREW WILLIAM MELLON 1855–1937
US financier
Remark, 1933

A small debt makes a man your debtor, a large one makes him your enemy.

LUCIUS ANNAEUS SENECA C. 4 BC–AD 65
Roman writer
Ad Lucilium

Words pay no debts.

WILLIAM SHAKESPEARE 1564–1616
English dramatist and poet
Troilus and Cressida

In Debtors' Yard the stones are hard,/ And the dripping wall is high.

OSCAR WILDE 1854–1900
Irish poet, dramatist, and wit
Ballad of Reading Goal

DECISIONS AND DECISION-MAKING

I must remind the Right Honourable Gentleman that a monologue is not a decision.

CLEMENT ATTLEE 1883–1967
British prime minister
Remark to Winston Churchill, quoted in
F Williams, *Prime Minister Remembers*

Nothing creates more self-respect among employees than being included in the process of making decisions.

JUDITH M BARDWICK
US academic
The Plateauing Trap

The man who never alters his opinions is like standing water, and breeds reptiles of the mind.

WILLIAM BLAKE 1757–1827
English poet and artist
Marriage of Heaven and Hell

Most of our executives make very sound decisions. The trouble is many of them have turned out not to have been right.

DONALD BULLOCK
US training director of C&P Telephone Co.
Seminar, Washington DC, 1980

Shelving hard decisions is the least ethical course.

ADRIAN CADBURY
Chairman of Cadbury Schweppes
Harvard Business Review 1987

Some people, however long their experience or strong their intellect, are temperamentally incapable of reaching firm decisions.

JAMES CALLAGHAN
British prime minister
Harvard Business Review 1986

Business leaders often get credit for the successful decisions that were forced on them.

OLIVER A FICK
US environmental services manager
Harvard Business Review 1986

I came to see that an objective view of the facts was one of the most important aspects of successful management. People go wrong most often when their decisions are based upon inadequate knowledge of the facts available.

HAROLD GENEEN
Business consultant and chairman of ITT
Managing

I'll give you a definite maybe.

SAMUEL GOLDWYN 1882–1974
Film producer and founder of Goldwyn Pictures
Corporation (later Metro-Goldwyn-Mayer),
famed for his off-beat sayings ('goldwynisms')
Attributed saying

Never make a decision. Let someone else make it and then if it turns out to be the wrong one, you can disclaim it, and if it is the right one you can abide by it.

HOWARD H HUGHES 1905–1976
Entrepreneur and founder of
Hughes Tool Co.
The Hughes Legacy: Scramble for the Billion

Procrastination is opportunity's natural assassin.

VICTOR KIAM
CEO of Remington
Going For It!

If someone tells you he is going to make a 'realistic decision', you immediately understand that he has resolved to do something bad.

MARY MCCARTHY 1912–1989
US novelist and critic
'American Realist Playwrights'

The man who is denied the opportunity of taking decisions of importance begins to regard as important the decisions he is allowed to take. He becomes fussy about filing, keen on seeing that pencils are sharpened, eager to ensure that the windows are open (or shut) and apt to use two or three different-coloured inks.

C NORTHCOTE PARKINSON
British historian, writer, and
formulator of Parkinson's law
Parkinson's Law and Other Studies in Administration

Our theory of management is that the time to get a decision doubles for every two levels of management; thus, parallel instead of serial decisions are best solutions.

EBERHARDT RECHTIN
President of Aerospace Corp.
Speech, Washington DC, 1978

Persuade the decision-takers that the decision you want is their idea.

MICHAEL SHEA
Director of public affairs at Hanson Trust plc
and former press secretary to the Queen
Influence

In many firms the technique is employed of having an executive vice president rule on an issue, the president remaining uninvolved so that appeals to him are still possible. If no one screams, the decision is allowed to stand.

ROSS STAGNER
US academic
Business Topics 1965

All decisions should be made as low as possible in the organization. The Charge of the Light Brigade was ordered by an officer who wasn't there looking at the territory.

ROBERT TOWNSEND
CEO of Avis
Up the Organization

There is a difference between attacking a decision and attacking the man who made the decision.

MAURICE S TROTTER
US academic
Supervisor's Handbook on Insubordination

If I make the decision and I am right, you will never remember. If I make the decision and I am wrong, you will never forget.

ROBERT WOOLSEY AND
HUNTINGTON SWANSON
US authors
Operations Research for Immediate Application:
A Quick and Dirty Manual

DELEGATION
(SEE ALSO INITIATIVE AND INDEPENDENCE)

The manager who supports the boss – the manager whom the boss can rely on and trust – is the one who will be given the most freedom and the least supervision.

MARY ANN ALLISON AND ERIC ALLISON
Vice-president of CitiCorp; financial writer
Managing Up, Managing Down

Effective delegation takes emotional courage as we allow, to one degree or another, others to make mistakes on our time, money, and good name. This courage consists of patience, self-control, faith in the potential of others, and respect for individual differences. Effective delegation must be two-way: responsibility given: responsibility received.

STEPHEN R COVEY
Founder of the Institute of
Principle-Centred Leadership
Principle-Centred Leadership

Delegating means letting others become the experts and hence the best.

TIMOTHY FIRNSTAHL
CEO of Restaurant Services, Inc.
Harvard Business Review 1986

Give up control even if it means the employees have to make some mistakes.

FRANK FLORES
CEO of Marsden Reproductions
Hispanic Business 1987

You have to do many things yourself. Things that you cannot delegate.

NADINE GRAMLING
CEO of Southeastern Metals Manufacturing Co.
Nation's Business 1988

You can delegate authority, but you can never delegate responsibility by delegating a task to someone else. If you picked the right man, fine, but if you picked the wrong man, the responsibility is yours – not his.

RICHARD E KRAFVE
President of Raytheon
Boston Sunday Globe 1960

I'm naturally a delegator. I guess I realized early in life that, unless you're going to be a violinist or something, your success will probably depend on other people.

WILLIAM G MCGOWAN
Chairman of MCI Communications Corp.
Inc. Magazine 1986

I was so busy doing things I should have delegated, I didn't have time to manage.

CHARLES PERCY
US senator and president of Bell & Howell
Quoted in R Alec Mackenzie, *The Time Trap*

Hire people and then delegate.

CAROL A TABER
US publisher of *Working Woman*
Management 1986

The only way for a large organization to function is to decentralize, to delegate real authority and responsibility to the man on the job. But be sure you have the right man on the job.

ROBERT E WOOD
President and chairman of Sear, Roebuck & Co.
Ordnance 1951

DESIGN

Why kick the man downstream who can't put the parts together because the parts really weren't designed properly?

PHILIP CALDWELL
CEO of Ford Motor Co.
Sky 1984

Retail is detail.

JAMES GULLIVER
Chairman of Argyll Group
You Magazine 1988

Never leave well enough alone.

RAYMOND LOEWY 1893–1986
US industrial designer
On new designs, quoted in *Business Week* 1990

You may never achieve zero defects. But if you want to avoid lawsuits, try to reach that goal.

MARISA MANLEY
US attorney at the Ginsberg Organization
Harvard Business Review 1987

The world is a complex place. Nonetheless, most of the things we admire, from the old Volkswagen Beetle to the 1985 Macintosh computer operating system, we admire because of their simplicity.

TOM PETERS
US international management consultant
and bestselling business author
Independent on Sunday 1995

DEVELOPING COUNTRIES

The South has got natural resources and the North has got capital. So huge sums of northern capital are going into natural resource extraction companies ... Because this money is in the private sector it goes without any form of environmental screening.

ANONYMOUS
Guardian 1995

I believe free trade, with sensitivity to the Third World's special problems, is the right answer.

COLIN CAMPBELL
Chairman of James Finlay plc
Speech at the Confederation of British Industry
annual conference, 1983

Energetic action on debt would make a radical difference to the prospects of many of the poorest countries in the world, at no practical cost to creditor countries.

KENNETH CLARKE
British chancellor of the Exchequer
Quoted in *Cosmopolitan* 1995

If I owe a million dollars, then I am lost. But if I owe fifty billion, the bankers are lost.

CELSO MING
Brazilian economist
On Third World debt, quoted in Anthony
Sampson, *The Money Lenders*

If development was measured not by Gross National Product, but a society's success in meeting the basic needs of its people, Vietnam would have been considered a model.

JOHN PILGER
Australian journalist, writer, and broadcaster
Guardian 1995

As we see nowadays in Southeast Asia or the Caribbean, the misery of being exploited by capitalists is nothing compared to the misery of not being exploited at all.

JOAN ROBINSON
British economist
Economic Philosophy 1962

DIPLOMACY AND TACT
(SEE ALSO INDUSTRIAL RELATIONS; NEGOTIATIONS; PUBLIC RELATIONS)

A want of tact is worse than a want of virtue.

BENJAMIN DISRAELI 1804–1881
British prime minister and novelist
The Young Duke

There's so much more to be gained with honey, so much more.

LORD HANSON
Business executive and chairman of Hanson plc
Financial Times 1983

It is much easier to apologize than to ask permission.

GRACE MURRAY HOPPER
US admiral
Observation made during *60 Minutes*,
CBS TV broadcast, 1986

Confrontation in any form of enterprise is damaging. What works is a dialogue between big investors and companies that continues through good times and bad.

GEOFF LINDLEY
Chairman of National Association of Pension Funds
Independent 1995

Make a suggestion or assumption and let them tell you you're wrong. People also have a need to feel smarter than you are.

MARK MCCORMACK
Founder of International Management Group
*What They Don't Teach You
at Harvard Business School*

Discretion is the tact not to see what can't be helped.

DAGOBERT D RUNES
US editor, publisher, and philosopher
A Book of Contemplation

If you're going to be a bridge, you've got to be prepared to be walked upon.

ROY A WEST
US school principal
The Washington Post 1988

EASY MONEY

Few women care to be laughed at and men not at all, except for large sums of money.

ALAN AYCKBOURN
English dramatist
Norman Conquests

Borrow fivers off everyone you meet.

RICHARD BRANSON
Entrepreneur and founder of Virgin Group
On the quickest way to become a millionaire

High premiums are being paid today not particularly for quality service or long-term building of a business but rather for making money quickly, getting rich, and getting out. And that's wrong.

WILLARD C BUTCHER
Chairman of Chase Manhattan Corp.
Speech, New Orleans, 1987

'My boy,' he says, 'always try to rub up against money, for if you rub up against money long enough, some of it may rub off on you.'

DAMON RUNYON 1884–1946
US writer
Furthermore

It is just like having a licence to print your own money.

LORD THOMSON 1894–1974
Newspaper proprietor
On the profits to be made from commercial television, quoted in R Braddon, *Roy Thomson*

ECONOMISTS, ECONOMICS, AND THE ECONOMY
(*SEE ALSO* INFLATION)

For the past 15 years or so, British governments have tried to persuade the rest of us that the best judges of the national interest are ... businessmen. This may be a ridiculous statement, but – ominously – fewer and fewer people laugh at it.

NEIL ASCHERSON
British journalist
Independent on Sunday 1995

The notion that big business and big labor and big government can sit down around a table somewhere and work out the direction of the American economy is at complete variance with the reality of where the American economy is headed. I mean, it's like dinosaurs gathering to talk about the evolution of a new generation of mammals.

BRUCE BABBIT
Governor of the state of Arizona
Inc. Magazine 1987

The single currency is like launching a rocket. Once you've got the boosters firing, you cannot put it into reverse.

YVES-THIBAULT DE SILGUY
EC commissioner of monetary affairs
Guardian 1995

According to [the Bank of England] the economy is growing too fast so interest rates must rise to counter the supposed inflationary threat. In lay terms, I interpret this to mean that people are working much harder, causing economic growth, and they're in danger of spending their money, which is what the recession-hit shops want them to do. But [the Bank] and the City seem to think this is wrong, and that if people work harder they should be punished by having their mortgages increased.

HARRY ENFIELD
British comedian
Independent on Sunday 1995

The rate of interest acts as a link between income-value and capital-value.

IRVING FISHER 1867–1947
US mathematician and economist
The Nature on Capital and Income 1923

One of the greatest pieces of economic wisdom is to know what you do not know.

J K GALBRAITH
US diplomat, economist, and writer
Time 1961

I always thought it was the first task of an economist to provide himself with a certain amount of money. The fact that I have been able to do so without too much strain has never bothered me.

J K GALBRAITH
US diplomat, economist, and writer
Evening Standard 1977

If we want stability we have to do what is necessary to achieve it. It is no good professing you believe in it and then shrinking from the action which is necessary to bring it about.

EDDIE GEORGE
Governor of the Bank of England
On the exchange rate, in a speech to the British
Chamber of Commerce Conference, Aberdeen, 1995

There is much of economic theory which is pursued for no better reason than its intellectual attraction; it is a good game. We have no reason to be ashamed of that, since the same would hold for many branches of mathematics.

JOHN HICKS 1904–1989
British economist
Causality in Economics

Please find me a one-armed economist so we will not always hear 'On the other hand ...'.

HERBERT HOOVER 1874–1964
31st president of the USA
Attributed

Old economists never die, they just change their assumptions.

GEOFFREY HOWE
British chancellor of the Exchequer
Sunday Times 1989

Nothing is esteemed a more certain sign of the flourishing condition of any nation than the lowness of interest.

DAVID HUME 1711–1776
Scottish philosopher
Essays

One of the most expensive things an economy can buy is economic trial, error, and development.

JANE JACOBS
US academic
The Economy of Cities

The theory of economics must begin with a correct theory of consumption.

WILLIAM STANLEY JEVONS 1835–1982
British economist and logician
Theory of Political Economy

Good economics is good politics.

PAUL KEATING
Australian prime minister
Quoted in *Sydney Morning Herald* 1988

If economists were any good at business, they would be rich men instead of advisers to rich men.

KIRK KERKORIAN
US business executive
Quoted in Robert W Kent, *Money Talks*

The ideas of economists and political philosophers, both when they are right and when they are wrong, are more powerful than is commonly understood. Indeed the world is ruled by little else. Practical men, who believe themselves to be quite exempt from any intellectual influences, are usually the slaves of some defunct economist.

JOHN MAYNARD KEYNES 1883–1946
English economist
The General Theory of Employment, Interest, and Money

Economists set themselves too easy, too useless a task if in tempestuous seasons they can only tell us that when the storm is long past the ocean is flat again

JOHN MAYNARD KEYNES 1883–1946
English economist
Tract on Monetary Reform

It would be a dreadful mistake to equate economics with real life.

PETER MIDDLETON
Permanent secretary to the Treasury
The Times 1988

Call a thing immoral, soul-destroying or a degradation of man, a peril to the peace of the world or to the well-being of future generations: as long as you have not shown it to be 'uneconomic' you have not really questioned its right to exist, grow and prosper.

E F SCHUMACHER 1911–1977
German-born British economist
Small Is Beautiful: Economics As If People Mattered

The British economy is suffering, like many well-heeled Americans, from too much analysis. Its every foible is picked up, picked over and turned upside down. And at the end of it all, we still don't understand that much about what makes it tick.

DAVID SMITH
British economics journalist
Sunday Times 1995

You and I come by road or rail – but economists travel on infrastructure.

MARGARET THATCHER
British prime minister
Quoted in *Observer* 1985

The economists are generally right in their predictions, but generally a good deal out in their dates.

SIDNEY WEBB 1859–1947
British economist and social historian
Quoted in *Observer* 1924

The first law of economics is that when the price goes up, consumption comes down. This is a divine law. You cannot change it.

SHEIK AHMED YAMANI
Saudi Arabian oil minister
Quoted in Jeffrey Robinson, *Yamani*

EDUCATION AND TRAINING
(*SEE ALSO* CAREERS; COMPETENCE; THEORY VERSUS PRACTICE)

My father and mother appreciated everything I was trying to do, encouraged me and gave me lots of love and praise. This sets you off on the right footing to become the leader of a large company.

RICHARD BRANSON
Entrepreneur and founder of Virgin Group
Today 1988

The mark of a true MBA is that he is often wrong but seldom in doubt.

ROBERT BUZZELL
Professor at Harvard Business School
Quoted in R Barron and J Fisk,
Great Business Quotations

We hire eagles and teach them to fly in formation.

D WAYNE CALLOWAY
CEO of PepsiCo
Fortune 1989

Mentoring is all about people – it's about caring, about relationships and sensitivity. As it becomes increasingly in vogue it is becoming too formulated – concerned with performance metrics, critical success factors, investment and spending. It'll be a disaster.

RENE CARAYOL
Director of IT at IPC magazines
Guardian 1995

Life at university, with its intellectual and inconclusive discussions at a postgraduate level is on the whole a bad training for the real world. Only men of very strong character surmount this handicap.

PAUL CHAMBERS 1904–1981
Chairman of ICI
Observer 1964

Information's pretty thin stuff, unless mixed with experience.

CLARENCE DAY 1874–1935
US writer
The Crow's Nest

A job in which young people are not given real training – though, of course, the training need not be a formal 'training program' – does not measure up to what they have a right and a duty to expect.

PETER F DRUCKER
US management expert
People and Performance

Imagination is more important than knowledge.

ALBERT EINSTEIN 1879–1955
Physicist and formulator of the theories of relativity
Quoted in Hurd, *Treasury of Great American Quotations*

Most owners of small businesses openly state that they believe in the value of skills and operational training. However, they also admit that they themselves undertake very little training, or offer only limited training to their employees, because of time restraints.

MOSHE GERSTENHABER
Chairman of Kall Kwik
Franchise World 1995

Learning is a double loop ... there is learning to solve a particular problem and then, more importantly, there is the habit of learning, the learning to learn to do such things, that second loop that can change the way you live.

CHARLES HANDY
Business executive and writer, and
professor at the London Business School
The Age of Unreason

'Don't tell me. Show me and I will be able to do it myself.' These words are hardly ever spoken but are very often seen in the eyes of an employee listening to directions and orders being barked out by a manager.

ROBIN LINNECAR
KPMG Career Consulting
Evening Standard 1995

When we describe skill failures we tend to speak of a lack of supply, but there is a lot of evidence to suggest that Britain's fundamental problem is a lack of demand.

KEN MAYHEW
Fellow of Pembroke College, Oxford University
Quoted in *People Management* 1995

Business schools, out of necessity, are condemned to teach the past.

MARK MCCORMACK
Founder of International Management Group
*What They Don't Teach You
at Harvard Business School*

It's too costly to learn from your own experience. You not only learn much faster, but it is also much cheaper to learn from other people's experiences.

ROBERT L MONTGOMERY
President of R L Montgomery & Associates
How to Sell in the 1980s

The sorry state of education and training means that, in effect, we confront panzer divisions with the home guard.

PETER MORGAN
Director general of the Institute of Directors
Speech on Britain and world trade at the Annual
Convention of the Institute of Directors, 1990

Education costs money, but then so does ignorance.

CLAUS MOSER
German-born British academic
Daily Telegraph 1990

Before asking someone to do something, you have to help them be something.

WILLIAM POLLARD
US partner of ServiceMaster
Quoted in James A Belasco, *Teaching
the Elephant to Dance*

The School of Hard Knocks, beloved of businessmen, is a somewhat unstructured comprehensive.

LORD VAIZEY 1929–1984
British company director
Quoted in *Observer* 1983

We don't have, but we desperately need, a training culture.

NORMAN WILLIS
General secretary of the TUC
'A Worker's Right to Train' in *National
Westminster Bank Quarterly Review* 1989

Anyone who wants to rebuild meritocracy must start by rebuilding education.

ADRIAN WOOLDRIDGE
British writer
Sunday Times 1995

EFFICIENCY

One of the great disadvantages of hurry is that it takes such a long time.

G K CHESTERTON 1874–1936
English writer
All Things Considered

Desire to have things done quickly prevents their being done thoroughly.

CONFUCIUS 551–479 BC
Chinese philosopher
Analects

You have to be efficient if you're going to be lazy.

SHIRLEY CONRAN
British writer
Superwoman

The first requirement for efficiency and economy ... is highly competent personnel.

JOHN F KENNEDY 1917–1963
35th president of the USA
Quoted in *Management* 1987

The myth of efficiency lies in the assumption that the most efficient manager is ipso facto the most effective; actually the most efficient manager working on the wrong task will not be effective.

R ALEC MACKENZIE
US management consultant and author
The Time Trap

Regardless of how 'efficient' the management operation is, it is not 'effective' unless it keeps clients happy.

SONIA RAPPAPORT
US lawyer
The Washington Lawyer 1987

I suspected it was time for a change when we hired those time-and-motion specialists to analyse our workers' routines. We thought these experts would help increase our workers' productivity. Much later, the workers told us they had quickly learned to slow down the analysts' timers, which made the study a washout.

RICARDO SEMLER
Brazilian CEO of Semco
Maverick

You can smell whether a factory is efficient.

LORD STOKES
Chairman of British Leyland
Interview, *The Times* 1969

The really efficient laborer will be found not to crowd his day with work, but will saunter to his task surrounded by a wide halo of ease and leisure.

HENRY DAVID THOREAU 1817–1862
US writer
Journal 1941

Whenever you have an efficient government you have a dictatorship.

HARRY S TRUMAN 1884–1972
33rd president of the USA
Speech, Colombia University, 1959

EMPLOYERS AND EMPLOYEES
(SEE ALSO PEOPLE AND PEOPLE MANAGEMENT; SECRETARIES AND PERSONAL ASSISTANTS; WORKER PARTICIPATION)

Most important for us is a good spiritual relationship between employees and management.

TATSUHIKO ANDOH
Japanese president of Okatoku Securities Co.
Cherry Blossoms and Robotics

Reliable office staff come in the shape of mature married women working from 9.30 to 3.30 (inside school hours) during which they will do more than the 9–5ers.

CHRIS BRASHER
British sports and business executive
Quoted in Ray Wild, *How to Manage*

It is your people who make the ultimate difference. You put the investment into training the people and then, when you get invited to the party with the big boys, that is a unique selling point.

PHIL DIXON
British founder of Newlife Cleaning Systems
Quoted in *Sunday Times* 1995

What we are looking for is what I call constructive no-men.

JOHN HARVEY-JONES
Business writer and former chairman of ICI
Making it Happen

I don't want men of experience working for me. The experienced man is always telling me why something can't be done. He is smart; he is intelligent; he thinks he knows the answers. The fellow who has not had any experience is so dumb he doesn't know a thing can't be done – and he goes ahead and does it.

CHARLES F KETTERING
US president of GM Research Group
How to Live with Life

It is hard being 'only a temp'. There are so many people who won't even learn your name. In the work environment you're never part of the group, even though half the time you're doing more work than anyone else.

ROSEMARY MACGUIRE
British accountancy temp
Cosmopolitan 1995

The investor and the employee are in the same position, but sometimes the employee is more important, because he will be there a long time whereas an investor will often get in and out on a whim in order to make a profit. The worker's mission is to contribute to the company's welfare, and his own, every day.

AKIO MORITA
Co-founder of Sony
Made in Japan

In the long run – and I emphasize this – no matter how good or successful you are or how clever or crafty, your business and its future are in the hands of the people you hire. To put it a bit more dramatically, the fate of your business is actually in the hands of the youngest recruits on the staff.

LORD SIEFF
Honorary president of Marks and Spencer plc
Management the Marks and Spencer Way

A worker is, first of all, a person who must fit into the social community in which he works.

GUY M WADSWORTH
US employment-test developer
Studies in Personnel Policy 1941

EMPLOYMENT
(*SEE ALSO* UNEMPLOYMENT; WORK)

Opportunities are everywhere. The recession might be drawing to a close, but its continuing legacy is employers' reliance on short-term staff. There may be fewer jobs for life, but there are more jobs in a lifetime.

LUCY BENINGTON
British journalist
Cosmopolitan 1995

In order to be irreplaceable one must always be different.

COCO CHANEL 1883–1971
French fashion designer
Quoted in Marcel Haedrich, *Coco Chanel,
Her Life, Her Secrets*

We may not be able to offer long-term employment, but we should try to offer long-term employability.

BRIAN CORBY
Chairman of Prudential Insurance
Retirement speech, quoted in *Independent* 1995

We've entered an era when very good, competent people aren't getting jobs. One remedy is to stand out, to self-promote. If you do, you're going to get the nod over some co-worker.

JEFFREY P DAVIDSON
US marketing consultant
Washington Post 1985

The old order of jobs for life has already passed. The uncertainty implicit in a flexible labour market needs to be countered by a certainty offered from a flexible welfare state.

FRANK FIELD
British politician
Making Welfare Work

For today's employers, a permanent work-force is a costly item in their inventory that, in conditions of intense global competition, they can no longer afford.

JOHN GRAY
British political theorist
Guardian 1995

There is no longer a residual loyalty to be relied on, no longer any implied promise of security in return for obedient labour. Good work must, in the long run, receive good rewards or it will cease to be good work. The contract is now more explicit, and in many respects more healthy for that.

CHARLES HANDY
Business executive and writer, and
professor at the London Business School
The Age of Unreason

If the economy expanded fast enough to mop up more unemployment so that companies couldn't be assured of hiring the skills they wanted, then permanent contracts could suddenly come back into fashion.

VICTOR KEEGAN
British economics columnist
Guardian 1995

We believe that if men have the talent to invent new machines that put men out of work, they have the talent to put those men back to work.

JOHN F KENNEDY 1917–1963
35th president of the USA
Speech, Whelling, West Virginia, 1962

The person who knows 'how' will always have a job. The person who knows 'why' will always be his boss.

DIANE RAVITCH
Professor at Columbia University Teachers College
Time 1985

ENTREPRENEURS AND ENTERPRISE

The sexist word 'businessman' has been upholstered into 'entrepreneur' or 'representative of local enterprise' or 'industrialist' or even 'wealth creator'. Notice the altruistic varnish of these terms. A businessman makes money, has too much lunch and waddles off to play golf – whereas your lean, fit entrepreneur is always seeking ways to make society leaner and fitter too.

NEIL ASCHERSON
British journalist
Independent on Sunday 1995

An entrepreneur tends to bite off a little more than he can chew knowing he'll quickly learn how to chew it.

ROY ASH
CEO of AM International
Remark during an interview, 1984

I believe Mrs Thatcher's emphasis on enterprise was right.

TONY BLAIR
British Labour Party leader
Sunday Times 1995

I never actually set out to see how I could make the most cash. I've always merely tried to make the figures fit the ideas I've had rather than the other way around. I guess that's doing it backwards.

RICHARD BRANSON
Entrepreneur and founder of Virgin Group
Quoted in Jeffrey Robinson, *The Risk Takers*

I see myself as a doer. I'm sure that other people have had ideas that were similar to mine. The difference is that I have carried mine into action, and they have not.

NOLAN BUSHNELL
Founder of Atari Computer Co.
Quoted in Roger von Oech, *A Whack on the Side of the Head*

I get a tremendous charge out of business. I get the same sort of feeling that women must have when their babies pop out.

TERENCE CONRAN
Design guru and founder of Habitat
Daily Express 1986

Entrepreneurs, the successful ones, have on average nine failures for every success. It is only the successes that you will hear about, the failures they credit to experience. Oil companies expect to drill nine empty wells for every one that flows. Getting it wrong is part of getting it right.

CHARLES HANDY
Business executive and writer, and
professor at the London Business School
The Age of Unreason

Good management and entrepreneurship are not synonymous.

JAMES L HAYES
President of the American Management Association
Memos for Management: Leadership

Entrepreneurship was the sacred mushroom of the 1980s. It seemed delusively greater and grander than it was.

TED LEVITT
Editor of *Harvard Business Review*
Thinking About Management

Anybody could have set up Sky Television. Anybody. And we started it. And people are still free to start against us. But they'd rather write articles, bitch and moan, lay around and say 'no, we'd rather just keep our lazy way of life. We don't want to compete'. You know, it's not until we get people being equally entrepreneurial and really driving at it that Britain is going to get going again.

RUPERT MURDOCH
Media baron
The Money Programme, BBC television, 1995

No entrepreneur I know is motivated by money. It's the idea. Seeing how far it will go.

ANITA RODDICK
British entrepreneur and founder
of The Body Shop
Interview, *Daily Telegraph* 1987

It would be difficult to exaggerate the importance of perception of potential opportunities created by social change either for the founders of new businesses or for entrepreneurs running relatively successful, well-established businesses.

LORD SIEFF
Honorary president of Marks and Spencer plc
Management the Marks and Spencer Way

The entrepreneur is like an eagle ... he soars alone, he flies alone and he hunts alone.

DR MICHAEL SMURFIT
Chairman of Jefferson Smurfit Ltd
Irish Independent 1986

An entrepreneur, if there is such a thing, is a born schemer and thinker-up of things.

ALAN SUGAR
Entrepreneur and founder of Amstrad plc
Quoted in David Thomas, *The Amstrad Story*

Enterprise is not greed.

LORD YOUNG
British business executive and politician
Speech at the Annual Convention
of the Institute of Directors, 1995

If you want to understand entrepreneurs, you have to study the psychology of the juvenile delinquent. They don't have the same anxiety triggers that we have.

ABRAHAM ZALEZNIK
Psychoanalyst and Matsushita Professor
of Leadership at Harvard Business School
US News & World Report 1992

EQUALITY AND DISCRIMINATION
(*SEE ALSO* EXPLOITATION)

When quarrels and complaints arise, it is when people who are equal have not got equal shares.

ARISTOTLE 384–322 BC
Greek philosopher
Nichomachaen

If you're not a white male, consider sales seriously. Most employers, regardless of how sexist or racist they may be, will pay for any sales they can get. And they care little for the color or gender of the person who brings that business to the firm. Most will be glad to get the business even if it comes from a green, bisexual Martian.

RAMONA ARNETT
President of Ramona Enterprises, Inc.
Speech, New York City, 1971

If school results were the key to power, girls would be running the world.

SARAH BOSELEY
British journalist
Guardian 1995

Discrimination is the act of treating differently two people ... under like circumstances.

LOUIS DEMBITZ BRANDEIS 1856–1941
US Supreme Court justice
National Life Insurance Co. v. USA 1927

There has to be positive action that allows the most disadvantaged people to get their fair share of job opportunities.

PAUL BURTON
British expert in urban studies
On the regeneration of inner cities, *Guardian* 1995

The mature woman ... after having raised her children has been a 'chief executive officer' at home for ten years or more. No one told her whether to dust first or make the beds first – and both chores got done. Yet when she starts working, she is put under a 'supervisor' who treats her as a moron who has never done anything on her own before when what she needs is a teacher and an assistant.

PETER F DRUCKER
US management expert
Management in Turbulent Times

The mandate for equal opportunity doesn't dictate disregard for the differences in candidates' qualities and skills. There is no constitutional right to play ball. All there is is a right to compete for it on equal terms.

TIM ELLIS III
US district court judge
Croteau v. Osbourne Park High School 1988

'The removal of all social and political inequalities' is a very dubious phrase with which to replace 'the removal of all class distinctions'. There will always be *certain* inequalities in the standard of life in different countries, provinces and places. They can be reduced to a minimum, but they can never be removed.

FRIEDRICH ENGELS 1820–1895
German socialist and political philosopher
Letter to August Bebel, founder of the League
of German Workers' Clubs, 1875

Generally, employees who file complaints of discrimination do so as a last resort.

RUBYE FIELDS
US president of Blacks in Government
Management Review 1987

I am free of all prejudice. I hate everyone equally.

W C FIELDS 1880–1946
US comedian
Attributed

The male human being is thousands of years in advance of the female in economic status.

CHARLOTTE PERKINS GILMAN 1860–1935
US writer on social and economic affairs
Women and Economics

The legacy of women's war work is our present post-industrial employment structure. It was the war that created the demand for a technologically advanced, de-skilled, low-paid, non-unionized female workforce and paved the way for making part-time work the norm for married women now. A generation later, it was the daughters of wartime women workers who completed their mothers' campaign for equal pay.

LINDA GRANT
British journalist
Guardian 1995

The destruction of the old world of work can be liberating for women, because the old work communities and structures were patriarchal. That's gone now, and it's a good thing.

JOHN GRAY
British political theorist
Cosmopolitan 1995

If seems that woman has more likelihood of success the higher she pitches her sights.

GERMAINE GREER
Australian academic and feminist writer
The Female Eunuch

That all men are equal is a proposition to which, at ordinary times, no sane individual has ever given his assent.

ALDOUS HUXLEY 1894–1963
English writer
Proper Studies

All of us do not have equal talent, but all of us should have an equal opportunity to develop our talents.

JOHN F KENNEDY 1917–1963
35th president of the USA
Speech, San Diego State College, California, 1963

Forget the paternity leave; most bosses would look askance if [a male employee] asked to leave work early to take their children to the dentist. The immediate assumption would be that their wife must just have died.

PENELOPE LEACH
British psychologist and childcare expert
Quoted in *Independent* 1988

Affirmative action can be viewed as the ultimate in risk reduction because it provides insurance against the 'bad luck' of having been born black or female.

JAMES O'TOOLE
US academic
Making America Work

Some people are trying very hard to set racial equality standards, and are succeeding in doing so. These standards have nothing to do with political correctness or political corruptness. They have everything to do with fairness, equality and justice. They need help, support and encouragement. Racial equality is good for business, good for our community, good for our society.

HERMAN OUSELEY
British chairman of the Commission
for Racial Equality
Quoted in *Guardian* 1995

Most hierarchies were established by men who now monopolize the upper levels, thus depriving women of the rightful share of opportunities for incompetence.

LAURENCE J PETER 1910–1990
Canadian writer, educationalist, and self-proclaimed
'researcher of remedies for incompetence'
The Peter Principle

Women cannot be expected to break the glass ceiling from below. Since men are the dominant group, they will have to remove the ceiling, and that will be difficult since for them it constitutes a floor – a feeling of security.

JUDY B ROSENER
US author
*America's Competitive Secret: Utilizing
Women as a Management Strategy*

We all decry prejudice, yet are all prejudiced.

HERBERT SPENCER 1820–1903
English philosopher
Social Statistics

Equality is equity.
NOAH HAYES SWAYNE 1804–1884
US Supreme Court justice
Pacific Insurance Co. v. Soule 1868

So far as natural law is concerned, all men are equal.
DOMITIUS ULPIAN C. AD 170–228
Roman jurist
Liber singularis regularum

The lack of the alternatives to the establishment's management style makes it difficult for minorities to progress.
PATTI WATTS
US assistant editor of *Management Review*
Management Review 1987

ETHICS
(*SEE ALSO* SOCIAL RESPONSIBILITIES OF BUSINESS)

Morality is a private and costly luxury.
HENRY BROOKS ADAMS 1838–1918
US historian and novelist
The Education of Henry Adams

Honesty is the cornerstone of all success, without which confidence and ability to perform shall cease to exist.
MARY KAY ASH
US entrepreneur and founder
of Mary Kay Cosmetics
Vital Speeches of the Day 1988

Damn it all, you can't have the crown of thorns and the thirty pieces of silver.
ANEURIN ('NYE') BEVAN 1897–1960
British politician
Quoted in Michael Foot, *Aneurin Bevan*

The world has achieved brilliance without conscience. But it is a world of nuclear giants and ethical infants.
OMAR NELSON BRADLEY 1893–1981
US general
Armistice Day speech, 1948

I think it's unethical to take money for poor quality performance.
ALVIN BURGER
Founder of 'Bugs' Burger Bug Killers, Inc.
Inc. Magazine 1984

The possibility that ethical and commercial considerations will conflict has always faced those who run companies. It is not a new problem. The difference now is that a more widespread and critical interest is being taken in our decisions and in the ethical judgements which lie behind them.
ADRIAN CADBURY
Chairman of Cadbury Schweppes
Harvard Business Review 1987

Those who cultivate moral confusion for profit should understand this: we will name their names and shame them as they deserve to be shamed.
BOB DOLE
Leader of the US Republican
Party and the US Senate
Quoted in *Guardian* 1995

Raising the subject of the company's values is like presenting someone parched and dying of thirst with an oasis. You can't take philosophy out of business, yet in so many companies it is neglected and there is no forum for discussion.
JOHN DRUMMOND
Managing director of Integrity Works
Independent 1995

The practice of declaring codes of ethics and teaching them to managers is not enough to deter unethical conduct.
SAUL W GELLERMAN
US academic
Harvard Business Review 1986

It horrifies me that ethics is only an optional extra at Harvard Business School.
JOHN HARVEY-JONES
Business writer and chairman of ICI
Quoted in Berry Ritchie and Walter Goldsmith,
The New Elite

If managers are careless about basic things – telling the truth, respecting moral codes, proper professional conduct – who can believe them on other issues?

JAMES L HAYES
President of the American Management Association
Memos for Management: Leadership

The ethics of dissent are a very real issue in profit center management. Is the good of the corporation the overriding concern? Or is it personal survival?

BRUCE HENDERSON
CEO of Boston Consulting Group, Inc.
Henderson on Corporate Strategy

A man is usually more careful of his money than he is of his principles.

EDGAR WATSON HOWE 1853–1937
US writer
Ventures in Common Sense

Money, and not morality, is the principle of commercial nations.

THOMAS JEFFERSON 1743–1832
3rd president of the USA
Letter to John Langdon, 1810

We talk endlessly about the economy but we don't talk enough about the moral economy. Yet the moral economy is always with us. People think about it all the time in their daily lives. They are always considering whether a price is right or they are getting enough reward for their effort. A lot of the time this boils down to questions of money. But the moral economy is not just about what you get and what you pay. It is also about quality of life, security, happiness, interesting ideas and beautiful things.

MARTIN KETTLE
British journalist
Guardian 1995

Executives have to start understanding that they have certain legal and ethical responsibilities for information under their control.

JIM LEEKE
US computer journalist
PC Week 1987

Like sex in Victorian England, the reality of big business today is our big dirty secret.

RALPH NADER
US lawyer and consumer campaigner
UK Press Gazette 1971

If companies cannot offer job security, the only way that they can weld together a structure is by being clear about their values and maintaining a high standard of corporate ethics. The example for the rest of the company must come from the top. Any suspicion about senior management, any rumour that they have their hands in the till, will destroy the fabric of the company.

JACK O'SULLIVAN
British journalist
Independent 1995

Being good is good business.

ANITA RODDICK
British entrepreneur and
founder of The Body Shop
Sunday Express Magazine 1986

A hierarchy based on what you sell makes people desperate to prove they're worth it and, in desperation, there's a very fine line between ethical and unethical.

DIANE SAUNDERS
British director of Women and Money
training organization
Cosmopolitan 1995

Sound principles do not change, though sound policy often must. Principles are sacrosanct – policy must be flexible.

LORD SIEFF
Honorary president of Marks and Spencer plc
Management the Marks and Spencer Way

An organized money-market has many advantages. But it is not a school of social ethics or of political responsibility.

R H TAWNEY 1880–1962
Economics historian
The Acquisitive Society

Prosperity is the best protector of principle.

MARK TWAIN 1835–1910
US writer
Pudd'nhead Wilson's New Calendar

Always do right! This will gratify some and astonish the rest.

MARK TWAIN 1835–1910
US writer
Speech to the Young People's Society, Greenpoint
Presbyterian Church, Brooklyn, New York, 1901

All business sagacity reduces itself in the last analysis to a judicious use of sabotage.

THORSTEIN VEBLEN 1857–1929
US economist
The Nature of Peace

EXPEDIENCE
(SEE ALSO HONESTY)

It is a fine thing to be honest, but it is very important for a prime minister to be right.

WINSTON CHURCHILL 1874–1965
British statesman and prime minister
Speech, Free Trade Hall, Manchester, 1932

He [Ramsay MacDonald] had sufficient conscience to bother him, but not sufficient to keep him straight.

DAVID LLOYD GEORGE 1863–1945
British prime minister
On Ramsay MacDonald, quoted in
A J Sylvester, *Life with Lloyd George*

Although it be detestable in everything to employ fraud, nevertheless in the conduct of war it is praiseworthy and admirable, and he is commended who overcomes the foe by stratagem, equally with him who overcomes by force.

NICCOLÒ MACHIAVELLI 1469–1527
Florentine statesman and writer
Discourses

You can't learn too soon that the most useful thing about a principle is that it can always be sacrificed to expediency.

W SOMERSET MAUGHAM 1874–1965
English writer
The Circle

The end must justify the means.

MATTHEW PRIOR 1664–1721
English poet and diplomat
Hans Carvel

The profession of exploiting loopholes is eminently respectable. Some of the nation's most erudite and honorable people do it.

ROBERT B REICH
US academic
Best of Business Quarterly 1987

No man is justified in doing evil on the grounds of expediency.

THEODORE ROOSEVELT 1858–1919
26th president of the USA
The Strenuous Life

EXPLOITATION
(SEE ALSO EQUALITY AND DISCRIMINATION)

If you allow men to use you for your own purposes, they will use you for theirs.

AESOP C. 620–564 BC
Greek author of fables
'The Horse, Hunter, and Stag'

Almost all our relationships begin and most of them continue as forms of mutual exploitation, a mental or physical barter, to be terminated when one or both parties run out of goods.

W H Auden 1907–1973
English-born US poet
The Dyer's Hand

A national minimum wage is the only way to end labour exploitation.

From the British Labour Party's policy document

When we apply it, you call it anarchy; and when you apply it, I call it exploitation.

G K Chesterton 1874–1936
English writer
The Scandal of Father Brown

Man does not only sell commodities, he sells himself and feels himself to be a commodity.

Erich Fromm 1900–1980
US psychologist, philosopher, and writer
Escape from Freedom

Let us distinguish between the creation of wealth for the community and the extortion of wealth from the community.

William Randolph Hearst 1863–1951
Newspaper tycoon and politician
Editorial, 1918

Failure
(*see also* Mistakes; Success)

It has been my experience that when an employee fails, he is the most uncomfortable with this fact.

Mary Kay Ash
US entrepreneur and founder
of Mary Kay Cosmetics
Mary Kay on People Management

There is much to be said for failure. It is more interesting than success.

Max Beerbohm 1872–1956
English wit, writer, broadcaster, and cartoonist
Mainly on the Air

Having left school without going to university, I decided to make money. I never really considered failure.

Richard Branson
Entrepreneur and founder of Virgin Group
International Management 1985

Failure is the condiment that gives success its flavor.

Truman Capote 1924–1984
US writer
The Dogs Bark

Failure must be but a challenge to others.

Amelia Earhart 1898–1937
US aviation pioneer and author
Last Flight

If all else fails, immortality can always be assured by spectacular error.

J K Galbraith
US diplomat, economist, and writer
Forbes 1985

My failures have been errors of judgement, not of intent.

Ulysses S Grant 1822–1885
18th president of the USA
Message to Congress, 1876

Failures are like skinned knees – painful but superficial.

H Ross Perot
US presidential candidate and founder
of Electronic Data Systems
Look 1970

I've had all my assumptions about organization ripped asunder as I've watched the Valley thrive. It has elbowed its way into the planet's consciousness, largely courtesy of failure after failure (and, along the way, many more than its fair share of successes – mostly by-products of the most exciting failures).

Tom Peters
US international management consultant
and bestselling business author
On Silicon Valley, *Liberation Management*

You gotta lose 'em sometime. When you do, lose 'em right.

CASEY STENGEL 1889–1975
US baseball player and manager
Quoted in Ira Berkow and Jim Kaplan,
The Gospel According to Casey

I cannot give you the formula for success, but I can give you the formula for failure, which is: Try to please everybody.

HERBERT B SWOPE 1882–1958
US journalist
Speech, 1950

FORECASTING AND PLANNING
(*SEE ALSO* FUTURE; VISION)

The seeds of every company's demise are contained in its business plan.

FRED ADLER
US CEO of Adler and Co.
Inc. Magazine 1987

The long term versus the short term argument is one used by losers.

LARRY ADLER
US founder of Fire & All Risk Insurances
Financial Times 1988

A trend is a trend is a trend/ But the question is, will it bend?/ Will it alter its course/ Through some unforeseen force/ And come to a premature end?

ALEC CAIRNCROSS
Scottish economist
'Economic Forecasting' in *Economics Journal* 1969

Any plan is bad which is not susceptible to change.

BARTOLOMMEO DE SAN CONCORDIO 1475–1517
Florentine painter and writer
Giunta agli Ammaestramenti degli Antichi

In complex situations, we may rely too heavily on planning and forecasting and underestimate the importance of random factors in the environment. That reliance can also lead to delusions of control.

HILLEL J EINHORN AND ROBIN M HOGARTH
US academics
Harvard Business Review 1987

It is important not to ignore forecasts that are uncongenial.

JIB FOWLES
US academic
New York Times 1988

There are two classes of people who tell you what is going to happen in the future: Those who don't know, and those who don't know they don't know.

J K GALBRAITH
US diplomat, economist, and writer
Washington Post 1988

I also discovered that we were spending so much time planning for the next year and the next five years that our units were not making the current quarterly earnings. They were falling prey to the old trap of saying, 'Oh, don't worry. I didn't make it this quarter, but I'll make it up before the end of the year.' I found that realistically it did not work that way ... I also issued the shortest memo on record at ITT, which said: 'There will be no more long-range planning'.

HAROLD GENEEN
Business consultant and chairman of ITT
Managing

If we can't figure something out in three weeks, we probably shouldn't bother.

STEVEN GILBERT
Managing partner of Chemical Ventures, Inc.
Venture 1988

Everything someone does on a daily basis should be traceable back to an annual or quarterly plan.

RICHARD E GRIGGS
US founder of MANFIT
Black Enterprise 1988

Good results without good planning come from good luck, not good management.

DAVID JAQUITH
President of Vega Industries, Inc.
Quoted in R Alec Mackenzie, *The Time Trap*

Business plans may be great for bankers and investors, but if companies really followed them, you might never have heard of Compaq, Lotus or Ben & Jerry's.

ERIK LARSON
US business writer
Inc. Magazine 1987

The weather forecast has no effect on the weather but the economics forecast may well affect the economy.

JOHN MASON
British diplomat and business executive
Presidential address made to the British
Association, 1983

Good people can fix a lot of flaws in poor planning, but it's never the other way round.

ROLAND SHMITT
Senior vice-president of General Electric Co.
Government Executive 1987

Men don't plan to fail – they fail to plan.

WILLIAM J SIEGEL
Vice-president of Printz-Biederman
Manufacturing Co.
Saying exhibited on desk

We *forecast*. Magicians and fortune-tellers *predict*.

ROBERT H SMITH
CEO of The Futures Group
Manhattan, Inc. 1990

Amid a multitude of projects, no plan is devised.

PUBLIUS SYRUS 1ST CENTURY BC
Roman writer
Maxims

What short-term CEO will take a long-term view when it lowers his own income? Only a saint, and there aren't very many saints.

LESTER C THUROW
US academic
Newsweek 1981

Somebody's got to be the guardian of the long term.

MARINA V N WHITMAN
Vice-president of General Motors
Forbes 1988

FRAUD
(SEE ALSO CRIME AND CORRUPTION; HONESTY; THEFT AND PIRACY)

There is incontrovertible evidence that the whole of the $17.5 million put up to develop the de Lorean two-seater sports-car was misappropriated. And nobody noticed. It is the only time in the whole of my professional career that I have met a case where the entire capital subscribed to develop a project was misappropriated. And nobody noticed. Because nobody looked ... We as receivers thought some of it was likely to go astray, but it never crossed our mind that the company had got nothing.

KENNETH CORK
British senior partner at Cork Gully
Cork on Cork

A man is his own easiest dupe, for what he wishes to be true he generally believes to be true.

DEMOSTHENES c. 384–322 BC
Greek orator
Third Olynthiac

Men have been swindled by other men on many occasions. The autumn of 1929 was, perhaps, the first occasion when men succeeded on a large scale in swindling themselves.

J K GALBRAITH
US diplomat, economist, and writer
The Great Crash, 1929

A bad forgery's the ultimate insult.

JONATHAN GASH
British writer
Remark by the antique-dealer hero of the
television series *Lovejoy* 1981

In the majority of fiddles, it is not the experts who discover them but disgruntled mistresses and colleagues.

KENNETH NEWMAN
Commissioner of the Metropolitan Police
Daily Mail 1988

It was beautiful and simple as all truly great swindles are.

O HENRY 1862–1910
US writer
'Octopus Marooned'

FREE MARKET ECONOMY

Protectionist barriers are to economies what steroids are to athletes – a temporary fix and a long term disaster.

ROBERT ALLEN
Chairman of ITT
Fortune 1990

The trouble about a free market economy is that it requires so many policemen to make it work.

NEIL ASCHERSON
British journalist
Observer 1985

The call for free trade is as unavailing as the cry of a spoiled child for the moon. It never has existed; it never will exist.

HENRY CLAY 1777–1852
US statesman
Speech before the Senate, 1832

We Asians are the original Conservatives because for thousands of years we have believed in free enterprise ... you have just stolen our philosophy.

JAYVANTSINNJI GOHEL 1915–1995
Chairman of the Anglo-Asian Conservative Society
Said to Margaret Thatcher, quoted in *Guardian* 1995

In the long run, free trade benefits everyone; in the short run it is bound to produce much pain.

HENRY HOBHOUSE
British writer
Seeds of Change

The right are in the contradictory position of endorsing the freedoms of the market while seeking to limit those freedoms when they are enacted socially. While the market promises flexibility, this flexibility puts unbearable pressure on the rigid moral system that they are currently proposing.

SUZANNE MOORE
British journalist
Guardian 1995

Free enterprise is a rough and competitive game. It is a hell of a lot better than a government monopoly.

RONALD REAGAN
40th president of the USA
Speech to the National Association of
Manufacturers, New York, 1972

The man who accepts the laissez-faire doctrine would allow his garden to run wild so that the roses might fight it out with the weeds and the fittest might survive.

JOHN RUSKIN 1819–1900
English art critic and social observer
Attributed

A woman whose dresses are made in Paris and whose marriage has been made in Heaven might be equally biased for and against free imports.

SAKI 1870–1916
Burmese-born British writer
The Unbearable Bassington

Japan's economic miracle was made possible because the rest of us were ready to keep our markets open to you.

MARGARET THATCHER
British prime minister
Quoted in *Financial Weekly* 1989

We've got so much taxation. I don't know of a single foreign product that enters this country untaxed except the answer to prayer.

MARK TWAIN 1835–1910
US writer
Speech, 1906

There is no power on earth like the power of the free marketplace and governments hate it because they cannot control it.

WALTER WRISTON
Chairman of Citicorp Bank
Quoted in Anthony Sampson, *The Money Lenders*

FRIENDS AND ENEMIES
(*SEE ALSO* COMPETITORS)

A friend in power is a friend lost.

HENRY BROOKS ADAMS 1838–1918
US historian and novelist.
Education of Henry Adams

Keep your friends close, but keep your enemies closer.

Sicilian proverb

There is little friendship in the world, and least of all between equals.

FRANCIS BACON 1561–1626
English politician, philosopher, and essayist
'Of Followers and Friends' in *Essays*

What matters is working with a few close friends, people you respect, knowing that if times did turn bad these people would hold together.

RICHARD BRANSON
Entrepreneur and founder of Virgin Group
Telegraph Weekend Magazine, 1980

From the foundation of character, we build and maintain Win/Win relationships. The trust, the Emotional Bank Account, is the essence of Win/Win. Without trust, the best we can do is compromise; without trust, we lack the basic credibility for open, mutual learning and communication and real creativity.

STEPHEN R COVEY
Founder of the Institute of
Principle-Centred Leadership
The Seven Habits of Highly Effective People

If you want to make peace, you don't talk to your friends. You talk to your enemies.

MOSHE DAYAN 1915–1981
Israeli general
Quoted in William and Leonard Safire, *Good Advice*

A man, Sir, should keep his friendship in constant repair.

SAMUEL JOHNSON 'DR JOHNSON' 1709–1784
English man of letters and lexicographer
Quoted in James Boswell, *Life of Johnson*

All things being equal, people will buy from a friend. All things being not quite so equal, people will *still* buy from a friend.

MARK McCORMACK
Founder of International Management Group
What They Don't Teach You At Harvard Business School

One doesn't have to be a stinker to be effective. But no chairman of Lloyd's can have any friends as such.

PETER MILLER
Chairman of Lloyd's
Today 1989

Money couldn't buy friends but you got a better class of enemy.

SPIKE MILLIGAN
British comic and humourist
Puckoon

One of our ironclad rules is 'Never do business with anybody you don't like.' If you don't like somebody, there's a reason. Chances are it's probably because you don't trust him, and you're probably right. I don't care who it is or what guarantees you get – cash in advance or whatever. If you do business with somebody you don't like, sooner or later you'll get screwed.

HENRY V QUADRACCI
US CEO of Quad/Graphics
Inc. Magazine 1987

It was a friendship founded on business, which is a good deal better than a business founded on friendship.

JOHN D ROCKEFELLER 1839–1937
US millionaire industrialist and philanthropist
John Ensor Harr and Peter J Johnson,
The Rockefeller Century

Don't hit at all if it is honorably possible to avoid hitting; but *never* hit soft.

THEODORE ROOSEVELT 1859–1919
26th president of the USA
Quoted in Bishop, *Theodore Roosevelt*

If you humiliate people publicly, they may support you publicly, but they will hate you privately.

VERNON WALTERS
US ambassador to the United Nations
Observation made during *American Interest*,
television broadcast, 1987

A man cannot be too careful in the choice of his enemies.

OSCAR WILDE 1854–1900
Irish poet, dramatist, and wit
The Picture of Dorian Gray

FUTURE
(*SEE ALSO* FORECASTING AND PLANNING; VISION)

I recalled an old epigram which had often comforted me, that the future comes one day at a time.

DEAN ACHESON 1891–1971
US politician
Present at the Creation

Prediction is very difficult, especially about the future.

NEILS BOHR 1885–1962
Danish Nobel laureate of physics
Favourite saying

You can never plan the future by the past.

EDMUND BURKE 1729–1797
Irish statesman and political theorist
A Letter ... to a Member of the National Assembly

Study the past, if you would divine the future.

CONFUCIUS 551–479 BC
Chinese philosopher
Analects

There is no data on the future.

LAUREL CUTLER
US vice-chairman of FBC/Leber Katz Partners
Inc. Magazine 1987

Predicting the future is easy. It's trying to figure out what's going on now that's hard.

FRITZ R S DRESSLER
US president of FRS Dressler Associates
New York Times 1987

The future never just happened. It was created.

WILL AND ARIEL DURANT
1885–1981; 1898–1981
US historians
The Lessons of History

I never think of the future. It comes soon enough.

ALBERT EINSTEIN 1879–1955
Physicist and formulator of the theories of relativity
Interview, 1930

The future is not inevitable. We can influence it, if we know what we want it to be. That conviction is the reason for this book. We can and should be in charge of our own destinies in a time of change.

CHARLES HANDY
Business executive and writer, and
professor at the London Business School
The Age of Unreason

Of all men's miseries the bitterest is this, to know so much and to have control over nothing.

HERODOTUS c. 484–424 BC
Greek historian
Histories

The best way to predict the future is to invent it.

ALAN KAY
Director of research at Apple Computer Co.
Quoted in Craig R Hickman and Michael A Silva,
Creating Excellence

GAMBLING AND LOTTERIES

The [UK] National Lottery is trash, a sleazy, low-life Treasury rip-off, a scummy exercise in triple taxation that demeans and infantilizes everything it touches.

BRYAN APPLEYARD
British journalist
Independent 1995

The urge to gamble is so universal and its practise so pleasurable that I assume it must be evil.

HEYWOOD BROUN 1888–1939
US writer
All About Money

At gambling, the deadly sin is to mistake bad play for bad luck.

IAN FLEMING 1908–1964
British writer and creator of James Bond
Casino Royale

Honest bread is very well – it's the butter that makes the temptation.

DOUGLAS JERROLD 1803–1857
British dramatist
The Catspaw

All life is six to five against.

DAMON RUNYON 1888–1946
US writer
Money from Home

There is no moral difference between gambling at cards or in lotteries or on the race track and gambling in the stock-market. One method is just as pernicious to the body politic as the other kind, and in degree the evil worked is far greater.

THEODORE ROOSEVELT 1858–1919
26th president of the USA
Message to Congress, 1908

Adventure upon all the tickets in the lottery, and you lose for certain; and the greater the number of your tickets the nearer your approach to this certainty.

ADAM SMITH 1723–1790
Scottish economist and philosopher
The Wealth of Nations

A lottery is a tax on imbeciles.

Traditional Italian saying

GOD AND MAMMON

If you would know what the Lord God thinks of money, you have only to look at those to whom He gives it.

MAURICE BARING 1874–1945
English writer
Quoted by Dorothy Parker in Malcolm Cowley
(ed, first series), *Writers at Work*

It is easier for a camel to go through the eye of a needle, than for a rich man to enter the kingdom of God.

BIBLE
Matthew 19:24

Mammon, the god of the world's leading religion. His chief temple is the holy city of New York.

AMBROSE BIERCE 1842–c. 1914
US writer
Devil's Dictionary

They [the clergy] can no more pontificate on economics than the Pope could correct Galileo on physics.

JOHN SELWYN GUMMER
British politician
Said with reference to the clergy's comments
on the Conservative Party's economic policy,
The Times 1984

Work hard and say your prayers.

CHRISTOPHER HEATH
Merchant banker with Barings Securities
Said when he was Britain's highest-paid executive,
Daily Mail 1987

I believe in God, family, and McDonald's and in the office that order is reversed.

RAY KROC 1902–1984
Founder of McDonald's
Quoted in John F Love, *McDonald's:
Behind the Arches*

Love your neighbour is not merely sound Christianity; it is good business.

DAVID LLOYD GEORGE 1863–1945
British prime minister
Quoted in *Observer* 1921

Better authentic mammon than a bogus god.

LOUIS MACNEICE 1907–1963
Irish-born English poet
Autumn Journal

Our ambition is not business, but to love God. To love God, one must live. To live, one must balance one's budget.

DOM SEBASTIAN
US abbot at Nôtre Dame des Dombes monastery
On the monastery's money-making business,
Fortune 1995

I was lucky. I learned about the business world at the feet of two outstanding men whose business ethos was their belief not that God helped those who helped themselves but that God helped those who helped their fellow men.

LORD SIEFF
Honorary president of Marks and Spencer plc
Management the Marks and Spencer Way

We have the highest authority for believing that the meek shall inherit the Earth; though I have never found any particular corroboration of this aphorism in the records of Somerset House.

F E SMITH 1872–1930
British politician, lawyer, and orator
'Marquess Curzon' in *Contemporary Personalities*

You find people ready enough to do the Samaritan, without the oil and twopence.

SYDNEY SMITH 1771–1845
English journalist, clergyman, and wit
Quoted in Lady Holland, *Memoirs*

It's very difficult to be a practising Hindu and a capitalist, but I try to put some of my spiritual beliefs into my business. I don't think God minds you making money as long as you spend it wisely.

ISAAC TIGRETT
Founder of Hard Rock Café
Evening Standard 1988

No one would have remembered the Good Samaritan if he'd only had good intentions. He had money as well.

MARGARET THATCHER
British prime minister
Quoted in *Observer* 1980

How different would our economy be if recruits were to 'seek first God's kingdom and his righteousness' instead of storing up treasure on earth.

RICHARD WILKINS
British general secretary of the
Association of Christian Teachers
Daily Telegraph 1995

'GOING FOR IT'
(SEE ALSO AMBITION; SUCCESS)

Every team needs a mad bomber with the conscience of a rattlesnake.

JOHNNY BACH
Coach with the Chicago Bulls basketball team
New York Times 1993

A lot of people have made a lot of money out of me, and I've decided that I'm going to be one of them.

JOAN COLLINS
British-born US actress
Observer 1085

Being aggressive is a lot less risky in the end. Are you going to eat your lunch, or have your lunch eaten for you?

WILLIAM T ESREY
US chairman of The Sprint Corporation
New York Times 1992

You've got to take the initiative and play *your* game. In a decisive set, confidence is the difference.

CHRIS EVERT
US tennis player
Quoted in William Safire, *Safire's Words of Wisdom*

A Three-Sentence Course on Business Management: You read a book from the beginning to the end. You run a business the opposite way. You start with the end, and then you do everything you must to reach it.

HAROLD GENEEN
Business writer and chairman of ITT
Managing

The idea is to grind the opposition into the ground. That's on and off the table.

BARRY HEARN
Snooker promoter
Interview, *Independent* 1989

God gives every bird his worm, but He does not throw it into the nest.

P D JAMES
British novelist
Devices and Desires

Mission statements are the operational, ethical and financial guiding lights of a company. They are not simply mottoes or slogans; they articulate the goals, dreams, behaviour, culture and strategies of companies.

PATRICIA JONES AND LARRY KAHANER
US authors
Say It and Live It: The 50 Corporate Mission Statements That Hit The Mark

When the going gets tough, the tough get going.

JOSEPH P KENNEDY 1888–1969
US industrialist and diplomat
Favourite saying of the Kennedy family, quoted in
J H Cutler, *Honey Fitz*

Aim higher. Network and support other people on the way – they might be the future leaders. Develop a thick skin. Get your image sorted: it matters. Always challenge things you don't understand or agree with. And be cheeky. Just go and ask, go and make yourself known.

CHRISTINE KING
Vice chancellor of Staffordshire University
Tips for getting to the top, *Cosmopolitan* 1995

Winning isn't everything, but wanting to win is.

VINCE LOMBARDI 1913–1970
US football coach
Esquire 1962

It is not enough to succeed; others must fail.

MAURICE SAATCHI
Advertising guru and co-founder of
Saatchi & Saatchi
Saying originally attributed to Genghis Khan,
adopted by Saatchi

Eagles come in all shapes and sizes, but you will recognize them chiefly by their attitudes. With things crumbling around them, they still will have some optimism. They haven't given up. They have ideas, plans and solutions to problems ... Remember, eagles don't flock.

CHARLES SCOTT
CEO of Intermark
Inc. Magazine's Guide to Small Business Success

There are two things to aim at in life: first, to get what you want; and, after that, to enjoy it. Only the wisest of mankind achieve the second.

LOGAN PEARSALL SMITH 1865–1946
US-born British writer
Afterthoughts

Never make concessions.

GERTRUDE STEIN 1874–1946
US author
Favourite saying, quoted in
Independent Magazine 1995

The trouble with the rat race is that even if you win, you're still a rat.

LILY TOMLIN
US comedienne and actress
Omni 1988

We're gonna stay on until the end of the world. And when that day comes we'll cover it, play *Nearer My God To Thee*, and sign off.

TED TURNER
US founder of CNN
Quoted in Douglas K Ramsey,
The Corporate Warriors

Nothing is impossible for the man who doesn't have to do it himself.

A H WEILER
US newspaper editor
Memorandum circulated at *New York Times*, 1968

We have only one enemy, and that in funk.

JAMES McNEILL WHISTLER 1834–1903
US painter
Favourite saying, quoted by Walter Sickert in
'The Naked and the Nude', *New Age* 1910

GOVERNMENT
(*SEE ALSO* POLITICS AND POLITICIANS; PUBLIC OFFICE)

The government solution to a problem is usually as bad as the problem.

MILTON FRIEDMAN
US economist
Attributed

Well, fancy giving money to the Government!/ Might as well have put it down the drain./ Fancy giving money to the Government!/ Nobody will see the stuff again.

A P HERBERT 1890–1971
British writer and politician
'Too Much!'

I think it's the most backbreaking job in government and indeed it has broken the back of nearly everyone who had held it since the war.

ROY JENKINS
British chancellor of the Exchequer
On being chancellor of the Exchequer,
Observer 1967

The Conservative party has never believed that the business of government is the government of business.

NIGEL LAWSON
British chancellor of the Exchequer
House of Commons, 1981

But the point about government is that no one has control. Lots of people have the power to stop something happening – but almost nobody has the power to *make* anything happen. We have a system of government with the engine of a lawn-mower and the brakes of a Rolls-Royce.

JONATHAN LYNN AND ANTHONY JAY
British writers
From the *Yes, Prime Minister* television series

One way to make sure crime doesn't pay would be to let the government run it.

RONALD REAGAN
40th president of the USA
Interview, 1967

Englishmen never will be slaves: they are free to do whatever the Government and public opinion allow them to do.

GEORGE BERNARD SHAW 1856–1950
Irish dramatist and critic
Man and Superman

You can't expect a viable economy if the only object of government policy is to be re-elected every four years.

LORD WEINSTOCK
Managing director of GEC
Independent 1986

The Treasury could not, with any marked success, run a fish and chip shop.

HAROLD WILSON 1916–1995
British prime minister
Quoted in *Observer* 1984

GREED AND SELF-INTEREST

Don't expect businessmen to protect any interest other than their own.

NEIL ASCHERSON
British journalist
Independent on Sunday 1995

Greed has been severely underestimated and denigrated – unfairly in my opinion. I mean there's nothing wrong with avarice as a motive, as long as it doesn't lead to dishonest or anti-social conduct.

CONRAD BLACK
Canadian newspaper proprietor
UK Press Gazette 1985

In an age of credulity, no authority can compare with that which promises to make you money. Management gurus can demand anything of their followers, starting with huge fees.

ANDREW BROWN AND PAUL VALLELY
British journalists
Independent 1995

All sensible people are selfish, and nature is tugging at every contract to make the terms of it fair.

RALPH WALDO EMERSON 1803–1882
US philosopher and poet
'Considerations by the Way' in *The Conduct of Life*

Spare all I have, and take my life.

GEORGE FARQUHAR 1677–1707
Irish dramatist
Beaux Stratagem

Proper responsible selfishness involves a purpose and a goal ... Diminish that goal, displace it or, worst of all, disallow it and we remove all incentive to learn or to change. Proper selfishness, however, recognizes that the goal needs to be tuned to the goals of the group, or the organization, or society, as well as being in line with our own needs and our own talents. Only improper selfishness sets goals at odds with the bits of humanity that matter to oneself.

CHARLES HANDY
Business executive and writer, and professor at the London Business School
The Age of Unreason

Even wisdom has to yield to self-interest.

PINDAR c. 518–438 BC
Greek poet
Pythian Odes

Why is altruism in business seen as suspect? Private greed never automatically translates into public benefit. The word love is never mentioned in big business.

ANITA RODDICK
British entrepreneur and founder
of The Body Shop
Daily Mail 1987

We have always known that heedless self-interest was bad morals; we now know that it is bad economics.

FRANKLIN D ROOSEVELT 1882–1945
32nd president of the USA
Speech, 1937

If human vices such as greed and envy are systematically cultivated, the inevitable result is nothing less than the collapse of intelligence. A man driven by greed and envy loses the power of seeing things as they really are, of seeing things in their roundness and wholeness, and his very successes become failures.

E F SCHUMACHER 1911–1977
German-born British economist
Small is Beautiful

Greed is right! Greed works! Greed will save the USA.

OLIVER STONE
US film director and writer
Said by Michael Douglas playing Wall Street
raider Gordon Gekko in the film *Wall Street* 1987

The greatest motivator known to man is greed and there's nothing wrong with greed as long as it's harnessed properly.

PETER WOOD
Chief executive of Direct Line Insurance
Quoted in *BusinessAge* 1995

GREEN CONSUMERISM

Undoubtedly competition involves waste. What human activity does not? ... There are wastes of competition which do not develop but kill. These the law can and should eliminate, by regulating competition.

LOUIS DEMBITZ BRANDEIS 1856–1941
US Supreme Court justice
Brandeis: A Free Man's Life

After one look at this planet any visitor from outer space would say 'I WANT TO SEE THE MANAGER.'

WILLIAM S BURROUGHS
US writer
'Women: A Biological Mistake?' in *Adding Machine*

The danger is that consumers will begin to see it all [promotion of environment-friendly goods] as a great green con. The cynicism of the majority is in danger of undermining the good work of a number of companies.

ANDREW DAVIDSON
Editor of *Marketing*
On companies that oversell the 'greenness' of
their products, *Sunday Times* 1989

The earth only has so much bounty to offer and inventing ever larger and more notional prices for that bounty does not change its real value.

BEN ELTON
British writer and comedian
Stark

No matter how well intentioned the consumer is ... [he or she] will not buy a product that doesn't taste good. Quality must come first.

JO FAIRLEY
Journalist and partner of Green and
Black's chocolate company
Importing Today 1995

It is difficult not to be extreme when one can see man's activity infecting the world like some horrible, pervasive and progressive disease.

JAMES GOLDSMITH
British financier
Financial Weekly 1989

I have to say that it is perfectly reasonable to me that we should need to destroy large parts of the beautiful countryside, because there isn't a single thing in this country – not a hospital, not a school, not a road – that you can build without destroying large parts of beautiful countryside.

LORD HANSON
Business executive and chairman of
Hanson plc
Spectator 1989

Of course it is better to buy recycled paper and lead-free petrol but it is even better to use less paper and less petrol. The logic of big business is that it must promote consumption. We suspect that however green tinted companies become, they will find it hard to encourage people to consume less.

LINDA HENDRY
Spokesperson for British Green Party
Guardian 1988

There is no wealth creation which doesn't take something out of the natural environment.

PRINCE PHILIP
Duke of Edinburgh
Speech at the Royal Society of Arts Environmental
Management Awards reception, 1995

Green consumerism is a target for exploitation. There's a lot of green froth on top, but murkiness lurks underneath.

JONATHAN PORRITT
Director of Friends of the Earth
Speech at a Friends of the Earth conference, 1989

Study how a society uses its land, and you can come to pretty reliable conclusions as to what its future will be.

E F SCHUMACHER 1911–1977
German-born British economist
Small is Beautiful

GROWTH AND EXPANSION

The greater the rate of company expansion, the easier it is to find valuable new jobs for people.

ED BERSOFF
Founder of BTG, Inc.
Inc. Magazine 1987

If it's not growing, it's going to die.

MICHAEL EISNER
CEO of Walt Disney Productions
Remark made during *60 Minutes*,
CBS TV broadcast, 1987

Size works against excellence.

BILL GATES
Founder of Microsoft
Quoted in Tom Peters, *Liberation Management*

If we have had a formula for growth it has been: start with the best; learn from the best, expand slowly and solidify our position; then horizontally diversify our expertise.

MARK MCCORMACK
Founder of the International Management Group
*What They Don't Teach You
at Harvard Business School*

Matushita's strategic assumption is that profits are linked to growth and that investments which promote growth will eventually pay off in profits *over the long term*.

**RICHARD T PASCALE AND
ANTHONY G ATHOS**
US academics
The Art of Japanese Management

We don't want to spend a lot of management time on things that don't fit our growth scenario.

PETER L SCOTT
Chairman of Emhart Corp.
Sky 1987

How does an industrial giant act as it grows? First, management concludes that a company cannot depend on individuals. After all, they have personalities and finite life spans. A corporation is supposed to be impersonal and eternal. Next thing you know, committees and task forces and working groups are spewing out procedures and regulations and stomping out individuality and spontaneity.

> **RICARDO SEMLER**
> Brazilian CEO of Semco
> *Maverick*

There will always be ... limiting processes. When one source of limitation is removed or made weaker, growth returns until a new source of limitation is encountered.

> **PETER M SENGE**
> Business academic and director of the
> organizational learning programme at MIT
> *The Fifth Discipline: The Art and Practice of the*
> *Learning Organization*

To achieve this growth, a short term orientation and dividend policy was bypassed in favour of an environment that supported a long term corporate strategy.

> **TOMOTSU YAMAGUCHI**
> Japanese banker
> On Japanese companies during the past 40 years,
> *The Academy of Management Executive* 1988

HEALTH
(*SEE ALSO* PRESSURE AND STRESS)

In business, paranoia is not a psychosis, it's reality; it's probably survival.

> **FRED ADLER**
> US CEO of Adler & Co.
> *Inc. Magazine* 1987

The best of wages will not compensate for excessively long working hours which undermine health.

> **LOUIS DEMBITZ BRANDEIS** 1856–1941
> US Supreme Court justice
> Quoted in Lief, *Brandeis: The Personal*
> *History of an American Ideal*

The trouble about always trying to preserve the health of the body is that it is so difficult to do without destroying the health of the mind.

> **G K CHESTERTON** 1874–1936
> English writer
> *Come to Think of It*

After the heart attack I thought: 'God all those years of not drinking and eating rice and this happens'. Kerry Packer [chairman of Consolidated Press Holdings] used to say to me: 'Your diet won't make you live longer, it will just seem longer'.

> **BRUCE GYNGELL**
> Chairman of TV-am
> *Daily Mail* 1988

A fit staff means a fit company. Fundamentally we are animals. We need exercise.

> **RALPH HALPERN**
> Chairman of Burton Group
> Commenting on the installation of a gymnasium
> for the company's directors, *Daily Mail* 1986

If you actually wanted an unhealthy life, the life of a leading businessman is just about as unhealthy as you can have. I don't have to, but I do eat caviar and chips at lunch time and dinner twice a day. I'm invariably entertaining. I drink and am offered drinks the whole time; I'm whisked from here to there by cars, by aeroplanes. I stagger to my feet and walk a few yards from time to time.

> **JOHN HARVEY-JONES**
> Business writer and chairman of ICI
> Quoted in David Lomax, *The Money Makers*

If you mean to keep as well as possible, the less you think about your health the better.

OLIVER WENDELL HOLMES SR 1809–1894
US physician, academic, and writer
Over the Teacups

Too much work and too much energy kill a man just as effectively as too much assorted vice or too much drink.

RUDYARD KIPLING 1865–1936
English writer
'Thrown Away' in *Plain Tales from the Hills*

I find that a change of nuisances is as good as a vacation.

DAVID LLOYD GEORGE 1863–1945
British prime minister
Attributed

The idea that ill-health is embodied in bricks and mortar is absurdly reductionist. Yes, poor air and dirty working conditions can undermine our strength and irritate us all. A grim office can be life-sappingly depressing. But the fault does not lie in the fabric alone. Instead of bulldozing 'sick' buildings, a better way of improving lives might be to quarantine the people running them.

EDWARD PILKINGTON
British journalist
On 'sick building syndrome', blamed by
many as the cause of a physical malaise
suffered by some office workers and thought
to be caused by such things as insulating
materials and paint, *Guardian* 1995

If I were a medical man, I should prescribe a holiday to any patient who considered his work important.

BERTRAND RUSSELL 1872–1970
English philosopher and mathematician
Conquest of Happiness

Executives feel pressure from their bosses to outwork colleagues and build their image and career. By this reasoning, having a heart attack because of work leads to true glory and keeling over at the office is even better – a sign, a Calvinist might say, of being among the Elect.

RICARDO SEMLER
Brazilian CEO of Semco
Maverick

Early to rise and early to bed makes a male healthy and wealthy and dead.

JAMES THURBER 1894–1961
US writer and cartoonist
'The Shrike and the Chipmunks' in
Fables for Our Time

HIRING AND FIRING
(*SEE ALSO* INTERVIEWS AND JOB HUNTING; REDUNDANCY AND RESIGNATION)

In hiring we almost never look at intrinsic motivation.

TERESA AMABILE
US academic
Journal of Personality and Social Psychology 1985

I have never been able to select quality employees in advance. I have learned, however, how to get rid of the poor and mediocre ones.

RAMONA E F ARNETT
President of Ramona Enterprises, Inc.
Speech, New York, 1979

Begin by recruiting meticulously. 'Garbage in – garbage out' applies to the people in your organization as well as data.

JAMES A BELASCO
US academic and management consultant
Teaching the Elephant to Dance

We hired the wrong people ... because we were in such a hurry to fill those positions.

LYNN TENDLER BIGNELL
US founder of Gilbert Tween Associates
Inc. Magazine 1987

I'm not hiring for where I am: I'm hiring for where I'll be.

FRED BRAMANTE JR
CEO of Daddy's Junky Music Shops, Inc.
Inc. Magazine 1987

In business there seems to be more excuses for not doing things. In the England team if you don't perform for a number of games, you get dropped. That's the big difference.

WILL CARLING
England rugby team captain and
management consultant
Quoted in *BusinessAge* 1995

I was told that the decision to demote me was taken in part because I was too polite to my staff – the Harrods policy of treating their staff was to tread on their fingers and clip their balls.

SUSAN CORKER
Employee of Harrods
On taking Harrods to an industrial tribunal,
quoted in *BusinessAge* 1995

Personnel selection is a political act and a proper concern for national policy.

LEE J CRONBACH
US industrial psychologist
Public Personnel Management 1980

When business is bad, always start weeding out at the top.

GRAHAM DAY
Chairman and CEO of The Rover Group plc
and director of Cadbury Schweppes plc
Sunday Times 1989

Well sometimes you just don't like somebody.

HENRY FORD II 1917–1987
US car manufacturer
On sacking Lee Iacocca from the chairmanship of
Ford Motor Company, quoted in Iacocca's
Autobiography

It is very seldom that you are fired for your own inadequacy. More often than not you are fired because your managers got it wrong.

JOHN HARVEY-JONES
Business writer and chairman of ICI
Managing to Survive

If you aren't fired with enthusiasm, you will be fired with enthusiasm.

VINCE LOMBARDI 1913–1970
US football coach
Quoted in Rowes, *The Book of Quotes*

People are rarely fired for incompetence. It's not getting along that's almost always the underlying reason for dismissal.

STUART MARGULIES
US industrial psychologist
Speech, New York, 1988

It is the inescapable duty of management to fire incompetent people. This duty is often shirked. When you have to fire, have the guts to get on with it. You will be surprised how often the victim is relieved.

DAVID OGILVY
Advertising guru and founder
of Ogilvy and Mather
Daily Telegraph 1969

A company in need of a messiah is also a company in a hurry. Eager to find a hero, the search committee often puts more energy into persuading the candidate to take the job than into considering how well he will mesh with the company.

PATRICIA O'TOOLE
US management consultant and business writer
Corporate Messiah

No particular method of selecting officials will produce officers who are best suited for the job.

C NORTHCOTE PARKINSON
British historian, writer, and
formulator of Parkinson's law
Parkinson's Law and Other Studies in Administration

Give a lot, expect a lot, and if you don't get it, prune.

TOM PETERS
US international management consultant
and bestselling business author
Thriving on Chaos

... hiring attitudes, not credentials.

TOM PETERS
US international management consultant
and bestselling business author
Recipe for success, *Independent on Sunday* 1995

Before people are hired or promoted to leadership positions, they are interviewed and approved by all who will be working for them. And every six months managers are evaluated by those who work under them. The results are posted for all to see. Does this mean workers can fire their bosses? I guess it does, since anyone who consistently gets bad grades usually leaves Semco, one way or another.

RICARDO SEMLER
Brazilian CEO of Semco
Maverick

I fired him [General MacArthur] because he wouldn't respect the authority of the President. That's the answer to that. I didn't fire him because he was a dumb son-of-a-bitch, although he was, but that's not against the law for generals. If it was, half to three-quarters of them would be in jail.

HARRY S TRUMAN 1884–1972
33rd president of the USA
On sacking General MacArthur, quoted
in *Plain Speaking*

Hire good people and let 'em do their jobs. Otherwise, why hire 'em?

BILL VEECK
US baseball club owner
Veeck as in Wreck

Hiring and firing are costly – but it is infinitely more costly to have a marginal or barely average man on the company rolls for 30 years.

GORDON W WHEELING
US personnel manager
Leadership in the Office

If the tests were rigorously applied across the board today, half of the most dynamic men in business would be out walking the streets for a job.

WALTER H WHYTE
US social critic and writer
On employment tests, *Fortune* 1954

HOME AND FAMILY LIFE

I need some peace and quiet at home.

BERNARD APPEL
US president, Radio Shack
Explaining why he refuses to go to meetings
before 8 am, *Computer and Software News* 1987

He that hath wife and children hath given hostages to fortune.

FRANCIS BACON 1561–1626
English politician, philosopher, and essayist
'Of Marriage and the Single Life' in *Essays*

Children sweeten labours, but they make misfortunes more bitter.

FRANCIS BACON 1561–1626
English politician, philosopher, and essayist
'Of Parents and Children' in *Essays*

Each [wife] was jealous and resentful of my preoccupation with business. Yet none showed any visible aversion to sharing in the proceeds.

J PAUL GETTY 1892–1976
US millionaire oil executive
Of his wives, in *As I See It*

What's the good of a home, if you are never in it?

GEORGE AND WEEDON GROSSMITH
1847–1912; 1854–1919
British writers and entertainers
Diary of a Nobody

To be happy at home is the ultimate result of all ambition, the end to which every enterprise and labour tends, and of which every desire prompts the persecution.

SAMUEL JOHNSON 'DR JOHNSON' 1709–1784
English man of letters and lexicographer
The Rambler

When I hear a man talk about how hard he works, and how he hasn't taken a vacation in five years, and how seldom he sees his family I am certain that this man will not succeed in the creative aspects of business ... and most of the important things that have to be done are the result of creative acts.

HERMAN KRANNERT
Chairman of Inland Container Corp
The Forum 1969

Let's face it – the family has had it ... It has changed (very fast I think) from being a unit of production to being a unit of consumption. Since consumption can be an individual activity, the family no longer meets a crucial need.

SARA MAITLAND
British journalist
Guardian 1995

It's about money and greed. Wealthy barons are robbing the people of their leisure and worship time. This Government is destroying family life. No wonder immorality is so rampant.

JOHN ROBERTS
General secretary of the Lord's Day Observance Society
On Home Office plans to legalize charging for admission to dances on Sundays *Guardian* 1995

Perpetual devotion to what a man calls his business is only to be sustained by perpetual neglect of many other things.

ROBERT LOUIS STEVENSON 1850–1894
Scottish novelist and poet
Virginibus Puerisque

The worst wives (from the standpoint of the effect on their husbands) in my experience are the overly ambitious ones. They seem to be constantly after their husbands to make more money. They don't understand that money, like prestige, if sought directly, is almost never gained. It must come as a byproduct of some worthwhile objective or result which is sought and achieved for its own sake.

ROBERT TOWNSEND
CEO of Avis
Up the Organization

Everybody's always talking about people breaking into houses ... but there are more people in the world who want to break out of houses.

THORNTON WILDER 1897–1975
US writer
The Matchmaker

What businessmen seem particularly bad at is realizing that you cannot buy relationships. Money and patronage will make a bad relationship bearable, or a mediocre one tolerable, but expensive presents and a gin and Jaguar environment do not of themselves make for love and understanding.

HENRY BERIC WRIGHT
Medical adviser to the Institute of Directors
Yorkshire Post 1973

HONESTY
(*SEE ALSO* CRIME AND CORRUPTION; EXPEDIENCE; FRAUD; THEFT AND PIRACY)

It is difficult but not impossible to conduct strictly honest business. What is true is that honesty is incompatible with the amassing of a large fortune.

MAHATMA GANDHI 1869–1948
Indian nationalist leader
Non-Violence in Peace and War

It is always the best policy to speak the truth, unless of course you are an exceptionally good liar.

JEROME K JEROME 1859–1927
English writer
The Idler

There are few ways in which a man can be more innocently employed than in getting money.

SAMUEL JOHNSON 'DR JOHNSON' 1709–1784
English man of letters and lexicographer
Quoted in James Boswell, *Life of Johnson*

Honesty is a good thing but it is not profitable to its possessor unless it is kept under control.

DON MARQUIS 1878–1937
US humorist and journalist
'archygrams'

Honesty is for the most part less profitable than dishonesty.

PLATO C. 427–347 BC
Greek philosopher
The Republic

I never heard of any real authority for any such proposition as that one owes full disclosure of the truth to all men at all times.

FREDERICK POLLOCK 1845–1937
English jurist and legal scholar
From the *The Holmes-Pollock Letters: The correspondence of Mr Justice Holmes and Sir Frederick Pollock 1874–1932*

If you tell the truth you don't have to remember anything.

MARK TWAIN 1835–1910
US writer
Notebook

IDEAS AND THE CREATIVE PROCESS

(*SEE ALSO* BRAINSTORMING; INNOVATION)

Never kill an idea, just deflect it.

Company slogan at 3M

Few ideas are in themselves practical. It is for want of imagination in applying them that they fail. The creative process does not end with an idea – it only starts with an idea.

JOHN ARNOLD
US academic
Business Week 1956

Even the 'best' ideas are only as good as their ability to attract attention in the social environment.

WARREN BENNIS AND BURT NANUS
Business academic and president of the University of Cincinnati; business academic and writer
Leaders: The Strategies for Taking Charge

The most creative ideas are those you can get other guys to think up.

LUD BOCK
US head councillor at Camp Arcady
Staff meeting, 1953

The contribution which the human mind makes to work and business is very much one of picking up information from tiny, seemingly insignificant trifles, and relating them to new concepts.

JOHN HARVEY-JONES
Business writer and chairman of ICI
Managing to Survive

We are trying to sell more and more intellect and less and less materials.

GEORGE HEGG
Vice-president of strategic planning, 3M
The Economist 1991

If it's a good idea ... go ahead and do it. It is much easier to apologize than it is to get permission.

GRACE MURRAY HOPPER
Retired US rear admiral
Speech, Washington DC, 1987

Never hesitate to steal a good idea.

AL NEUHARTH
US chairman of Gannett Company
Confessions of an S.O.B.

The best way to have a good idea is to have a lot of ideas.

LINUS PAULING
US chemist and peace activist
Quoted in John Peers, *1,001 Logical Laws*

Inspiring visions rarely (I'm tempted to say never) include numbers.

TOM PETERS
US international management consultant
and bestselling business author
Thriving on Chaos

Steve Wozniak couldn't get Hewlett-Packard to take an interest in small computers. He very reluctantly left to join Steve Jobs, who couldn't sell a similar idea to Atari. They formed Apple Computers.

GIFFORD PINCHOT III
The International Institute of Intrapreneurs
Intrapreneuring

Good ideas are not adopted automatically. They must be driven into practice with courageous patience.

HYMAN RICKOVER 1900–1989
US admiral
Quoted in Warren Bennis and Burt Nanus, *Leaders: The Strategies for Taking Charge*

You look at any giant corporation, and I mean the biggies, and they all started with a guy with an idea, doing it well.

IRVINE ROBBINS
Co-founder of Baskin-Robbins Ice Cream
Quoted in Carter Henderson, *Winners: The Successful Strategies Entrepreneurs Use to Build New Businesses*

IMAGE AND SELF-IMAGE

I don't change my style of dress when I go to lunch with my bankers.

RICHARD BRANSON
Entrepreneur and founder of the Virgin Group
who habitually wears jeans,
sports shirt, and sweater.
Quoted in Jeffrey Robinson, *The Money Makers*

It is the height of bad taste to have anything business-related in your briefcase. Briefcases are for taking the contents of the stationery cupboard home with you at the end of the day. Only photocopier repairmen have their work in their briefcases – 15 different screwdrivers, a copy of the *Sun* and a list of exotic, faraway locations where the vital missing part will have to be supplied from.

GUY BROWNING
British humorist
Guardian 1995

The more important, clear cut and highly paid the job, the shorter the title. The formula works for those born into roles which transcend pension schemes and annual holidays: Queen, princes and gods are the best examples. It also works for those like PMs, MDs, CEOs, VPs and DGs, who have earned their titles. (The latter group prefers abbreviations to stress they're too busy for time-consuming things like syllables.)

PAUL FISHER
British employment columnist
Guardian 1995

Many a man has busted in business because his necktie did not match his socks.

FRANK MCKINNEY ('KIN')
HUBBARD 1868–1930
US writer
Epigrams

As a general rule it is advisable to have your business dress say nothing about you – other than perhaps that your clothes fit.

MARK MCCORMACK
Founder of International Management Group
What They Don't Teach You at Harvard Business School

These guys don't write you a check just for wearing the right tie.

JOSEPH R PARELLA
US partner of Wasserstein, Parella & Co.
New York Times 1988

Women have a high lack of confidence ... It seems to be ingrained in our subconscious. But, in fact, women are just as capable. They just think they know less.

FIONA PRICE
British women's financial adviser
Cosmopolitan 1995

Trust the man who hesitates in his speech and is quick and steady in action, but beware of long arguments and long beards.

GEORGE SANTAYANA 1863–1952
Spanish-born American philosopher
Soliloquies in England

Dress codes are all about conformity. People want to feel secure, and dressing like everyone else is one way to accomplish it. If everyone at IBM wears blue suits and white shirts, then even a trainee will feel he is part of the company if he is so attired. But the flip side is that these same people will come to depend on other forms of artificially imposed unity, such as uniform language, uniform behavior, maybe even uniform thinking ... The more elaborate they are, the worse it is for flexibility and, ultimately, profits.

RICARDO SEMLER
Brazilian CEO of Semco
Maverick

'Think the unthinkable but wear a dark suit' is a handy maxim for the city.

KATHERINE WHITEHORN
British journalist
Observer 1987

Remember the City never forgives casual clothes. Whenever so-and-so's name comes up, people don't mention the quality of his thought or the pungency of his prose. They say: 'Wasn't he the fellow who wore suede shoes to the Bank of England?'.

L D WILLIAMS
City editor for the *Daily Mail*
Said to his successor, Patrick Sergeant,
quoted in *Daily Mail*

INCENTIVE AND MOTIVATION
(*SEE ALSO* BONUSES AND GIFTS)

By receiving praise for each small achievement, an individual gains confidence to try harder ... I believe that in order to be a good manager you must understand the value of *praising people to success*.

MARY KAY ASH
US entrepreneur and founder
of Mary Kay Cosmetics
Mary Kay on People Management

People want to feel that they have contributed to those things that affect their lives. When they don't, they feel slighted and manipulated.

MARY KAY ASH
US entrepreneur and founder
of Mary Kay Cosmetics
Mary Kay on People Management

Motivation will almost always beat mere talent.

NORMAN R AUGUSTINE
President and CEO of Martin Marietta Corp.
Augustine's Laws

If anything goes bad, I did it. If anything goes semi-good, then we did it. If anything goes real good, then you did it. That's all it takes to get people to win football games.

PAUL 'BEAR' BRYANT 1913–1983
US football coach
Quoted in *Bits & Pieces* 1987

If I understood too clearly what I was doing, where I was going, then I probably wasn't working on anything very interesting.

PETER CARRUTHERS
US physicist
New York Times

I praise loudly, I blame softly.

CATHERINE II 'THE GREAT' 1729–1796
Empress of Russia
Complete Works of Catherine II

To be truly motivated, one must make personal commitments.

WILLIAM G DYER
US academic
Strategies for Managing Change

Ego gratification is one of the worst traps devised to ensnare the successful businessman.

HAROLD GENEEN
Business consultant and chairman of ITT
Managing

You must keep people scared every day.

PETER GRACE
US CEO of W R Grace Co.
Financial World 1988

As an entrepreneurial startup company you look at the business like a racer doing a sprint. But as a company gets successful, you've got to get your people to realize that it's a marathon they're in.

TRIP HAWKINS
President of Electronic Arts, Inc.
Computer & Software News 1987

Favors are used to reward. Favors also are used to punish by reducing the initiative available to others. Giving or withholding favors is the lever of organizational power.

BRUCE HENDERSON
CEO of Boston Consulting Group, Inc.
Henderson on Corporate Strategy

Good words are worth much, and cost little.

GEORGE HERBERT 1593–1633
English cleric and writer
Jacula Prudentum

Speak softly and carry a big carrot.

HOWARD C LAUER
US assistant executive vice-president
of United Jewish Appeal Federation
Draft notes for his book

It's a company's responsibility to allow each individual to be as good as he or she is capable of being. People basically want to do a good job. I have never heard anybody walk out of this building and say, 'Boy, I feel great! I did a lousy job today.'

HARVEY MILLER
Co-owner of Quill Corp.
Nation's Business 1988

What we in industry learned in dealing with people is that people do not work just for money and that, if you are trying to motivate them, money is not the most effective tool. To motivate people you must bring them into the family, and treat them like respected members of it.

AKIO MORITA
Co-founder of Sony
Made in Japan

In order that people be happy in their work, these three things are needed: They must be fit for it: They must not do too much of it: And they must have a sense of success in it.

JOHN RUSKIN 1819–1900
English art critic and social observer
Pre-Raphaelitism

Using money as a motivator leads to a progressive degradation in the quality of everything produced.

PHILIP SLATER
US sociologist and writer
Wealth Addiction

While industrial psychologists have insisted for years that motivation must lie in positive things, not in the threat of firing, somehow that idea has never really caught on with some bosses.

JOHN TARRANT
US business consultant and writer
Perks and Parachutes

A person who has a good boss and congenial fellow workers will not change jobs for a few dollars more.

MAURICE S TROTTER
US academic
Supervisor's Handbook on Insubordination

People are like dogs: they love praise. If you can't pay more, praise more.

BJÖRN WAHLSTRÜM
Chairman of CKAB
International Management 1986

INCOME
(SEE ALSO PAY; POVERTY)

My problem lies in reconciling my gross habits with my net income.

ERROL FLYNN 1909–1959
Actor
Quoted in Jane Mercer, *Great Lovers of the Movies*

What's the point of taking all these risks as businessmen, what's the point of making all these decisions and getting them right, if we're not going to be rewarded? If we're not going to be rewarded we'll go back to the situation when no one bothers, they all go and play golf.

RALPH HALPERN
Chairman of Burton Group
International Management 1987

Some of the nicest fellows I have known in my life have experienced ... confusion between capital and

income, but they usually ended up in rather dreary lodging houses.

HAROLD MACMILLAN 1894–1986
British prime minister
Speech, House of Lords, 1985

Few people would assert that a man with fifty thousand a year is likely to have a very much happier life than if he had only a thousand.

ALFRED MARSHALL 1842–1924
British economist
'The Social Possibilities of Economic Chivalry' in *Economic Journal* 1907

All decent people live beyond their incomes nowadays, and those who aren't respectable live beyond other peoples'. A few gifted individuals manage to do both.

SAKI 1870–1916
Burmese-born British writer
'Match-Maker' in *The Chronicles of Clovis*

There are few sorrows, however poignant, in which a good income is of no avail.

LOGAN PEARSALL SMITH 1865–1946
US-born British writer
'Afterthoughts'

Solvency is entirely a matter of temperament and not of income.

LOGAN PEARSALL SMITH 1865–1946
US-born British writer
'Afterthoughts'

Share it fairly but don't take a slice of my pie.

ROGER WATERS/PINK FLOYD
British rock musician
From the song 'Money'

INDUSTRIAL RELATIONS
(SEE ALSO DIPLOMACY AND TACT; NEGOTIATIONS; STRIKES)

Had the employers of past generations dealt fairly with men,

there would have been no trade
unions.

STANLEY BALDWIN 1867–1947
British prime minister
Quoted in *Observer* 1931

The quality of employees will be
directly proportional to the quality of
life you maintain for them.

CHARLES E BRYAN
US trade unionist
New York Times 1988

I never understood how
'confrontation' came to be a dirty
word. It should be the rule of
industrial relations *every* day.

KENNETH CORK
British senior partner at Cork Gully
Cork on Cork

With all their faults, trades unions have
done more for humanity than any other
organization of men that ever existed.
They have done more for decency, for
honesty, for education, for the
betterment of the race, for the
developing of character in man, than
any other association of men.

CLARENCE DARROW 1857–1938
US lawyer and reformer
The Railroad Trainman 1909

Industrial relations are like sexual
relations. It's better between two
consenting parties.

VIC FEATHER 1908–1976
British trade unionist
Guardian Weekly 1976

The strike and the picket are
implements of the 19th century. As
we move towards the year 2000 we
must fashion new, more civilized,
more responsible means of
conducting industrial relations.

WALTER GOLDSMITH
Director general of the Institute of Directors
Speech at the Institute of
Directors annual convention, 1983

You can't force good industrial
relations. Just as you can't force
people to be good neighbours.

JOE GORMLEY
British president of the NUM
Sunday Times 1972

The real question is why employers
and employees have such divergent
perceptions of their goals.

BETTY HARTZELL
US publisher
Personnel Journal 1988

Trade unions are the only means
by which workmen can protect
themselves from the tyranny of those
who employ them. But the moment
that trade unions become tyrants in
their turn they are engines for evil:
they have no right to prevent people
from working on any terms that they
choose.

LORD LINDLEY 1828–1921
British law lord
Lyons v. *Wilkins* 1896

All the members of a company must
always work together to make their
company competitive. In a Japanese
company everybody knows they are
in the same boat. It is not an old
Japanese tradition; it is a basic
principle of the economic system and
a very simple principle. I am
wondering why you in Britain have
forgotten it.

AKIO MORITA
Co-founder of Sony
The Times 1982

Employers generally get the kind of
labor relations they ask for.

PHILIP MURRAY
Director of the Congress of
Industrial Organizations
Organized Labor and Production

It is one of the characteristics of a free and democratic modern nation that it have free and independent labor unions.

FRANKLIN D ROOSEVELT 1882–1945
32nd president of the USA
Speech addressed to the Teamsters' Union, 1940

I think it's ludicrous that it takes seventeen unions to build a motor car in Britain.

HUGH SCANLON
British president of the AUEW
Quoted in *Observer* 1979

Our experience proves that a policy of good human relations results in self-discipline, staff stability, good service to the customer, high productivity and good profits in which we all share; employees, shareholders, pensioners and the community.

LORD SIEFF
Honorary president of Marks and Spencer plc
Financial Times 1982

I had come to believe labour unions were more than a necessary evil. They are one of the few legitimate agents of workplace change.

RICARDO SEMLER
Brazilian CEO of Semco
Maverick

They [management] make us feel unimportant, as if the managers are so busy they can barely fit us into their schedules. We become impatient and irritated, and are less attentive when the negotiations begin.

WALTER SCHIAVON
Brazilian union leader
On typical strategies adopted by Brazilian management in dealings with unions, quoted in
Ricardo Semler, *Maverick*

Anyone who hasn't understood that business has a social responsibility is someone I would accuse of

incompetence, because the supreme reward for good industrial relations is to make more money.

BERNARD TAPIE
French business executive and politician
Sunday Correspondent Magazine 1990

The facts show that politically independent trade unions do not exist anywhere. There have never been any. Experience and theory say that there never will be any.

LEON TROTSKY 1879–1940
Russian communist revolutionary
Communism and Syndicalism

Let us work together without disputing; it is the only way to render life tolerable.

FRANÇOIS MARIE VOLTAIRE 1694–1778
French writer
Candide

Bad relationships in a company must be laid at the door of management just as much as at the door of trade unions.

LORD WATKINSON
Chairman of Cadbury Schweppes
Yorkshire Post 1969

The two sides of industry have traditionally always regarded each other in Britain with the greatest possible loathing, mistrust and contempt. They are both absolutely right.

AUBERON WAUGH
British writer
Private Eye 1983

INDUSTRY AND MANUFACTURING

Basically, as I see it, there is a total lack of interest from the South East, the middle classes, the university educated classes, in the process of *manufacturing*. Too often, design and marketing skills are to be found in these classes. But the other form of brilliance that goes into *making* the actual goods is separated from them by a terrible chasm.

EMMA BRIDGEWATER
British executive and founder of
Bridgewater Designs
Interview in Carol Dix, *Enterprising Women*

Modern industry needs visionary heroes more than ever before, not only to build new worlds but also to invent better mousetraps.

TERENCE E DEAL AND ALLEN A KENNEDY
US writers
Corporate Cultures

A business that makes nothing but money is a poor kind of business.

HENRY FORD 1863–1947
Pioneering industrialist and car
manufacturer
Attributed

The purpose of industry is to create wealth. It is not, despite belief to the contrary, to create jobs. The jobs are created from the wealth that industry produces.

JOHN HARVEY-JONES
Business writer and chairman of ICI
Making It Happen

Industry is a bit like the human body. The cells are continuously dying and unless new cells are created, sooner or later the whole thing will collapse and disappear.

JOHN HARVEY-JONES
Business writer and chairman of ICI
Making It Happen

Manufacturing is as vital for the United Kingdom as it is for any nation wanting to compete and prosper in the modern world. Historically, modern nations have

won supremacy only through manufacturing excellence.

TREVOR HOLDSWORTH
Chairman of National Power
The Times 1988

The starting point of any economy is manufacturing – the making of things. Money not backed up by manufacturing is nothing more than wastepaper.

HAJIMA KARATSU
Japanese economic spokesman
Financial Post 1990

Industry is limited by capital.

JOHN STUART MILL 1806–1873
English philosopher and economist
Principles of Political Economy

INFLATION
(*SEE ALSO* ECONOMISTS, ECONOMICS, AND THE ECONOMY)

Most people favour an incomes policy – provided it doesn't apply to them.

FRANK COUSINS 1904–1986
British trade union leader
Quoted in *Observer* 1969

Inflation is a form of taxation that can be imposed without legislation.

MILTON FRIEDMAN
US economist
The Times 1981

Inflation is never ultimately tamed. It only becomes subdued.

DR ALAN GREENSPAN
Chairman of the Federal Reserve Board
Financial Times 1987

Inflation is like sin; every government denounces it and every government practices it.

FREDERICK LEITH-ROSS 1887–1968
British economist and financier
Observer 1957

Inflation isn't an Act of God. High inflation is a man-made disaster, like southern beer and nylon shirts.

ROLAND LONG
British industrial relations consultant
Speech at the Confederation of
British Industry Conference, 1990

Inflation is like toothpaste. Once it's out you can hardly put it back in.

CARL OTTO PÖHL
President of Bundesbank
Newsweek 1980

Inflation is the parent of unemployment and the unseen robber of those who have saved.

MARGARET THATCHER
British prime minister
Speech at the Conservative Party conference, 1980

From now the pound abroad is worth 14% or so less in terms of other currencies. It does not mean, of course, that the pound here in Britain, in your pocket or purse, or in your bank, has been devalued.

HAROLD WILSON 1916–1995
British prime minister
Broadcast speech, popularly rendered 'The Pound
in Your Pocket', following the government's
devaluation of the pound, 1967

One man's wage rise is another man's price rise.

HAROLD WILSON 1916–1995
British prime minister
Speech, Blackburn, 1970

INFORMATION AND INFORMING
(*SEE ALSO* COMMUNICATION)

Most MIS designers 'determine' what information is needed by asking managers what information they would like to have. This is based on the (often erroneous) assumption that managers know what information they need.

RUSSELL L ACKOFF
US scientist with Management
Information Systems
Management Science 1967

When you are drowning in numbers you need a system to separate the wheat from the chaff.

ANTHONY ADAMS
Vice-president of Campbell Soup Co.
New York Times 1988

Try as far as possible to pass on information rather than your conclusions. Your conclusions, if they are right, are part of your competitive advantage. If they are wrong and you pass them on they may come back to haunt you.

MARY ANN ALLISON AND ERIC ALLISON
Vice-president of CitiCorp; financial writer
Managing Up, Managing Down

Information may be accumulated in files, but it must be retrieved to be of use in decision making.

KENNETH J ARROW
US economist
The Limits of Organization

If you get all the facts, your judgement can be right; if you don't get all the facts, it can't be right.

BERNARD BARUCH 1970–1965
US presidential advisor and investment broker
St Louis Post-Dispatch 1965

There is nothing more deceptive than an obvious fact.

ARTHUR CONAN DOYLE 1859–1930
British writer
'The Bascombealley Mystery' in
The Adventures of Sherlock Holmes

There is an especially efficient way to get information, much neglected by most managers. That is to visit a particular place in the company and observe what's going on there.

ANDREW S GROVE
CEO of Intel Corp.
High Output Management

Facts do not cease to exist because they are ignored.

ALDOUS HUXLEY 1894–1963
English writer
'A Note on Dogma' in *Proper Studies*

Every person seems to have a limited capacity to assimilate information, and if it is presented to him too rapidly and without adequate repetition, this capacity will be exceeded and communication will break down.

R DUNCAN LUCE
US academic
Developments in Mathematical Psychology

It is more important for the manager to get his information quickly and efficiently than to get it formally.

HENRY MINTZBERG
Canadian professor of management
at McGill University
The Nature of Managerial Work

If you don't give people information, they'll make up something to fill the void.

CARLA O'DELL
US president of O'Dell & Associates
CFO 1987

Immediate memory is limited to about seven 'chunks' of information. Most people can remember about seven numbers in a row, seven colors, seven shapes or seven of any other item. So if you need to remember more than seven items, it's better to organize them into a smaller number of chunks.

PETER RUSSELL
US psychologist and management consultant
The Brain Book

We now had an accounting department full of people who only stopped cranking out numbers to pick up their paychecks. And we had so damn many numbers, inside so damn many folders, that almost no one was looking at them. But no one would admit it. Everyone just bluffed their way through meetings, pretending to be familiar with every little detail.

RICARDO SEMLER
Brazilian CEO of Semco
Maverick

The tendency to hide unfavourable information often occurs in companies that are quick to reward success and equally quick to punish failure.

ROBERT M TOMASKO
Principal of Temple, Barker & Sloan, Inc.
Downsizing

You don't just wait for information to come to you.

ROBERT H WATERMAN
US management consultant and writer
The Renewal Factor

INFORMATION TECHNOLOGY
(*SEE ALSO* COMPUTERS AND COMPUTING; TECHNOLOGY)

Technology is so much fun but we can drown in our technology. The fog of information can drive out knowledge.

DANIEL J BOORSTIN
US writer, academic, and librarian of Congress
New York Times 1983

In the information society nobody thinks. We expected to banish paper, but we actually banished thought.

MICHAEL CRICHTON
US science-fiction writer
Jurassic Park

To have customer care, you need a database to recognize who to care for. You won't be able to exist in five years without a database, because everybody else will have one.

STEVE GAPPER
Direct-marketing manager at Scottish Widows
Marketing 1995

It saddens me that when people look at the impact of information technology they think so frequently in terms of organizing business in the ways that we have in the past. The enormous powers that are now within our grasp are used merely, so to speak, to mechanize what we have done rather imperfectly before. I see the advent of information technology in a rather different way. The whole nature of selling, and the relationship between the customer and supplier, will be changed by information technology.

JOHN HARVEY-JONES
Business writer and chairman of ICI
Making It Happen

Practically all large corporations insure their databases against loss or damage or against their inability to gain access to them. Some day, on the corporate balance sheet, there will be an entry which reads, 'Information'; for in most cases, the information is more valuable than the hardware which processes it.

GRACE MURRAY HOPPER
Retired US rear admiral
Speech, Washington DC, 1987

Computer science has many applications but the information technology – the 'super highway' we hear so much about – is essentially a marketing medium.

COLIN MARSHALL
President of the Chartered Institute of Marketing
Nottingham Evening Post 1995

No industry has been – or will be – more affected by information technology than financial services.

TOM PETERS
US international management consultant
and bestselling business author
Liberation Management

INITIATIVE AND INDEPENDENCE
(SEE ALSO DELEGATION)

As we become independent – proactive, centred in correct principles, value-driven, and able to organize and execute around the priorities in our life with integrity – we can choose to become interdependent: capable of building rich, enduring, productive relationships with other people.

STEPHEN R COVEY
Founder of the Institute of
Principle-Centred Leadership
Principle-Centred Leadership

True freedom is not the absence of structure – letting the employees go off and do whatever they want – but rather a clear structure that enables people to work within established boundaries in an autonomous and creative way.

ERICH FROMM 1900–1980
US psychologist, philosopher, and writer
Escape from Freedom

All employees ... deserve to be treated as responsible adults, if that is the behavior we expect of them.

ERIC HARVEY
Executive director of Performance
Systems Corp.
Management Review 1987

It's one of those irregular verbs, isn't it? 'I have an independent mind, you are eccentric, he is round the twist?'.

JONATHAN LYNN AND ANTHONY JAY
British writers
From the *Yes, Prime Minister* television series

Use your own best judgement at all times.

NORDSTROM CORP.
The single sentence to be found in the contents of
the company's policy manual

You have to have people free to act, or they become dependent. They don't have to be told, they have to be allowed.

JOHN R OPEL
Chairman of IBM
Quoted in Robert Heller, *The Supermanagers*

We like the freedom to make a successful decision, or even an unsuccessful one, without having to explain it to some analyst.

JOHN OREN
US president of Eastway Delivery Service
Best of Business Quarterly 1987

We have always found that people are most productive in small teams with tight budgets, time lines and the freedom to solve their own problems.

JOHN ROLLWAGEN
US CEO of Cray Research
Quoted in Adams, *Transforming Work*

The point is, if we can't trust a manager to use good judgment about such things, we sure as hell shouldn't be sending him off to do business in our name.

RICARDO SEMLER
Brazilian CEO of Semco
On petty rules for expenses on business trips,
Maverick

Initiative is doing the right thing without being told.

WILLIAM J SIEGEL 1910–1966
US business executive
Saying displayed in his office

You can't tell people you trust them – and be believed – if you have a lot of inspectors and auditors running around.

LOUIS SPRINGER
CEO of Campbell Soup Co.
Government Executive 1987

If we devise too elaborate a system of checks and balances, and have too many inspectors going out as representatives of the parent organization, it will be only a matter of time before the self-reliance and initiative of our managers will be destroyed and our organization will be gradually converted into a huge bureaucracy.

ROBERT E WOOD 1879–1969
US president and chairman of
Sears, Roebuck & Co.
Memo, 1938

INNOVATION
(*SEE ALSO* IDEAS AND THE CREATIVE PROCESS; INVENTORS AND INVENTIONS)

The function of genius is to furnish cretins with ideas twenty years later.

LOUIS ARAGON 1897–1982
French poet and novelist
'Le Porte-Plume' in *Traitè du Style*

We must beware of needless innovations, especially when guided by logic.

WINSTON CHURCHILL 1874–1965
British statesman and prime minister
House of Commons, 1942

We keep moving forward, opening up new doors, and doing new things, because we're curious and curiosity keeps leading us down new paths.

WALT DISNEY 1901–1966
Filmmaker, animator, and pioneer
of family entertainment
The Man Behind the Magic

Innovation is the new conservatism.

PETER F DRUCKER
US management expert
Quoted in Jeremy Turnstall, *The Advertising Man*

Most managers are rewarded if their unit operates efficiently and effectively. A highly creative unit, in contrast, might appear ineffective and uneven, and rather crazy to an outside or inside observer.

WILLIAM G DYER
US academic
Strategies for Managing Change

If you see a bandwagon, it's too late.

JAMES GOLDSMITH
British financier
Quoted in Jeffrey Robinson, *The Risk Takers*

William Webb Ellis, who invented rugby by picking up the ball during a soccer match, may now be seen as an innovator; but normally those who behave like that are treated as cheats who should not be allowed to play. Success in business mostly comes from being like Ellis: modifying the rules to match one's own particular strengths.

JOHN KAY
British economics columnist
Daily Telegraph 1995

Innovations never happen as planned.

GIFFORD PINCHOT III
The International Institute of Intrapreneurs
Intrapreneuring

'Almost nothing new works' is a common expression among innovative persons. This phrase is not spoken, however, in a defeatist tone of voice, but rather in simple recognition of the fact that innovation is a high risk venture.

LYLE E SCHALLER
US academic
The Change Agent

The desire for rules and the need for innovation are, I believe, incompatible ... Rules freeze companies inside a glacier; innovation lets them ride sleighs over it.

RICARDO SEMLER
Brazilian CEO of Semco
Maverick

Innovation comes from creative destruction.

YOSHIHISA TABUCHI
CEO of Nomura Securities
Harvard Business Review 1989

A recent study of product innovation in the scientific instruments and tool machinery industries indicates that 80% of all product innovations are initiated by the customer.

ERIC VON HIPPLE
US management consultant and computer analyst
Technology Review

Never be a pioneer. It's better to be second or third.

MARK WEINBERG
Chairman of Allied Dunbar Assurance
Quoted in William Kay, *Tycoons*

INSURANCE

When the praying does no good, insurance does help.

BERTOLT BRECHT 1898–1956
German dramatist and poet
The Mother

In the insurance business, there is no statute of limitations on stupidity.

WALTER BUFFETT
US CEO of Berkshire Hathaway
Annual Report, 1991

The Act of God designation on all insurance policies ... means roughly that you cannot be insured for the accidents that are most likely to happen to you. If your ox kicks a hole in your neighbour's Maserati, however, indemnity is instantaneous.

ALAN COREN
British writer
The Lady from Stalingrad Mansions

Down went the owners – greedy men whom hope of gain allured:/ Oh, dry the starting tear, for they were heavily insured.

W S GILBERT 1836–1911
British humorist, dramatist, and librettist
Etiquette

We don't think it's up to the insurance industry to try and dictate or influence what the compensation for pain and suffering should be ... You can't have it both ways. If we want to be a high compensation society then we have to pay the price.

MIKE KEMP
Non-life insurance manager of
Irish Insurance Federation
Post Magazine 1995

INTERVIEWS AND JOB HUNTING
(SEE ALSO HIRING AND FIRING; REDUNDANCY AND RESIGNATION)

There are people who interview extremely well and perform poorly. But the reverse is also true. There are lots of people who interview terribly but have done a great job.

PAUL W BARADA
President of Barada Associates, Inc.
Insight 1988

When you are all done, you'll discover there are no perfect candidates. No one fits the profile perfectly. Selection is a process of trade-offs ... Choose the least flawed person – or at least the person whose flaws you can most easily live with.

JAMES A BELASCO
US academic and management consultant
Teaching the Elephant to Dance

When you walk through the door to meet a prospective employer, in many cases that person will have made up their mind about whether you are right for the job by the time you have sat down.

LYN CECIL
British managing director of Secretaries Plus
Evening Standard 1995

Many of the best jobs do not really exist until someone is hired for them.

JAMES E CHALLENGER
US president of Challenger, Gery, & Christmas
Working Woman 1988

Obviously, the interviewer learns little or nothing when he is talking.

JOHN D DRAKE
US president of Behavioral Sciences Technology
Interviewing for Managers

Some candidates seem to think an interviewer wants to hear what an unprofessional hell-hole of a company they work for ... or how their current boss keeps a bottle of gin in her bottom drawer – [this] always makes me suspicious. Will they be whispering unsavoury gossip about *me* six months down the line?

FIONA GIBSON
British editor
More! 1992

We don't approve of high-pressure techniques used by some City banks, such as conducting the interview by the noisy trading floor to unnerve the person. Interviewers have power: if you ask someone to sing, they probably will.

PAULA GRAYSON
British chairman of Institute
of Personnel Management
Cosmopolitan 1992

A résumé is a balance sheet without any liabilities.

ROBERT HALF
US president of Robert Half International
Robert Half on Hiring

Asking the right questions takes as much skill as giving the right answers.

ROBERT HALF
US President of Robert Half International
Half on Hiring

The first essential in any job interview is to feel good about yourself. The second is to be ready to communicate that confidently and cheerfully.

ROS MILES
British editor
Cosmopolitan 1995

Your best asset is still *you* and no one can take that away. Your chief skills will always be your intelligence, your experience and your nerve. And they're all portable.

ROS MILES
British editor
Cosmopolitan 1995

Employers' frequent complaint is that applicants for any position lack specific skills. Raising the profile of acquiring these general skills and making it easier for everyone to acquire them – at whatever age and level of formal qualification – is a central element.

BRIDGET ROSEWALL
British financial columnist
Guardian 1995

Businessmen aren't writers, your honour. There's only one businessman in a thousand that can write a good letter of recommendation.

THORNTON WILDER 1897–1975
US writer
The Matchmaker

INVENTORS AND INVENTIONS
(*SEE ALSO* INNOVATION)

Small firms are more prolific inventors than giant companies; small firms exert significantly greater research and development effort than large ones; small firms devise and develop inventions at substantially lower costs than large firms.

WALTER ADAMS AND JAMES BROCK
US academics
The Bigness Complex

I am proud of the fact that I never invented weapons to kill.

THOMAS ALVA EDISON 1847–1931
US inventor and entrepreneur
New York Times 1915

Time and again we find, in ICI, that inventions, or discoveries we have made, and regarded as interesting technical developments, require the stimulation of a perceived need before they are developed and exploited, so often in ways quite different from the original perception.

JOHN HARVEY-JONES
Business writer and chairman of ICI
Making It Happen

Never let an inventor run a company. You can never get him to stop tinkering and bring something to market.

ROYAL LITTLE
US founder of Textron
Best of Business Quarterly 1987

Laziness, rather than necessity, is often the mother of invention.

ROBERT NOYCE
Vice-chairman of Intel Corp
Remark during *Silicon Valley*, PBS
TV broadcast, 1987

One so inclined may lament the decline of the free-ranging independent and his replacement by the captive inventor of the corporate laboratory. Yet in the face of team research, expensive equipment, and lengthy projects needed to exploit the potentialities of modern science, such a shift was inevitable.

JACOB SCHMOOKLER
US academic
Technological Progress and the
Modern American Corporation

INVESTORS AND INVESTMENT

It has always been my contention that a tribe of monkeys throwing darts at the financial pages are going to come up with advice as good or better than the manager of a unit trust.

BOB BECKMAN
Investment adviser
Daily Mail 1985

People feel investment companies have a duty to inform them about ethical investments. For many, the ethical profile of an investment may be just as important as the risk profile.

FRANK BLIGHE
Senior unit-trust manager at Friends Provident
Sunday Times 1995

The wise man understands equity; the small man understands only profits.

CONFUCIUS 551–479 BC
Chinese philosopher
Analects

In an information-based economy much of what we now consider 'expenditure' or 'social overhead' is actually 'capital investment' and should – perhaps, must – produce a high return and be self-financing.

PETER F DRUCKER
US management expert
Quoted in Walter Wriston, *Risk and*
Other Four-Letter Words

Knowledge work, unlike manual work, cannot be replaced by capital investment. On the contrary, capital investment creates the need for more knowledge work.

PETER F DRUCKER
US management expert
Management in Turbulent Times

If you like something, check out who makes it, owns it or sells it. If you still like it, buy some shares.

KEVIN GOLDSTEIN JACKSON
Founder of Television South West
Sunday Times 1995

'Induce your competition not to invest in those products, markets and services where you expect to invest the most.' That is the fundamental rule of strategy.

BRUCE HENDERSON
CEO of Boston Consulting Group, Inc.
Henderson on Corporate Strategy

Put not your trust in money, but put your money in trust.

OLIVER WENDELL HOLMES SR 1809–1894
US physician, academic, and writer
Autocrat of the Breakfast Table

The real crisis facing the British economy as it starts the long slide into the next recession is not inflation but pathetically inadequate levels of investment.

KEN LIVINGSTONE
British politician
Guardian 1995

It is one thing to find well-managed companies with exciting products in fast-growing markets but often they are too overpriced. The boring solid companies with the dull products often offer the best bargain.

MATTHEW OAKENSHOTT
Co-founder of OLIM investment managers
Sunday Times 1995

Never invest your money in anything that eats or needs repairing.

BILLY ROSE 1899–1966
Broadway producer and songwriter
New York Post 1957

When presented with freedom of choice, investors often behave in ways that reveal that what they really want is freedom *from* choice.

MEIR STATMAN
US professor of finance
Quoted in Daniel Kehrer, *Doing Business Boldly:*
Essential Lessons in the Art of Taking Intelligent Risks

To turn around our national fortunes, we need to be fully committed to investing in our long-term future – not just peripherally involved. What's the difference? Consider a meal of ham and eggs: the hen is involved, the pig is committed.

CAROL VORDERMAN
British television presenter and columnist
Radio Times 1995

JARGON VERSUS PLAIN ENGLISH

You ask me what I do. Well actually, you know,/ I'm partly a liaison man and partly P.R.O./ Essentially I integrate the current export drive/ And basically I'm viable from ten o'clock till five.

JOHN BETJEMAN 1906–1984
English poet and essayist
'The Executive'

Incomprehensible jargon is the hallmark of a profession.

KINGMAN BREWSTER 1919–1988
President of Yale University
Speech, 1977

Negative expectation thwarts realization, and self-congratulation guarantees disaster. (Or, simply put: if you think of it, it won't happen quite that way.)

MICHAEL DONNER
US editor of *Games machine*
Games Magazine 1979

Combining IBM and Lotus represents a truly unique opportunity. Our goal is to accelerate the creation of a truly open, scalable collaborative computing environment so people can work and communicate across enterprise and across corporate and national borders.

LOU GERSTNER
CEO of IBM
Explaining his company's hostile
bid for Lotus, *Independent* 1995

There is something monstrous in commands couched in invented and unfamiliar language; an alien master is worst of all. The language of the law must not be foreign to those who are to obey it.

LEARNED HAND 1872–1961
US judge
Speech, Washington DC, 1929

Petrol retailers should recognize that they are not selling a product but offering a branded experience.

GERARD LECOEUR
British design consultant
Quoted in *Sunday Correspondent*

Maladjustment co-extensive with problem areas ... alternative but nevertheless meaningful minimae ... utilization of factors which in a dynamic democracy can be channelized into both quantitative phrases ...

MAURY MAVERICK 1895–1954
US Congressman
Words written by the head of a government
agency during World War II, quoted by Maverick
when he coined the term 'gobbledegook'

The great enemy of clear language is insincerity. When there is a gap between one's real and one's declared aims, one turns as it were instinctively to long words and exhausted idioms, like a cuttlefish squirting out ink.

GEORGE ORWELL 1903–1950
English writer
Shooting an Elephant

Never use a long word where a short one will do, and never use jargon if you can think of an everyday English equivalent.

GEORGE ORWELL 1903–1950
English writer
Shooting an Elephant

Words are the litmus paper of the mind. If you find yourself in the power of someone who will use the word 'commence' in cold blood; go somewhere else very quickly. But if they say 'enter', don't stop to pack.

TERRY PRATCHETT
British writer
Small Gods

The manufacture of a five-pronged implement for digging results in a fork even if the manufacturer, unfamiliar with the English language, insists that he intended to make and has made a spade.

LORD TEMPLEMAN
English judge
Street v. *Mountford* 1985

It is no exaggeration to describe plain English as a fundamental tool of government.

MARGARET THATCHER
British prime minister
Quoted in *Observer* 1988

JUSTICE AND INJUSTICE

Justice is not capable of being measured out by an accountant's computer.

NICHOLAS BROWNE-WILKINSON
British law lord
Quoted in *Observer*

To those who are engaged in commercial dealing, justice is indispensable for the conduct of business.

MARCUS TULLIUS CICERO 106–43 BC
Roman orator, writer, and politician
De Officiis

Capitalism thrives on the first definition of distributive justice – those who achieve most should get most. But it will not long be credible or tolerated if it ignores its opposite, that those who need most should have their needs met.

CHARLES HANDY
Business executive and writer, and
professor at the London Business School
The Empty Raincoat

Injustice is relatively easy to bear; what stings is justice.

H L MENCKEN 1880–1956
US essayist and critic
Prejudices

The big print giveth, and the small print taketh away.

J FULTON SHEEN 1895–1979
US archbishop and writer
Attributed

LAWYERS, LAW, AND LITIGATION

Law is a bottomless pit, it is a cormorant, a harpy, that devours everything.

JOHN ARBUTHNOT 1667–1735
Scottish writer and physician.
The History of John Bull

American scientists, runs one joke, are starting to use lawyers in their experiments instead of white rats. They give three reasons: first, there are more lawyers than white rats; second, you can't become emotionally attached to a lawyer; and third, there are some things a white rat just won't do.

BRIAN CATHCART
British journalist
Independent on Sunday 1995

No man has ever yet been hanged for breaking the spirit of the law.

GROVER CLEVELAND 1837–1908
22nd and 24th president of the USA
Quoted in Hibben, *Peerless Leader*

It is not a presumption of law that a hire-purchase finance company cannot be innocent.

LORD DIPLOCK 1907–1985
English judge
Snook v. London and West Riding
Investments 1967

The law exists to protect us all, whether we are union members, union leaders, employers or merely long-suffering members of the public. We cannot do without it. But the law is not a one-way street. Part goes our way, part goes against us. We have either to accept it all or else opt for anarchy.

JOHN DONALDSON
English Master of the Rolls
Con-Mech (Engineers) Ltd v. AUEW 1973

People say law but they mean wealth.

RALPH WALDO EMERSON 1803–1882
US philosopher and poet
Journals

Litigation is the pursuit of practical ends, not a game of chess.

FELIX FRANKFURTER 1882–1965
US judge
Indianapolis v. Chase National Bank 1941

As in law so in war, the longest purse finally wins.

MAHATMA GANDHI 1869–1948
Indian nationalist leader
From a paper read to the Bombay Provincial
Co-operative Conference, 1917

I cannot resist saying that I regard our profession as one of the obstacles to national reform.

LORD HAILSHAM
British lord chancellor, politician, and lawyer
On lawyers, quoted in *Observer* 1986

The Common Law of England has been laboriously built about a mythical figure – the figure of 'The Reasonable Man'.

A P HERBERT 1890–1971
British writer and politician
'Reasonable Man'

Lawyers' houses are built on the heads of fools.

GEORGE HERBERT 1593–1633
English cleric and writer
Jacula Prudentum

If your lawyers tell you that you have a very good case, you should settle immediately.

RICHARD INGRAMS
British editor and founder of *Private Eye*
On losing a major libel case brought by Robert
Maxwell, quoted in Tom Bower,
Maxwell, the Outsider

The law, by any standards, is an extraordinary profession. Its practitioners are always anxious to voice the highest principles of fairness and impartiality in relation to everyone but themselves.

ROBERT MARK
Commissioner of the Metropolitan Police
In the Office of Constable

I don't know as I want a lawyer to tell me what I cannot do. I hire him to tell me how to do what I want to do.

JOHN PIERPONT MORGAN 1837–1913
US banker and business executive
Quoted in Tarbell, *The Life of Elbert H Gary*

The whole system is absurd. There seems to be no commitment to the idea of swift simple justice.

FRANK PEDLEY
British magistrate
On the small claims court, in *Guardian* 1995

Judges, as a class, display, in the matter of arranging alimony, that reckless generosity that is found only in men who are giving away someone else's cash.

P G WODEHOUSE 1881–1975
English novelist
Louder and Funnier

LEADERS AND LEADERSHIP

Failing organizations are usually over-managed and under-led.

WARREN BENNIS
Business academic and president of the
University of Cincinnati
University of Maryland symposium, 1988

Leadership is like the Abominable Snowman, whose footprints are everywhere but who is nowhere to be seen.

WARREN BENNIS AND BURT NANUS
Business academic and president of the University of Cincinnati; business academic and writer
Leaders: The Strategies for Taking Charge

Leaders acquire and wear their visions like clothes. Accordingly, they seem to enrol themselves (and then others) in the belief of their ideals as attainable, and their behavior exemplifies the ideals in action.

WARREN BENNIS AND BURT NANUS
Business academic and president of the University of Cincinnati; business academic and writer
Leaders: The Strategies for Taking Charge

A leader must have the courage to act against an expert's advice.

JAMES CALLAGHAN
British prime minister
Harvard Business Review 1986

A leader has to *appear* consistent. That doesn't mean he has to *be* consistent.

JAMES CALLAGHAN
British prime minister
Harvard Business Review 1986

We don't need any more leadership training; we need some followership training.

MAUREEN CARROLL
Senior vice-president of University
Research Corp.
Management meeting, 1985

The man who commands efficiently must have obeyed others in the past, and the man who obeys dutifully is worthy of being some day a commander.

MARCUS TULLIUS CICERO 106–43 BC
Roman orator, writer, and politician
On Law

All great businesses understand that enterprise involves risk, that occasionally there will be mistakes and that the true test of leadership is the ability to guide people through those moments of crisis.

NIALL FITZGERALD
Management executive at Unilever, UK
Quoted in *Sunday Times* 1995

The ability to lead and inspire others is far more instinctual than premeditated and it is acquired somehow through the experience of one's everyday life, and the ultimate nature and quality of the leadership comes out of the innate character and personality of the leader himself.

HAROLD GENEEN
Business consultant and chairman of ITT
Managing

The person who heads a company should realize that his people are really not working for him; they are working *with him* for themselves.

They have their own dreams, their own need for self-fulfilment. He has to help fill their needs as much as they do his.

HAROLD GENEEN
Business consultant and chairman of ITT
Managing

Leadership is a two-way street, loyalty up and loyalty down. Respect for one's superiors; care for one's crew.

GRACE MURRAY HOPPER
Retired US rear admiral
Speech, Washington DC, 1987

We have no difficulty finding the leaders: They have people following them.

WILLIAM L GORE
US CEO and founder of W L Gore and Associates
Quoted in Gifford Pinchot III, *Intrapreneuring*

Leadership is the priceless gift that you earn from the people who work for you. I have to earn the right to that gift and have to continuously re-earn that right.

JOHN HARVEY-JONES
Business writer and chairman of ICI
International Management 1985

It is a paradox that the greater the decentralization, the greater the need for both leadership and explicit policies from the top management.

BRUCE HENDERSON
CEO of Boston Consulting Group, Inc.
Henderson on Corporate Strategy

Strategic leadership requires ... It is a readiness to look personally foolish; a readiness to discuss half-baked ideas, since most fully baked ideas start out in that form; a total honesty, a readiness to admit you got it wrong.

JOHN HOSKYNS
Chairman of Burton Group
Financial Times 1987

The final test of a leader is that he leaves behind him in other men the conviction and the will to carry on.

WALTER LIPPMANN 1889–1974
US liberal political commentator
New York Herald Tribune 1945

Contrary to the opinion of many people, leaders are not born. Leaders are made, and they are made by effort and hard work.

VINCE LOMBARDI 1913–1970
US football coach
Quoted in Wiebusch, *Lombardi*

It isn't necessary to have original ideas to be a successful leader.

JONELLE LONG
President of Maid-To-Order, Inc.
Speech, Washington DC, 1987

It was just the day for Organizing Something, or for Writing a Notice signed Rabbit ... It was a Captainish sort of day when everybody said 'Yes, Rabbit' and waited until he had told them.

A A MILNE 1882–1958
English writer
The House at Pooh Corner

Effective leaders have agendas; they are totally results-oriented. They adopt challenging new visions of what is both possible and desirable, communicate their visions, and persuade others to become so committed to these new directions that they are eager to lend their resources and energies to make them happen.

BURT NANUS
US business academic and writer
Visionary Leadership

The first rule of leadership is to save yourself for the big decision. Don't allow your mind to be cluttered with the trivia.

RICHARD NIXON 1919–1994
37th president of the USA
Quoted in Michael Shea, *Leadership Rules*

A person of bourgeois origin goes through life with some expectation of getting what he wants, within reasonable limits. Hence the fact that in times of stress 'educated' people tend to come to the front.

GEORGE ORWELL 1903–1950
English writer
The Road to Wigan Pier

No man is fit to command another that cannot command himself.

WILLIAM PENN 1644–1718
English Quaker leader and founder of Pennsylvania
No Cross, No Crown

Leadership, above all, consists of telling the truth, unpalatable though it may be. It is better to go down with the truth on one's lips that to rise high by innuendo and doubletalk.

LORD ROBENS
Chairman of the National Coal Board
Speech at the Institute of Directors annual convention, 1974

Image in leadership matters just as much as, if not more than, reality.

MICHAEL SHEA
British director of public affairs at Hanson Trust plc
and former press secretary to the Queen
Leadership Rules

Either lead, follow, or get out of the way.

TED TURNER
Founder of CNN
Sign displayed on his desk

Who sees leadership more clearly than subordinates?

JOHN H ZENGER
President of Zenger-Miller, Inc.
Training 1985

Time deals gently only with those who take it gently.

ANATOLE FRANCE 1844–1944
French writer
The Crime of Sylvestre Bonnard

Most people work the greater part of their time for a mere living; and the little freedom which remains to them so troubles them that they use every means of getting rid of it.

JOHANN WOLFGANG VON GOETHE 1749–1832
German poet, novelist, and dramatist
The Sorrows of Young Werther

It is impossible to enjoy idling thoroughly unless one has plenty of work to do.

JEROME K JEROME 1859–1927
English journalist and writer
'On Being Idle' in *Idle Thoughts of an Idle Fellow*

I must confess that I am interested in leisure in the same way that a poor man is interested in money.

PRINCE PHILIP
Duke of Edinburgh
Quoted in Martin Manser, *Chambers Book of Business Quotations*

My idea of relaxation is to sit in the sunshine reading *Management Today* or *The Director*. Fascinating. On holiday I do that for hours.

CYRIL STEIN
Chairman of Ladbroke Group plc
Sun 1967

Good friends, good books and a sleepy conscience: this is the ideal life.

MARK TWAIN 1835–1910
US writer
Notebooks

LEISURE
(SEE ALSO TIME)

Making a living is only part of life.

CECIL ANDRUS
Governor of Idaho
Wall Street Journal 1988

LOYALTY

Most good managers inspire loyalty.

MARY ANN ALLISON AND ERIC ALLISON
Vice-president of CitiCorp; financial writer
Managing Up, Managing Down

Retailers are moaning all the time about customers being promiscuous, but who is training them to be that way?

MARCUS EVANS
Managing director of The Ogilvy
Loyalty Centre
Marketing Week 1995

The qualities that companies offered to employees of security and the qualities of loyalty they expected in return have been swept aside by global competition ... Old loyalties towards a corporation will tend to be replaced by new ones towards a group of colleagues.

HAMISH MCRAE
Scottish journalist
Independent 1995

When your employer says sales are down this year and there won't be a raise, you're not supposed to look around and say, 'Well, where would I be better off?' But it also means that when the company is hurting, it doesn't start firing people. Loyal employees have to believe that the company will support them and I don't find very many employees who believe that anymore.

MARK PASTEN
US academic
Washington Post 1988

There is a great deal of talk about loyalty from the bottom to the top. Loyalty from the top down is even more necessary and much less prevalent.

GEORGE PATTON 1885–1945
US general
War as I Knew It

There is a time when integrity should take the rudder from team loyalty.

THOMAS J WATSON JR
US ambassador to the former Soviet
Union and CEO of IBM
Fortune 1977

LUCK
(*SEE ALSO* OPPORTUNITY)

We must believe in luck. For how else can we explain the success of those we don't like?

JEAN COCTEAU 1889–1963
French writer
Quoted in Robert Byrne, *The Other 637
Best Things Anybody Ever Said*

Luck's rather like a sponge cake; it's always better if you make it yourself.

TOM HOLT
British writer
Faust Among Equals

I am a great believer in luck, and I find the harder I work the more I have of it.

STEPHEN LEACOCK 1869–1944
Canadian humorist
Quoted in Robert W Kent, *Money Talks*. A similar
statement has been attributed to others,
including golfer Gary Player

Anyone who says luck is not an essential element in business is a fool – luck permeates every transaction.

CRAIG MCKINNEY
Chairman of Woodchester Investments
Sunday Press 1989

Luck is infatuated with the efficient.
Persian proverb

MACHINERY
(*SEE ALSO* TECHNOLOGY)

The factory of the future will have only two employees, a man and a dog. The man will be there to feed the dog. The dog will be there to keep the man from touching the equipment.

WARREN G BENNIS
Business academic and president of the
University of Cincinnati
University of Maryland symposium, 1988

Man will never be enslaved by machinery if the man tending the machine be paid enough.

KAREL CAPEK 1890–1938
Czech writer
News Chronicle

Automation simply provides more efficient ways of doing the wrong kinds of things.

MICHAEL HAMMER AND JAMES CHAMPY
US international management consultants and business authors
Reengineering the Corporation

One machine can do the work of fifty ordinary men. No machine can do the work of one extraordinary man.

ELBERT HUBBARD 1856–1915
US writer and printer
Thousand and One Epigrams

The technology of *mass production* is inherently violent, ecologically damaging, self-defeating in terms of non-renewable resources, and stultifying for the human person.

E F SCHUMACHER 1911–1977
German-born British economist
Small is Beautiful

Engineering is the ability to do for $1 what any damn fool can do for $5.

ARTHUR MELLEN WELLINGTON 1847–1895
US engineer
Quoted in *Washington Business Journal* 1987

Let us remember that the automatic machine is the precise economic equivalent for slave labor. Any labor that competes with slave labor must accept the economic conditions of slave labor.

NORBERT WIENER 1894–1964
US computer pioneer
The Human Use of Human Beings

MANAGEMENT AND MANAGERS

(SEE ALSO BOSSES)

Managers who are skilled communicators may also be good at covering up real problems.

CHRIS ARGYRIS
US academic
Harvard Business Review 1986

Good managers should never have dollar signs in their eyes, regarding their people merely in terms of profit.

MARY KAY ASH
US entrepreneur and founder of Mary Kay Cosmetics
Mary Kay on People Management

There's a lot of nonsense talked about democracy. I believe management democracy is everybody agreeing to do what the leader wants.

JOHN ASHCROFT
Chairman of Coloroll Group plc
Telegraph Magazine 1988

The most successful managers are those that can quickly grasp how their bosses think.

AMY BERMAR
US business and computer journalist
PC Week 1987

At too many companies, the boss shoots the arrow of managerial performance, and then hastily paints the bullseye around the spot where it lands.

WALTER BUFFETT
Chairman of Berkshire Hathaway Inc.
Shareholder 1989

Most companies spend all their time looking for another management concept and very little time following up the one they have just taught their managers.

KENNETH H BLANCHARD
AND ROBERT LORBER
US business executives
Putting the One Minute Manager to Work

The worst rule of management is 'If it ain't broke, don't fix it.' In today's economy, if it ain't broke, you might as well break it yourself, because it soon will be.

D WAYNE CALLOWAY
CEO of PepsiCo
Fortune 1991

British management doesn't seem to understand the importance of the human factor.

PRINCE CHARLES
Speech at a Parliamentary and Scientific
Committee lunch, 1979

The basic task of management is to make people productive.

PETER F DRUCKER
US management expert
Financial Times 1986

Managing a business requires a great deal of frankness and openness and you actually lead by being very honest with people.

MICHAEL EDWARDES
South African-born British industrialist
Quoted in *Observer* 1983

The first job of a manager is convincing themselves and others that nobody, lower paid staff in particular, can manage without them.

PAUL FISHER
British employment columnist
Guardian 1995

It is practically impossible for a top management man, or even middle management, to be doing the degree and level of work that he should be doing and, at the same time, have a clean desk.

HAROLD GENEEN
Business consultant and chairman of ITT
Managing

Performance is your reality. Forget everything else. That is why my definition of a manager is what it is: one who turns in the performance.

HAROLD GENEEN
Business consultant and chairman of ITT
Managing

If the new manager doesn't fit the culture, the business, or you, chances are the [employees] he brings in won't either.

RICHARD GOULD
Vice-president for Human Resources,
General Host Corp.
Management Review 1987

Basically I try to jolly things along. After all, the problems can only be solved by the people who have them. You have to try and coax them and love them into seeing ways in which they can help themselves.

JOHN HARVEY-JONES
Business writer and chairman of ICI
Independent on Sunday 1990

I believe that management is an art – and possibly one of the most difficult ones. Just as the artist constantly and consciously works to perfect his technique and to gain mastery of his relevant skills, so must the manager.

JOHN HARVEY-JONES
Business writer and chairman of ICI
Managing to Survive

There can never be any single correct solution for any management problem, or all-embracing system which will carry one through a particular situation or period of time.

JOHN HARVEY-JONES
Business writer and chairman of ICI
Managing to Survive

Effective managers live in the present – but concentrate on the future.

JAMES L HAYES
President and CEO of the American
Management Association
Memos for Management: Leadership

The first myth of management is that it exists. The second myth of management is that success equals skill.

ROBERT HELLER
US business writer and editor of *Manager Today*
The Great Executive Dream

Effective management always means asking the right questions.

ROBERT HELLER
US business writer and editor of *Manager Today*
The Supermanagers

Start with good people, lay out the rules, communicate with your employees, motivate them and reward them. If you do all those things effectively, you can't miss.

LEE IACOCCA
CEO of Chrysler Corporation
Talking Straight

Things were run on a need-to-know principle: if you needed to know, you weren't told.

PETER JAY
Writer, broadcaster and executive at
Maxwell Communications
On Robert Maxwell's management style, *Newsweek*

There is no grade of 'perfect' in crisis management – it is a matter of reducing pain and damage – but the results are measurable in big dollar savings and protection of human resources.

GERALD C MEYERS
Chairman of American Motors
When It Hits the Fan

No manager is an island.

WILLIAM JR ONCKEN
US management writer
Success 1988

I don't believe top management should be in the business of strategy setting at all, except as creators of a general business mission. Strategies must be set from below.

TOM PETERS
US international management consultant and
bestselling business author
Liberation Management

Most managers, most of the time, treat the happenings of the past as if they were the permanent or given nature of things, rather than simply things that occurred in the past.

KENNETH AND LINDA SCHATZ
US leadership and management consultants
Management By Influence

Managers don't have problems. Managers solve problems.

BERNARD SCHULMAN
President of Hot Pink Party Services, Inc.
Favourite saying

Today I am a big believer in MBWA, or Management by Wandering Around. Popularized at Hewlett-Packard, it simply means taking time each week to walk around with, as Bob Dylan said, no destination known.

RICARDO SEMLER
Brazilian CEO of Semco
Maverick

I think we're proving that worker involvement doesn't mean that bosses lose power. What we do strip away is the blind, irrational authoritarianism that diminishes productivity.

RICARDO SEMLER
Brazilian CEO of Semco
On worker participation in management, *Maverick*

The secret of managing is to keep the five guys who hate you away from the guys who are undecided.

CASEY STENGEL 1889–1975
US baseball player and manager
Quoted in Ira Berkow and Jim Kaplan, *The Gospel
According to Casey*

It's only the companies that you're unfamiliar with that are well managed.

FRED VANDERSCHMIDT
Director of Abt Associates, Inc.
Managers' conference, 1974

I don't dictate. I sit in my office and watch them start to get frightened when things go badly. When they're frightened enough they ask my help. I give it and they take it.

EARL WEAVER
Manager at Baltimore Orioles
New York Times 1992

Line managers ... are prone to faddism, the quickie solution and the latest utterance from management gurus.

VICKY WRIGHT
British managing director of Hay
Management Consultants
Speech at the Society of Chief Personnel Officers
in Local Government annual conference, 1995

MARKETING AND MARKET RESEARCH

The concept of mass marketing may be unfashionable but the mass market is still there.

EMILY BELL
British journalist
Guardian 1995

The whole point about marketing goods I already knew: what makes a piece of pottery worth £7.99 rather than 99p is all in the *design*. The basic cost need hardly change.

EMMA BRIDGEWATER
British executive and founder of
Bridgewater Designs
Interview in Carol Dix, *Enterprising Women*

Pile it high, sell it cheap.

JOHN 'JACK' COHEN 1898–1979
Founder and chairman of Tesco's
Marketing slogan

Market research will always tell you why you can't do something. It is a substitute for decision making, for guts.

LAUREL CUTLER
US vice chairman of FCB/Leber Katz Partners
Inc. Magazine 1987

Given that marketing has inherited the world, the luxury industry has a continuing problem in coming up with a design vocabulary with which to provide the essential clues that suggest luxury.

SUDJIC DEJAN
British journalist
Guardian 1995

Everyone says a business should stick to its niche. Niches, however, are usually quite dark and very confining.

MELVYN ESTRIN
CEO of Human Service Group Inc.
Speech, Washington DC, 1983

Communication is the most important form of marketing.

AKIO MORITA
Co-founder of Sony
The Times 1982

Once you have created a market, you are faced with the necessity of re-creating it continually.

WILLIAM OLSTEN
CEO of Olsten Services Corp.
Success 1988

Promotional items are not trendsetters, but trend followers. The secret of a blockbusting promotion is to be aware of forthcoming trends and plan ahead.

TONY REID
Director of Supreia International
Marketing Week 1995

Market research is like driving along looking in the rear view mirror. You are studying what has gone.

ANITA RODDICK
British entrepreneur and
founder of The Body Shop
The Times 1987

Market research is now a sophisticated technique, but, however much it can tell you about how many people *might* buy what you have to offer, it can never *make* people buy what you have to sell.

LORD SIEFF
Honorary president of Marks and Spencer plc
Management the Marks and Spencer Way

If there was a market in mass-produced portable nuclear weapons, we'd market them too.

ALAN SUGAR
Entrepreneur and founder of Amstrad plc
Quoted in *Observer* 1986

50% of Japanese companies do not have a marketing department, and 90% have no special section for marketing research. The reason is that everyone is considered to be a marketing specialist.

HIROTAKA TAKEUCHI
Japanese academic
Cherry Blossoms and Robotics

Marketing relies on pseudo-scientific language that proves nothing at all about the benefits of the product.

BERNADETTE VALLELY
British director of Women's
Environmental Network
The Times 1990

It's just called the *Bible* now – we dropped the word 'Holy' to give it more mass-market appeal.

JUDITH YOUNG
Spokeswoman at Hodder & Stoughton Ltd
Quoted in *Financial Times* 1989

MARKET FORCES AND SUPPLY AND DEMAND
(*SEE ALSO* FREE ENTERPRISE; TRADE)

Price in the market is not always the same thing as market price.

THOMAS DE QUINCEY 1785–1859
English writer
Logic of Political Economy

A friend in the market is better than money in the chest.

THOMAS FULLER 1654–1734
English physician and writer
Gnomologia

The only salvation ... is for a company to produce several different products, so that when the demand for one goes down, the company can deploy its assets to the products for which there is a demand.

HAROLD GENEEN
Business consultant and chairman of ITT
Managing

Private enterprise and the unregulated market has one inevitable outcome – the rich get richer at the expense of the poor.

ROY HATTERSLEY
British politician
Guardian 1995

If you have a lot of what people want and can't get, then you can supply the demand and shovel in the dough.

MEYER LANSKY 1902–1983
Russian-born US bootlegger and gangster
Attributed saying, known as 'Lansky's Law'

If you want a really dynamic, effective economy, the only damn thing you can do is pursue the market logic completely. Whole hog, not halfway.

MICHAEL MANLEY
Vice-president of the Socialist International
and prime minister of Jamaica
New Perspectives Quarterly 1992

The market is a wonderful servant, but a cruel, destructive and wasteful master.

DAVID MARQUAND
British director of the Political Economy
Research Centre, Sheffield University
Guardian 1995

MAVERICKS

Doing business with Alan Bond is like wrestling with a pig. You both get sprayed with mud and the pig loves it.

ANONYMOUS TEXAN BANKER
Sunday Times 1989

Rebels are imaginative, creative and confident, making them indispensable at work ... Independent and irreverent, they are brilliant both in a crisis and in stressful jobs.

ALBERT J BERNSTEIN AND
SYDNEY CRAFT ROZEN
British authors
Neanderthals at Work

You really have to be an idiot not to be successful in this country.

PAUL HAMLYN
British publishing guru
Evening News 1965

I do not want as my epitaph that I was a successful Attila for a few years of my career, I want to be known as a forward-looking publisher, a modernizer, and a builder.

TIM HELY HUTCHINSON
Managing director of Hodder Headline plc
publishers and campaigner for the
end of the net book agreement
Interview, *Independent* 1994

If we had ten men like Robert Maxwell, Britain would not have suffered from the economic problems that have plagued it since the war.

LORD KEARTON
Chairman of Courtaulds
Defending Maxwell's business methods,
Current Biography 1988

Making a billion dollars on a new deal is not difficult for me. Making it in a way that gives me satisfaction is the real challenge.

ADNAN KHASOOGI
Saudi arms dealer and international deal maker
Daily Express 1986

All I say is, if you cannot ride two horses you have no right in the circus.

JAMES MAXTON 1885–1946
British politician
On being told that he could not be in two
political parties, quoted in *Daily Herald* 1932

I've come down flat on my arse, but I'm going up again and this time I'm staying up.

ROBERT MAXWELL 1923–1991
Czech-born British publishing and
newspaper magnate, whose death
prompted an investigation into his
business empire revealing bankrupty
and the misappropriation of millions of
pounds from pension funds
After his first bankruptcy, quoted in Tom Bower
Maxwell, The Outsider

When I pass a belt, I cannot resist hitting below it.

ROBERT MAXWELL 1923–1991
Czech-born British publishing and
newspaper magnate, whose death
prompted an investigation into his
business empire revealing bankrupty
and the misappropriation of millions of
pounds from pension funds
Quoted in *New York Times* 1991

I defy anyone who's ever done a deal with Bob Maxwell to say he didn't get a full 12 annas for his rupee.

ROBERT MAXWELL 1923–1991
Czech-born British publishing and
newspaper magnate, whose death
prompted an investigation into his
business empire revealing bankrupty
and the misappropriation of millions of
pounds from pension funds
There are 16 annas to the rupee. Quoted in Jeffrey
Robinson, *The Risk Takers*

Every society honors its live conformists and its dead troublemakers.

MIGNON MCLAUGHLIN
US writer and editor
The Neurotic's Notebook

Tap the energy of the anarchist and he will be the one to push your company ahead.

ANITA RODDICK
British entrepreneur and
founder of The Body Shop
Quoted in Tom Peters, *Liberation Management*

My commitment to Guinness is total. With the team I have and the many opportunities I see for Guinness worldwide there is no way I am not going to be part of this group until I retire.

ERNEST SAUNDERS
CEO and chairman of Guinness plc later found guilty of a share supporting operation in the Guinness takeover bid for Distillers
Guardian 1984

He is of course a pirate; the kind of man who would walk into a revolving door behind you and emerge, the other side, in front.

STEWART STEVEN
British journalist
Of Tiny Rowland, *Daily Mail* 1973

If Max gets to Heaven he won't last long. He will be chucked out for trying to pull off a merger between Heaven and Hell ... after having secured a controlling interest in key subsidiary companies in both places, of course.

H G WELLS 1866–1946
English writer
Of Max Beaverbrook, quoted in
A J P Taylor, *Beaverbrook*

Early in life I had to choose between honest arrogance and hypocritical humility. I chose honest arrogance and have seen no occasion to change.

FRANK LLOYD WRIGHT 1869–1959
US architect
Quoted in Herbert Jacobs, *Frank Lloyd Wright*

MEDIA COVERAGE

Basically you're all overpaid and we hate you.

Press officer at the Department of Trade and Industry
Anonymous comment on journalists,
Money Marketing 1989

The printing-press is either the greatest blessing or the greatest curse of modern times, one sometimes forgets which.

JAMES M BARRIE 1860–1937
Scottish playwright and novelist
Sentimental Tommy

Nothing is real unless it happens on television.

DANIEL J BOORSTIN
US writer, academic, and librarian of Congress
New York Times 1978

I won't eat anything that has intelligent life, but I'd gladly eat a network executive or a politician.

MARTY FELDMAN 1933–1983
British comedian
Quoted in Michael Cader and Debby Roth, *Eat These Words*

The Government couldn't have done less for the movies unless they had made them illegal, and under the principle of prohibition maybe more would have been made if they had been banned.

CHRISTOPHER HAMPTON
British dramatist and film producer
Guardian 1995

I would not like to comment on whether the press have been fair or unfair. Over a long career I've always found they get the last word.

LORD KEITH
British merchant banker and industrialist
Financial Times 1986

The media projection of the union–employer relationship is a travesty of the truth.

GAVIN LAIRD
Scottish general secretary of the AUEW
Quoted in David Clutterbuck and Stuart Cranier, *The Decline and Rise of British Industry*

I shall resist the temptation to dwell on the golden age of the fifties and sixties when I was a financial journalist. But I must say I am struck by the modern obsession with inevitably speculative forecasts of the short term future, at the expense of informing the reader about what is actually happening in the present.

NIGEL LAWSON
British chancellor of the Exchequer
Financial Times 1984

The media are as eco-friendly as anybody in their desire to recycle stories endlessly.

JONATHAN MARGOLIS
British journalist
Sunday Times 1995

Gutenberg made everybody a reader. Xerox makes everybody a publisher.

MARSHALL MCLUHAN 1911–1980
Canadian communications theorist
Guardian Weekly 1977

Early in life I had noticed that no event is ever correctly reported in a newspaper.

GEORGE ORWELL 1903–1950
English writer
Collected Essays, Journalism and Letters

Television? No good will come of this device. The word is half Greek and half Latin.

C P SCOTT 1846–1932
British editor of *Manchester Guardian*
Attributed

Freedom of the press in Britain means freedom to print such of the proprietor's prejudices as the advertisers don't object to.

HANNEN SWAFFER 1879–1962
British journalist
Quoted in Tom Driberg, *Swaff*

We write frankly and freely but then we 'modify' before we print.

MARK TWAIN 1835–1910
US writer
Life on the Mississippi

However vast your media empire, if you haven't got a string of cable stations emitting the grunts and writhings of their birth pangs today, the ruthless tenets of capitalism dictate you'll not be up and running in the 21st century.

SALLY VINCENT
British journalist
Guardian 1995

You cannot hope to bribe or twist, thank God! the British journalist./ But, seeing what the man will do unbribed, there's no occasion to.

HUMBERT WOLFE 1886–1940
English poet
'Over the Fire'

MEETINGS
(*SEE ALSO* COMMITTEES; CONFERENCES)

Never let the other fellow set the agenda.

JAMES BAKER
US secretary of state
Quoted in *Observer* 1988

If a problem causes many meetings, the meetings eventually become more important than the problem.

ARTHUR BLOCH
US writer and humorist
Murphy's Law

Feeling that you have to attend every meeting may mean that you don't trust someone on your staff to cover them well enough.

HARRIET BRAIKER
US psychologist and management consultant
Working Woman 1988

I leave Messina happy because if you continue meeting you will not agree; even if you agree, nothing will result;

and even if something results, it will be a disaster.

RUSSELL BRETHERTON
British observer at the conference of EU member states held in Messina to review working of Maastricht Treaty
Guardian 1995

Meetings are indispensable when you don't want to do anything.

J K GALBRAITH
US diplomat, economist, and writer
Ambassador's Journal 1969

In a good meeting there is a momentum that comes from the spontaneous exchange of fresh ideas, while interests are high, that produces extraordinary results, and that momentum relies upon the freedom and flexibility permitted to the participants. To my mind that is the essence of good management.

HAROLD GENEEN
Business consultant and chairman of ITT
Managing

It does not matter if there are two or ten people in my office, just as we are breaking up someone will remark, 'Oh, incidentally...' and the most important point of the whole meeting emerges. Only a fool would cut a man off at that point.

HAROLD GENEEN
Business consultant and chairman of ITT
Managing

When you're walking together, there is no head of the table. People mingle. And you have to wear sensible clothes; tracksuits and gumboots, no ties. With everybody dressed as ordinary people there's no hierarchy. It is liberating.

LARRY GOULD
British chairman and managing director of Link Up
On his policy of holding senior management meetings whilst hiking, *Sunday Times* 1995

Once somebody asked me to identify the single most useful management technique that I learned through my years of managing. My answer was: the practice of regularly scheduled *one-to-one* meetings.

ANDREW S GROVE
CEO of Intel Corp.
One-to-One with Andy Grove

A good sign that either the meeting or some of the people are superfluous is when they try to get out of coming.

ROBERT HELLER
US business writer and editor of *Manager Today*
The Supermanagers

While the staff meeting may not be the best place to solve complex problems, it surely is a place to express opinions.

HARRY D KOLB
US head of personnel development at Humble Oil & Refining Co.
Leadership in the Office

Meetings force you to do your job. You'll find that there are issues that you don't think of and someone else will.

EDWARD KOPCZYNSKI
Senior vice-president of Shearson Lehman Brothers
New York Times 1988

Many meetings should not be called at all. Among them are those a manager calls because he is unable or unwilling to make a decision.

R ALEC MACKENZIE
US management consultant and author
The Time Trap

The purpose of a meeting is to bring depth and breath of discussion to a problem that merits the attention and effort of every member present.

ALFRED J MARROW
US chairman of Harwood Manufacturing Corp.
Leadership in the Office

When the result of a meeting is to schedule more meetings, it usually signals trouble.

MIKE MURPHY
US management writer
Effective Listening

The success of a meeting often depends on having the right documents – proofs, artwork, schedules, research charts, etc. – present at the start of the meeting. All too often we arrive like plumbers, leaving our tools behind.

DAVID OGILVY
Advertising guru and founder
of Ogilvy and Mather
The Unpublished David Ogilvy

The Law of Triviality ... means that the time spent on any item on the agenda will be in inverse proportion to the sum involved.

C NORTHCOTE PARKINSON
British historian, writer, and
formulator of Parkinson's law
Parkinson's Law and Other Studies in Administration

For lots of business people, meetings (meetings, and more meetings) are politics at its worst, and an epic waste ... But the point many miss is that meetings really aren't about doing things. They are about figuring out the way so-and-so is thinking, and feeling, paving the way for an initiative that is still months off, edging towards some eventual consensus about this and that.

TOM PETERS
US international management consultant
and bestselling business author
Independent on Sunday 1995

Some do use meetings to grandstand, intimidate, and establish their power vis-à-vis someone else. But in my experience, these people usually get their comeuppance.

TOM PETERS
US international management consultant
and bestselling business author
Independent on Sunday 1995

The length of a meeting rises with the square of the number of people present.

EILEEN SHANAHAN
US journalist
Quoted in *New York Times Magazine* 1968

Some meetings should be long and leisurely. Some should be mercifully brief. A good way to handle the latter is to hold the meeting with everybody standing up. The 'meetees' won't believe you at first. Then they get very uncomfortable and can hardly wait to get the meeting over with.

ROBERT TOWNSEND
CEO of Avis
Up the Organization

MEMORABLE LINES

I never forgive but I always forget.

ARTHUR BALFOUR 1848–1930
British prime minister
Quoted in R Blake, *Conservative Party*

I have been told that when in charge, ponder; when in trouble, delegate; when in doubt, mumble.

BARONESS CUMBERLEDGE
Working member of the House of Lords
Speech, House of Lords, 24 April 1995

A son can bear with equanimity the loss of his father, but the loss of his inheritance may drive him to despair.

NICCOLÒ MACHIAVELLI 1469–1527
Florentine statesman and writer
The Prince

Don't leap to conclusions, you will only rupture yourselves.

ALASTAIR MORTON
Co-chairman of Eurotunnel
Said after Eurotunnel's public announcement
that the cost of servicing the company's
debts would far outweigh projected revenue
for the next year, 1995

I have a brain and a uterus and I use both.

PATRICIA SCHROEDER
US Congresswoman
On combining motherhood and
office, *New York Times* 1977

Let us leave the labels to those who have little else wherewith to cover their nakedness.

WALTER SICKERT 1860–1942
German-born British painter
The New Age 1914

You don't have to be nice to people on the way up if you're not planning to come back down.

DAN G STONE
Vice-president of Institutional Equity
Sales, Drexel Burnham
April Fools

Recession is when you tighten your belt. Depression is when you have no belt to tighten. When you have lost your trousers you are in the airline business.

ADAM THOMPSON
Chairman of British Caledonian Airlines
High Risk: The Politics of the Air

'If you want a job done right, do it yourself'. Not unless you want an ulcer.

DEBORAH THORP
British editor
Company 1993

The most important man in the room is the one who knows what to do next.

JAMES L WEBB
First administrator of NASA
Favourite saying

MISTAKES
(*SEE ALSO* COMPETENCE; CRITICISM; FAILURE)

A little known fact is that the Apollo moon missions were on course less than 1% of the time. The mission was composed of almost constant midcourse corrections. That's also true of most business situations. Yet few business people have the guts to own up to that reality.

JAMES A BELASCO
US academic and management consultant
Teaching the Elephant to Dance

The man who never makes any blunders is a very nice piece of machinery – that's all.

JOSH BILLINGS (HENRY
WHEELER SHAW) 1818–1885
US writer and auctioneer
Josh Billings: His Book

It is just when you are most successful that you are most vulnerable.

ROGER FOSTER
British entrepreneur and founder
of Apricot Computers
Sunday Times 1988

You've got to have an atmosphere where people can make mistakes. If we're not making mistakes we're not going anywhere.

GORDON FORWARD
US president of Chaparral Steel
Quoted in Tom Peters, *Thriving on Chaos*

Most men who run large corporations are primarily concerned with how not to make mistakes, not even little ones. Their jobs depend upon it. In sizeable corporations, where steady annual gains are expected, mistakes are not easily forgiven.

HAROLD GENEEN
Business consultant and chairman of ITT
Managing

We become uncompetitive by not being tolerant of mistakes. The moment you let avoiding failure become your motivator, you're down the path of inactivity. You can stumble only if you're moving.

ROBERTO GOIZUETA
CEO of Coca-Cola Company
Fortune 1995

No one can be right all of the time, but it helps to be right most of the time.

ROBERT HALF
US president of Robert Half International
Robert Half on Hiring

I asked an American friend the secret of his firm's obviously successful development policy. He looked me straight in the eye. 'Forgiveness', he said. 'We give them big jobs and big responsibilities. Inevitably they make mistakes, we can't check them all the time and don't want to. They learn, we forgive, they don't make the mistake again.' He was unusual. Too many organizations use their appraisal schemes and their confidential files to record our errors and our small disasters. They use them to chastise us with, hoping to inspire us, or to frighten us to do better. It might work once but in future we will make sure that we do not venture far enough from the beaten track to make any mistake.

CHARLES HANDY
Business executive and writer, and
professor at the London Business School
The Age of Unreason

I am humble enough to recognize that I have made mistakes, but politically astute enough to know that I have forgotten what they are.

MICHAEL HESELTINE
British politician
The Economist 1992

In the average [plant] 20–25% of the cost of goods sold is spent on finding and correcting errors. And many of the workers do not actually produce anything – they just correct mistakes.

HENRY J JOHANSSON
US head of manufacturing practice
at Coopers & Lybrand
New York Times 1988

It's a good thing to make mistakes so long as you're found out quickly.

JOHN MAYNARD KEYNES 1883–1946
English economist
Attributed

If something goes wrong it is considered bad taste for management to enquire who made the mistake ... The important thing, in my view, is not to pin the blame for a mistake on somebody, but rather to find out what caused the mistake.

AKIO MORITA
Co-founder of Sony
Made in Japan

We tell our young managers: 'Don't be afraid to make a mistake. But be sure you don't make the same mistake twice'.

AKIO MORITA
Co-founder of Sony
Quoted in Nick Lyons, *The Sony Vision*

You know, by the time you reach my age, you've made plenty of mistakes if you've lived your life properly.

RONALD REAGAN
40th president of the USA
Observer 1987

Experience is the name every one gives to their mistakes.

OSCAR WILDE 1854–1900
Irish poet, dramatist, and wit
Lady Windermere's Fan

MONEY

(*SEE ALSO* GOD AND MAMMON;
INCOME; WEALTH)

Money is better than poverty, if only
for financial reasons.

WOODY ALLEN
US film writer, actor, director
Without Feathers 'Early Essays'

Making money ain't nothing exciting
to me. You might be able to buy a
little better booze than the wino on
the corner. But you get sick just like
the next cat and when you die you're
just as graveyard dead.

LOUIS ARMSTRONG 'SATCHMO' 1900–1971
US jazz trumpeter, bandleader, and singer
Quoted in *Observer* 1970

Money, it turned out, was exactly like
sex, you thought of nothing else if
you didn't have it and thought of
other things if you did.

JAMES BALDWIN 1924–1987
US writer
'Black Boy Looks at White Boy' in *Esquire* 1961

I'm tired of Love: I'm still more tired
of Rhyme./ But Money gives me
pleasure all the time.

HILAIRE BELLOC 1870–1953
French-born English politician and
writer, best known for his nonsensical
verse for children
'Fatigued'

Money doesn't not talk, it swears.

BOB DYLAN
US singer-songwriter
From the song 'It's Alright, Ma'

Money is of no value; it cannot
spend itself. All depends on the skill
of the spender.

RALPH WALDO EMERSON 1803–1882
US philosopher and poet
The Young American

Money is like an arm or a leg – use
it or lose it.

HENRY FORD 1863–1947
Pioneering industrialist and car manufacturer
New York Times 1931

There's no money in poetry; but then
there's no poetry in money.

ROBERT GRAVES 1895–1985
British poet and writer
Quoted in George Plimpton, *The Writer's Chapbook*

Bad money drives out good money.

THOMAS GRESHAM 1519–1579
English financier
'Gresham's Law', contained in a royal
proclamation of 1560

I don't believe money is no object.
Money is the object.

JAMES GULLIVER
Chairman of Argyll Group
You Magazine 1988

If you want to make money, go
where the money is.

JOSEPH P KENNEDY 1888–1969
US business executive and politician
Quoted in A M Schlesinger, *Robert Kennedy
and his Times*

The importance of money essentially
flows from its being a link between
the present and the future.

JOHN MAYNARD KEYNES 1883–1946
English economist
The General Theory of Employment, Interest, and Money

The importance of money essentially
flows from its being a link between
the present and the future.

JOHN MAYNARD KEYNES 1883–1946
English economist
The General Theory of Employment, Interest, and Money

I don't like money actually, but it
quiets my nerves.

JOE LOUIS 1914–1981
US champion boxer
Attributed

Money is like a sixth sense without which you cannot make a complete use of the other five.

W SOMERSET MAUGHAM 1874–1965
English novelist
Of Human Bondage

Money is like manure. If you spread it around, it does a lot of good.

CLINT W MURCHISON
US oil man and financier
Time 1961

But it is pretty to see what money will do.

SAMUEL PEPYS 1633–1703
English diarist
Diary 1667

What is the use of money if you have to work for it?

GEORGE BERNARD SHAW 1856–1950
Irish dramatist and critic
Major Barbara

From birth to 18 a girl needs good parents. From 18 to 35, she needs good looks. From 35 to 55, good personality. From 55 on, she needs good cash. I'm saving my money.

SOPHIE TUCKER 1884–1966
Russian-born US singer and entertainer
Quoted in M Freedland, *Sophie*

MONOPOLY
(SEE ALSO FREE MARKET ECONOMY)

There is unfortunately no good solution for technical monopoly. There is only a choice among three evils: private unregulated monopoly, private monopoly regulated by the state, and government operation.

MILTON FRIEDMAN
US economist
Capitalism and Freedom

Cartels are like babies: we tend to be against them until we have one of our own.

LORD MANCROFT 1914–1987
British business executive
Attributed

A monopoly is a terrible thing until you've got one.

RUPERT MURDOCH
Media baron
Guardian 1995

You learn it on the first day of your first economics class: Smart persons seek monopolies. Because as Willie Sutton said about banks, that's where the money is. (Which is why smart governments try to keep smart businesspersons from achieving monopolies.)

TOM PETERS
US international management consultant
and bestselling business author
Liberation Management

Like many businessmen of genius he learned that free competition was wasteful, monopoly efficient.

MARIO PUZO
US novelist
The Godfather

NATIONALIZATION VERSUS PRIVATIZATION

The private sector is that part of the economy the Government controls and the public sector is the part that nobody controls.

JAMES GOLDSMITH
British financier
Quoted in *Observer* 1979

I don't know anywhere else in the world where every five years I face the possibility of nationalization and then five years later face the probability of privatization.

JOHN HARVEY-JONES
Business writer and chairman of ICI
The Times 1985

Frankly, I'd like to see the government get out of war altogether and leave the whole field to private industry.

JOSEPH HELLER
US writer
Catch-22

First all the Georgian silver goes, and then that nice furniture that used to be in the saloon. Then the Canalettos go.

HAROLD MACMILLAN 1894–1986
British prime minister
Speech attacking privatization, often dubbed
'Selling off the Family Silver', 1985

The major privatizations have involved a gift to the wealthy of more than £323 from every British adult.

ROWLAND MORGAN
British journalist
Guardian 1995

It's not just a goldfish bowl in a nationalized industry, it's a piranha bowl.

PETER PARKER
Chairman of British Rail
The Times 1978

Under our system of parliamentary rule, nationalized industries have a built-in trend towards bankruptcy ... the more an industry is identified with government the less chance it has to economize on salaries and wages. Every man sacked is a voter. Every man hired is a voter.

C NORTHCOTE PARKINSON
British historian, writer, and formulator
of Parkinson's law
Speech, 'Aims of Industry', 1964

Business has a freedom to experiment [that is] missing in the public sector and, often, in nonprofit organizations. It also has a clear 'bottom line,' so that experiments can be evaluated, at least in principle, by objective criteria.

PETER M SENGE
Business academic and director of the
organizational learning programme at MIT
*The Fifth Discipline: The Art and Practice of the
Learning Organization*

It has always seemed to me it's [privatization's] purpose was to put those industries which were hamstrung and restricted into the freedom of the private sector for the benefit of the British public as a whole – not just the shareholders, and certainly not just the management.

KEITH STUART
British chairman of Seeboard
On privatization, *Evening Standard* 1995

Successful businessmen do not take jobs in nationalized industries.

MARGARET THATCHER
British prime minister
Remark to Peter Parker, chairman of British Rail,
quoted in *Observer* 1982

One of the dreadful things about privatization is that service is no longer possible.

UNISON SPOKESPERSON
On the sale of Powerhouse electrical
shops, *Guardian* 1995

Regulators are public officials who know the rate for the job when they accept it. It seems that anybody doing the job now expects a six figure sum. It's like paying referees the same salaries as Eric Cantona.

BRIAN WILSON
British Labour Party trade
and industry spokesman
Guardian 1995

NEGOTIATIONS

(*SEE ALSO* DEALS; DIPLOMACY AND TACT; INDUSTRIAL RELATIONS)

'Frank and explicit' – that is the right line to take when you wish to conceal your own mind and to confuse the minds of others.

BENJAMIN DISRAELI 1804–1881
British prime minister and novelist
Sybil

Let little things go. Never loose your temper.

JOE GORMLEY
British president of the NUM
Sunday Times 1972

It's a well known proposition that you know who is going to win a negotiation: it's he who pauses the longest.

ROBERT HOLMES À COURT 1937–1990
Australian business executive
Sydney Morning Herald 1986

When a man tells me he's going to put all his cards on the table, I always look up his sleeve.

LORD HORE-BELISHA 1893–1957
British politician
Quoted in Martin Manser, *Chambers Book of Business Quotations*

You should not convey to an opponent, whether by word or action, that you want whatever the opponent has.

JOHN ILICH
US professional negotiator
Power Negotiating

Let us never negotiate out of fear, but let us never fear to negotiate.

JOHN F KENNEDY 1917–1963
35th president of the USA
Inaugural address, 1961

Whenever you're sitting across from some important person, always

picture him sitting there in a suit of long red underwear. That's the way I always operated in business.

JOSEPH KENNEDY 1888–1969
US business executive and politician
Quoted in Martin Manser, *Chambers Book of Business Quotations*

A negotiator should observe everything. You must be part Sherlock Holmes, part Sigmund Freud.

VICTOR KIAM
CEO of Remington
Going For It!

I never back down. And so far, what I have determined I shall have the gods have been kind enough to grant me, after some trepidation.

ROBERT MAXWELL 1923–1991
Czech-born British publishing and newspaper magnate, whose death prompted an investigation into his business empire revealing bankruptcy and the misappropriation of millions of pounds from pension funds,
Current Biography 1988

In a successful negotiation, everybody wins.

GERARD NIERENBERG
US president of the Negotiation Institute
Wall Street Journal 1987

Concentrate on the issues that are most important to you and minimize or ignore the nonessentials.

JAMES C NUNAN AND THOMAS J HUTTON
US businessmen
Personnel Journal 1987

Don't negotiate with yourself. Have the patience to wait for the other fellow to make a counter-offer after you've made one.

RICHARD SMITH
US partner of Smith, McWorter & Pacher
Speech, Washington DC, 1988

I do not find myself being confrontational. I try to find a way of avoiding people who are getting in my way. It's all about making your opponent's line of least resistance coincide with what you want.

PATRICIA VAZ
Director of BT payphones and 'Veuve Cliquot
Businesswoman of the Year' 1995
Interview, *Independent* 1995

NON-EXECUTIVE DIRECTORS
(*SEE ALSO* BOARD AND BOARDROOM; CHAIRMEN, CHAIRWOMEN, AND CEOs; TOP EXECUTIVES)

A non-executive director is only as good as the information he is given.

JONATHAN AITKEN
British politician and non-executive
director of BMARC
Question Time, BBC1 television broadcast, 1995

All too often it is the non-executive director who has the unhappy task of blowing the whistle, and demonstrating that the company is in serious trouble. Hence the title of this chapter – The Emperor's Clothes – [in *Making It Happen*] for it is the non-executive director who, above all, is best placed to observe that the Emperor he is serving actually hasn't got any, or at best many less and of a different style and cut than the Emperor believes.

JOHN HARVEY-JONES
Business writer and chairman of ICI
Making It Happen

The non-executive director has a very small range of weapons and powers although he has a wide range of responsibilities. It is in learning to deploy these limited assets that the problems of becoming a good non-executive director lie. All too often

you only get one kick at the ball – and you have to learn on the run.

JOHN HARVEY-JONES
Business writer and chairman of ICI
Making It Happen

I suspect we are in the early stages of redefining the way in which boards of quoted companies will work, with non-execs having to act in the public as well as the shareholder interest.

HAMISH MCRAE
Scottish journalist
Independent 1995

[Non-executive directors can be compared to] Christmas tree decorations.

TINY ROWLAND
Entrepreneur and CEO of Lonrho
Expressing his view about the role of non-executive directors, quoted in Richard Hall *My Life with Tiny*

OFFICE LIFE

Plants are to offices what goalkeepers are to football. They look ridiculous and their only function is to get in your way.

GUY BROWNING
British journalist
Guardian 1995

It's been my impression through the years that when I come upon a man who has a gleaming, empty, clean desk top, I am dealing with a fellow who is so far removed from the realities of his business that someone else is running it for him.

HAROLD GENEEN
Business consultant and chairman of ITT
Managing

Staff unhappiness is largely ignored because the people with the most power tend to have the most control. They sit next to windows, they have cellular offices and comfortable working conditions. Control also goes with being male. Women tend to sit in the middle of buildings, away from the window seats. So they are more sensitive to poorer conditions.

ADRIAN LEAMAN
British expert on 'sick building syndrome'
Independent 1995

Being away from the office is very therapeutic.

ROYAL LITTLE
US founder of Textron
Best of Business Quarterly 1987

Some gravitate to small firms to avoid politics. Forget it. The only place to avoid politics is in a cabin, by yourself, with no electricity, somewhere deep in the wilderness ... All organizations with more than one employee are political. And all companies with three or more employees have cliques.

TOM PETERS
US international management consultant
and bestselling business author
Independent on Sunday 1995

A man who has no office to go to – I don't care who he is – is a trial of which you can have no conception.

GEORGE BERNARD SHAW 1856–1950
Irish dramatist and critic
Irrational Knot

The office is a fine place for day-to-day activity. But it's not the best place for big thinking.

W E UZZELL
US president of Royal Crown Cola Co.
Quoted in Mackenzie, *The Time Trap*

I yield to no one in my admiration

for the office as a social centre, but it's no place actually to get any work done.

KATHERINE WHITEHORN
British journalist
Sunday Best

OPPORTUNITY
(SEE ALSO LUCK)

It cannot be ignored that *Luck* and *Opportunity* often win the race, while *Merit* and *Ability* lag behind, but those who have 'greatness thrust upon them' are few and far between.

ANONYMOUS
'Business Habits' in *The Universal Self-Instructor* 1883

For most of us, our speed of reaction to opportunity is a tithe of our speed of reaction to adversity.

JOHN HARVEY-JONES
Business writer and chairman of ICI
Managing to Survive

Entrepreneurs are simply those who understand that there is little difference between obstacle and opportunity and are able to turn both to their advantage.

VICTOR KIAM
CEO of Remington
Going For It!

You must believe the unbelievable, snatch the possible out of the impossible.

DON KING
US boxing promoter
Daily Telegraph 1977

One can present people with opportunities. One cannot make them equal to them.

ROSAMOND LEHMANN 1901–1990
British novelist
Ballad and the Source

ORGANIZATIONS

Every organization has a Siberia.

WARREN G BENNIS
Business academic and president of the
University of Cincinnati
Symposium, University of Maryland, 1988

We can assume that an organization possesses a healthy structure when it has a clear sense of what it is and what it is to do.

WARREN BENNIS AND BURT NANUS
Business academic and president of the
University of Cincinnati; business
academic and writer
Leaders: The Strategies for Taking Charge

I'm surprised that a government organization could do it that quickly.

JIMMY CARTER
39th president of the USA
Attributed remark on hearing that the building of
the Great Pyramid took 20 years

Every company has two organizational structures: the formal one is written on the charts; the other is the living relationship of the men and women in the organization.

HAROLD GENEEN
Business consultant and chairman of ITT
Managing

In the old style of organization, managers needed the skills of command and control, and workers needed the technical skills that related to their jobs. In the modern organization, however, everybody needs skills that enable them to work as a team, to solve problems and to make decisions jointly, to be creative and, above all, to communicate.

TERRY GILLEN
Training consultant
Sunday Times 1995

The bigger the headquarters the more decadent the company.

JAMES GOLDSMITH
British financier
Quoted in *Financial Weekly* 1990

A organization with an indispensable man is guilty of management failure.

HAROLD S HOOK
CEO and chairman of American General Corp.
Forbes 1987

Organizations exist to enable ordinary people to do extraordinary things.

TED LEVITT
Editor of *Harvard Business Review*
Thinking About Management

Parkinson's Third Law: expansion means complexity, and complexity, decay. Or: the more complex the sooner dead

C NORTHCOTE PARKINSON
British historian, writer, and formulator
of Parkinson's law
In-Laws and Outlaws

I've developed what I call 'the rule of five': no more than five central staffers per billion dollars in revenue booked! Funny thing, I'm serious. Only a fickle, decentralized operation will survive in a fickle, decentralized global economy. One essential element of decentralization is the demise of central staffs.

TOM PETERS
US international management consultant
and bestselling business author
Liberation Management

The people who really run organizations are usually found several levels down, where it's still possible to get things done.

TERRY PRATCHETT
British writer
Small Gods

People think the president has to be the main organizer. No, the president is the main *dis*-organizer. Everybody 'manages' quite well: whenever anything goes wrong, they take immediate action to make sure nothing'll go wrong again. The problem is, nothing new will ever happen, either.

HENRY V QUADRACCI
US CEO of Quad/Graphics
Quoted in Tom Peters, *Liberation Management*

In times of robust economic growth we have found our divided plants make more money than they did when they were larger. And we have also found that smaller plants bounce back from bad times or a crisis much faster than larger ones.

RICARDO SEMLER
Brazilian CEO of Semco
On company policy of keeping factory units small, *Maverick*

Middle managers make nothing but the organization.

EARL SHORRIS
US manager and writer
The Oppressed Middle

All organizations engage in the three basic activities of strategy, tactics, and logistics. Strategy defines the job. Tactics does the job. Logistics provides the resources to get the job done – not only material resources, but also manpower, funds, and data.

ROBERT L SIEGEL
Branch manager of McLaughlin Research Corp.
Speech, Arlington, Virginia, 1987

The difference between 'structure' and 'stricture' is 'I'.

MARLENE SOLOMON
US publisher of *Magna Magazine*
Sales meeting, 1988

Big seems to breed bigger. As total employment increases, so does the number of management layers required to keep things under control.

ROBERT TOMASKO
Principal of Temple, Barker & Sloane, Inc.
Downsizing

Organizations exist for only one purpose: to help people reach ends together that they could not achieve individually.

ROBERT H WATERMAN
US management consultant and writer
The Renewal Factor

ORGANIZING

This island is made mainly of coal and surrounded by fish. Only an organizing genius could produce a shortage of coal and fish at the same time.

ANEURIN ('NYE') BEVAN 1897–1960
British politician
Speech, Blackpool, 1945

Organization can never be a substitute for initiative.

LOUIS DEMBITZ BRANDEIS 1856–1941
US Supreme Court justice
Business – A Profession

The company with the second-best organization ends up second place in the market.

D WAYNE CALLOWAY
CEO of PepsiCo
Harvard Business Review 1987

Don't agonize. Organize.

FLORYNCE R KENNEDY
US writer and feminist
Ms. Magazine 1973

Necessary Disorganization.

TOM PETERS
US international management consultant
and bestselling business author
Chapter heading and theme
in *Liberation Management*

Structure is not organization.

ROBERT H WATERMAN
US management consultant and writer
Business Horizons 1980

PAY
(SEE ALSO INCOME)

One man's definition of excessive is another's derisory sum.

JOHN ASHCROFT
Chairman of Coloroll plc
Quoted in *Financial Times* 1988

If our people develop faster than a competitor's people, then they're worth more.

JAMES M BIGGAR
US CEO of Nestlè Enterprises
USA Today 1988

If there are many applicants for a few jobs, the job is overpaid.

MILTON FRIEDMAN
US economist
Daily Mirror 1981

In the business world, everyone is paid in two coins: cash and experience. Take the experience first; the cash will come later.

HAROLD GENEEN
Business consultant and chairman of ITT
Managing

It is but a truism that labor is most productive where its wages are largest. Poorly paid labor is inefficient labor, the world over.

HENRY GEORGE 1839–1897
US economist
Progress and Poverty

I know of no salary plan that will guarantee against eventual employee dissatisfaction with pay.

FREDERICK HERZBERG
US academic
The Managerial Choice

The most effective way to use money is to give outstanding performers spectacular rewards at rare intervals. Nothing is too good for our make-or-break individuals.

DAVID OGILVY
Advertising guru and founder
of Ogilvy and Mather
Daily Telegraph 1969

The two most beautiful words in the English language are 'Cheque Enclosed'.

DOROTHY PARKER 1893–1967
US writer and wit
Attributed

The highest salary the EDS ever paid me was $64,000, because I tied my fate to the stockholders' fate. Today many companies pay their chief executives obscene salaries and treat customers and stockholders as a nuisance.

H ROSS PEROT
US presidential candidate and founder
of Electronic Data Systems
Life 1988

Reward workers while the sweat's still on their brow.

H ROSS PEROT
US presidential candidate and founder
of Electronic Data Systems
Life 1988

Only in our dreams are we free. The rest of the time we need wages.

TERRY PRATCHETT
British writer
Wyrd Sisters

Some of you have the gall to increase your own salaries by 25% and introduce bonus systems for yourselves worth millions of kroner. How, during these times, can you do this? Are you living on another planet?

MONA SAHLIN
Swedish deputy prime minister
from an open letter to Swedish business leaders
printed in *Expressen*, quoted in *Guardian* 1995

The price of ability does not depend on merit, but on supply and demand.
GEORGE BERNARD SHAW 1856–1950
Irish dramatist and critic
'Socialism and Superior Brains' in *Fortnightly Review* 1894

A man should never endeavour to price himself, but should accept the price which others put on him, – only being careful that he should learn what that price is.
ANTHONY TROLLOPE 1815–1882
English novelist
The Prime Minister

It isn't the sum you get, it's how much you can buy with it that's the important thing; and it's that that tells you whether your wages are high in fact or only high in name.
MARK TWAIN 1835–1910
US writer
A Connecticut Yankee at King Arthur's Court

'For two days' labour, you ask two hundred guineas?' 'No, I ask it for the knowledge of a lifetime'.
JAMES MCNEILL WHISTLER 1834–1903
US-born English painter
Quoted in D C Seitz, *Whistler Stories*

We need to think more about earning money and less about making it.
HAROLD WILSON 1916–1995
British prime minister
Quoted in *Observer* 1964

PEOPLE AND PEOPLE MANAGEMENT
(*SEE ALSO* EMPLOYERS AND EMPLOYEES)

Treat employees like partners, and they act like partners.
FRED ALLEN
US Chairman, Pitney-Bowes Co.
Leaders Magazine 1979

My experience with people is that they generally *do what you expect them to do!* If you expect them to perform well, they will; conversely, if you expect them to perform poorly, they'll probably oblige.
MARY KAY ASH
US entrepreneur and founder of Mary Kay Cosmetics
Mary Kay on People Management

A good people manager will never put someone down: not only is it nonproductive – it's counterproductive. You must remember that your job is to play the role of problem solver, and that by taking this approach instead of criticizing people you'll accomplish considerably more.
MARY KAY ASH
US entrepreneur and founder of Mary Kay Cosmetics
Mary Kay on People Management

The worst mistake a boss can make is not to say 'well done'.
JOHN ASHCROFT
Chairman of Coloroll plc
Sunday Telegraph Magazine 1988

Dealing with people is the biggest problem you face, especially if you are a business man.
DALE CARNEGIE 1888–1955
US writer and teacher of public speaking
How to Win Friends and Influence People

There's no substitute for personal contact ... People want to be recognized as people.
PATRICIA M CARRIGAN
Plant manager for General Motors Corp.
MTS Digest 1987

A great business is really too big to be human.
HENRY FORD 1863–1947
Pioneering industrialist and car manufacturer
Quoted in Ricardo Semler, *Maverick*

What you manage in business is people.

HAROLD GENEEN
Business consultant and chairman of ITT
Managing

Getting results through people is a skill that cannot be learned in the classroom.

J PAUL GETTY 1892–1976
US millionaire oil executive
Quoted in Martin Manser, *Chambers Book of Business Quotations*

A personnel officer should possess a sensitive ear, a caring heart and the skin of a rhinoceros.

PRISCILLA GOSS
Vice-president for Human Resources,
American Management Association
Management Review 1987

Treat others as ends, never as means.

DAG HAMMERSKJÖLD 1905–1961
Secretary-General of the United Nations
Markings

The organization which treats people like assets, requiring maintenance, love and investment, can behave quite differently from the organization which looks upon them as costs, to be reduced wherever and whenever possible.

CHARLES HANDY
Business executive and writer, and
professor at the London Business School
The Age of Unreason

Management, above everything else, is about people. It is about accomplishment of ends and aims by the efforts of groups of people working together.

JOHN HARVEY-JONES
Business writer and chairman of ICI
Managing to Survive

I wonder how often chairmen visit their telephone exchanges, or actually thank those on the switchboard for the way in which they respond for the company. It really is an essential port of call, at least once a year, because, just like everybody else in your business, the telephone exchange like to feel that they are working for people who care, and it means a lot to them to know that a quick response or pleasant manner is valued.

JOHN HARVEY-JONES
Business writer and chairman of ICI
Making It Happen

Effort is nourished by appreciation and appreciation is something that the workers and management in our manufacturing industry have not had for a long time.

LORD KEARTON
Chairman of Courtaulds
Daily Mail 1983

Suffer fools gladly. They may be right.

HOLBROOK JACKSON 1874–1948
British writer and editor
Platitudes in the Making

We know more about the motives, habits, and most intimate arcana of the primitive peoples of New Guinea or elsewhere, than we do the denizens of the executive suites in Unilever House.

ROY LEWIS AND ROSEMARY STEWART
US authors
The Boss

People influence people.

ROBERT F MAGER
US psychologist and educational technologist
Developing Attitude Toward Learning

Many of the job failures, nervous breakdowns, and 'battles with the bottle' almost certainly have their causes in vocational misplacement and subsequent mishandling by well-intentioned but often unqualified personnel people.

ROBERT N McMURRY
US management expert
'Clear Communications for Chief Executives' in
Harvard Business Review 1965

When white-collar people get jobs, they sell not only their time and energy, but their personalities as well. They sell by the week, or month their smiles and their kindly gestures, and they must practice that prompt repression of resentment and aggression.

C WRIGHT MILLS
US sociologist
White Collar

The mere act of showing people you're concerned about them spurs them to better job performance.

JEROME PELOQUIN
President of Performance Control Corp.
Training 1986

The ability to deal with people is as purchasable a commodity as sugar and coffee. And I will pay more for that ability than for any other under the sun.

JOHN D ROCKEFELLER 1839–1937
US millionaire industrialist and philanthropist
Quoted in Dale Carnegie, *How to Win Friends and Influence People*

Self confidence is important. Confidence in others is essential.

WILLIAM A SCHREYER
CEO of Merrill Lynch & Co.
American Heritage

Factories that have become too large for their own good should be broken into units small enough to insure that the people who worked in them would feel human again. In a small factory, it is possible to know everyone by their first name, to

debate plans and strategies, to feel involved. *To belong*.

RICARDO SEMLER
Brazilian CEO of Semco
Maverick

One of the hallmarks of a well-organized and attractive business, large or small, is the impression created by the response of its staff to a telephone call ... You should also consider your own behaviour on the telephone and to the telephone operator. It does not matter who you are or how important you are in the business, correct treatment of telephone operators is essential – they are an important asset.

LORD SIEFF
Honorary president of Marks and Spencer plc
Management the Marks and Spencer Way

A personnel man with his arm around an employee is like a treasurer with his hand in the till.

ROBERT TOWNSEND
CEO of Avis
Up the Organization

Put your personnel work first because it is the most important.

ROBERT E WOOD 1879–1969
US chairman and president of
Sears, Roebuck & Co.
Memo to territorial officers, 1931

POINT OF SALE

Food-retailer labels like to concentrate on positive attributes, making a plus point out of giving us what we always thought we were getting. Thus we now live in the world of 'flavour-grown' tomatoes and 'ripe-and-ready-to-eat' fruit – frequently the same duff stuff elaborately over-packaged, retailing at twice the price.

JO BLYTHMAN
British journalist
Guardian 1995

The forthcoming, virtual, three-dimensional teleshopping may well stimulate interest in buying valuable articles, but the potential customers sitting at home will continue to use the television primarily as a source of information. The actual purchasing of such valuable and premium-priced items will still take place in the shop.

RAINER BRUDERLE
German government minister
Retail Jeweller 1995

In retailing the first consideration in the design of a shop should be ease of shopping for the customer. Being able to find what you want is the key thing, and only after that do aesthetics come into it.

SIMON HORNBY
Chairman of W H Smith & Son
Telegraph Magazine 1988

Out-of-town centres and factory villages are all car-borne. City centres that want to thrive have to attract the car-borne shopper.

IAN LAWRIE
British department-store manager
Nottingham Evening Post 1995

POLITICS AND POLITICIANS
(*SEE ALSO* GOVERNMENT)

Controlling public spending is a long and gruelling slog. But the alternative is far worse.

TONY BLAIR
British Labour Party leader
Mais Lecture, City University, London, 1995

We urgently need a government equivalent of Weight Watchers.

ROD CARNEGIE
Australian business executive
Quoted in *Sydney Morning News* 1985

That fabulous animal formally called 'economic policy' and more familiarly called political interference.

G A DUNCAN
Irish economist
Economic Journal 1961

There are times in politics when you must be on the right side and lose.

J K GALBRAITH
US diplomat, economist, and writer
Quoted in *Observer* 1968

Politics is not the art of the possible. It consists in choosing between the disastrous and the unpalatable.

J K GALBRAITH
US diplomat, economist, and writer
Ambassador's Journal

The future of Europe, and the future of the UK in Europe, is vital for the competitiveness of British industry. Businesses do not seek to become embroiled in the political process, but they are citizens of Europe too.

ROBIN GELDARD
President of the British Chambers of Commerce
Guardian 1995

In a race for global competitiveness, the nation-state has no option but to accept the lowest common global denominator – whether of TV standards or employment.

WILL HUTTON
British economics columnist
Guardian 1995

The political problem of mankind is to combine three things: economic efficiency, social justice, and individual liberty.

JOHN MAYNARD KEYNES 1883–1946
English economist
Attributed

Bankers sometimes look on politicians as people who, when they see light at the end of the tunnel, order more tunnel.

JOHN QUINTON
British banker
Independent 1989

We consider donations to Party funds to be similar to buying a round of drinks. If you want to be welcome at a party or a pub, it is policy and polite to pay your round.

ROY RICHARDSON
British property developer and
Conservative Party supporter
Sunday Times 1995

POVERTY
(*SEE ALSO* INCOME; PAY)

Poverty is the parent of revolution and crime.

ARISTOTLE 348–322 BC
Greek philosopher
Politics

Anyone who has ever struggled with poverty knows how extremely expensive it is to be poor.

JAMES BALDWIN 1924–1987
US writer and civil-rights activist
'Fifth Avenue, Uptown: a letter from Harlem'
in *Nobody Knows My Name*

You cannot sift out the poor from the community. The poor are indispensable to the rich.

HENRY WARD BEECHER 1813–1897
US cleric and writer
Proverbs from Plymouth Pulpit

The poor always ye have with you.

BIBLE
John 12:8

It has been said that the love of money is the root of all evil. The want of money is so quite as truly.

SAMUEL BUTLER 1835–1902
English writer
Erewhon

Almost every desire a poor man has is a punishable offence.

LOUIS-FERDINAND CÉLINE 1894–1961
French writer
Journey to the End of the Night

The rich man may never get into heaven, but the pauper is already serving his term in hell.

ALEXANDER CHASE
US journalist
Perspectives

To be poor and independent is very nearly an impossibility.

WILLIAM COBBETT 1762–1835
English social critic and writer
Advice to Young Men

Extreme poverty destroys man altogether.

MILOVAN DJILAS
Yugoslav socialist author and dissident
The New Class

Poverty wastes the energy and talents of individuals and imperils the security of liberty and property.

ALAN DUNCAN AND DOMINIC HOBSON
British writers
Saturn's Children

Can anybody remember when the times were not hard, and money not scarce?

RALPH WALDO EMERSON 1803–1882
US writer and philosopher
'Works and Days' in *Society and Solitude*

New kings will rule and the poor will toil/ And tear their hands as they tear the soil/ But a day will come in the dawning age/ When an honest man sees an honest wage.

DAVID EVANS 'THE EDGE'/U2
Irish rock musician
From the song 'Van Dieman's Land '

I used to think I was poor. Then they told me I wasn't poor. I was needy. Then they told me it was self-defeating to think of myself as needy. I was underprivileged. Then they told me that underprivileged was overused. I was disadvantaged. I still don't have a dime. But I have a great vocabulary.

JULES FEIFFER
US cartoonist
Village Voice 1965

They [the poor] have to labour in the face of the majestic equality of the law, which forbids the rich as well as the poor to sleep under bridges, to beg in the streets, and to steal bread.

ANATOLE FRANCE 1844–1924
French writer
Red Lily

If a free society cannot help the many who are poor, it cannot save the few who are rich.

JOHN F KENNEDY 1917–1963
35th president of the USA
Inaugural address, 1961

If poverty is the mother of crime, stupidity is its father.

JEAN DE LA BRUYÈRE 1645–1696
French writer
'Of Man' in *Characters*

Poverty is no disgrace to a man, but it is confoundedly inconvenient.

SYDNEY SMITH 1771–1845
English journalist, cleric, and wit
His Wit and Wisdom

A beggar hates his benefactor as much as he hates himself for being a beggar.

FATHER OSKAR WERMTER
German Jesuit missionary in Zimbabwe
Sunday Times magazine 1995

When the poor feel as poor as the rich do, there will be bloody revolution.

REBECCA WEST 1892–1983
British writer
The Thinking Reed 1935

To recommend thrift to the poor is both grotesque and insulting. It is like advising a man who is starving to eat less.

OSCAR WILDE 1854–1900
Irish poet, dramatist, and wit
The Soul of Man under Socialism

POWER
(*SEE ALSO* BOSSES)

Power tends to corrupt and absolute power corrupts absolutely.

LORD ACTON 1834–1902
British historian and Liberal politician
Letter to Mandell Creighton, first professor of ecclesiastical history at Cambridge University
(later bishop of London), 1887

Men in great place are thrice servants: servants of the sovereign or state, servants of fame, and servants of business.

FRANCIS BACON 1561–1626
English politician, philosopher, and essayist
'Of Great Place' in *Essays*

Money is economical power.

WALTER BAGEHOT 1826–1877
English writer and economist
Lombard Street

Influence those who influence others.

JOHN FAIRCHILD
US publisher
Motto

Lipstick isn't sexy. Lipstick is power. I hate wearing lipstick, but it's important. They've done studies on it.

BARBARA FOLLETT
British political activist and style consultant
Interview, *Independent Magazine* 1995

Men of power have no time to read; yet men who do not read are unfit for power.

ISAAC FOOT 1880–1960
British Liberal politician
Debts of Honour

I spent my youth and early manhood worrying about corporate power. Now I worry about corporate incompetence.

J K GALBRAITH
US diplomat, economist, and writer
Fortune 1992

Power is where power goes.

LYNDON BAINES JOHNSON 1908–1973
36th president of the USA
Response to journalists' questions about his decision to step down from Senate majority leader to run for the comparatively powerless job of vice-president

Power corrupts, but lack of power corrupts absolutely.

ADLAI STEVENSON 1900–1968
US statesman and presidential candidate
Quoted in Tom Bower, *Maxwell, The Outsider*

What do I care about the law. H'aint I got the power?

CORNELIUS VANDERBILT 1794–1877
US shipping and railroad magnate
Quoted in Josephson, *The Robber Barons*

PRESSURE AND STRESS
(*SEE ALSO* HEALTH)

Always do one thing less than you think you can do.

BERNARD BARUCH 1870–1965
US presidential advisor and financial analyst
Quoted in Laurence J Peter, *The Peter Principle*

It is not work that kills men; it is worry. Work is healthy; you can hardly put more upon a man than he can bear. Worry is rust upon the blade. It is not the revolution that destroys the machinery, but the friction.

HENRY WARD BEECHER 1813–1887
US cleric and writer
Proverbs from Plymouth Pulpit

People react defensively to situations in which they feel both threatened and under pressure. The threat is usually not physical ... In the workaday world, the blows we receive most frequently are psychological, and the deepest wounds we get from them are to our motivation and our feelings of self-worth.

ROBERT M BRANSON
US psychologist and management consultant
Coping With Difficult People

Leaders make mistakes when they're too tired and overwhelmed with paper.

JAMES CALLAGHAN
British prime minister
Harvard Business Review 1986

I don't have ulcers; I give them.

HARRY COHN 1891–1958
US film mogul and president of Columbia Pictures
Quoted in Ringo, *Nobody Said It Better*

I'm sure the problem is connected with control of events. The lower in the chain of command you are, the less you can influence the events around you, and the more you may suffer.

CARY L COOPER
British stress-management consultant
The Times 1985

You can have the best systems in the world, but if your people aren't fresh, if they're burned out, it won't matter. They won't provide the kind of service that customers expect.

BOB DANIELS
Owner of Copperfield Chimney Supply, Inc.
Inc. Magazine 1987

I enjoy pressure, can't do without it, almost seek it out.

GEORGE DAVIES
Chairman of Next plc
Observer Magazine 1986

When you are under pressure to deny you are under pressure, then you are under pressure.

JIM DUNNE
Financial journalist
Business and Finance 1986

As a cure for worrying, work is better than whiskey.

THOMAS ALVA EDISON 1847–1931
US inventor
Radio interview, 1931

Every manager knows the problem of battling the daily, even hourly, barrage of operating data that assaults the mind. The realization that I could not track every detail of my business came as my days got longer, my nights got shorter, and my leaden briefcase seemed increasingly likely to unhinge my right shoulder.

AXEL L GRABOWSKY
US CEO of Harte & Co.
Inc. Magazine's Guide to Small Business Success

Burnout is one of the costliest factors ... We're beating guys up so hard for results, that all the human resource guidelines just go to hell in a handbasket.

ROBERT GUERRA
US executive at Federal Data Systems
Computer & Software News 1987

Executive stress is difficult to overstate when there is a conflict among policy restrictions, near-term performance, long-term good of the company, and personal survival.

BRUCE HENDERSON
CEO of Boston Consulting Group, Inc.
Henderson on Corporate Strategy

If you're not scared, you're too stupid to work here.

LEE IACOCCA
CEO of Chrysler Corporation
Said in a senior management meeting, 1990

If you can keep your head when all about you are losing theirs, it's just possible you haven't grasped the situation.

JEAN KERR
US writer
Please Don't Eat the Daisies

Mental toughness wins more games than great skill and fancy game plans.

VINCE LOMBARDI 1913–1970
US football coach
Quoted in James A Belasco, *Teaching the Elephant to Dance*

Just as the body becomes exhausted by hard labour and is reinvigorated by rest, so the mind needs its weariness relieved by rest.

MOSES MAIMONIDES 1135–1204
Spanish-born Egyptian philosopher and personal physician to Sultan Saladin
The Eight Chapters on Ethics

I don't know any executive who ever thought about stress, although a lot of other people do. No one ever dies of hard work. But a lot of people die once they retire from an active job.

IAN McGREGOR
Chairman of the National Coal Board
Daily Mail 1980

Just as the body can be trained to tolerate physiological stress, so presumably can the mind be trained to tolerate psychological stress.

HENRY MINTZBERG
Canadian professor of management at McGill University
The Nature of Managerial Work

One quality that has brought many executives up to their present positions is their ability to handle emergencies and to work under pressure. But an executive, in order to grow and endure, will soon find it imperative to concentrate on the elimination of emergencies.

E B OSBORN
President of Economics Laboratory Inc.
Executive Development Manual

Twenty-five years ago, we had more intermittent stress. We had a chance to bounce back before we encountered another crisis. Today, we have chronic, unremitting stress.

GENEVA ROWE
US psychotherapist
Newsweek 1988

Some senior managers are the toxic carriers of stress.

ROBERT L SWAIN
US outplacement expert
Fortune 1988

The nineties will be a decade in a hurry, a nanosecond culture. There'll be only two kinds of managers: the quick and the dead.

DAVID VICE
US vice chairman of Northern Telecom
Quoted in Tom Peters, *Liberation Management*

PRICES AND VALUE

A fair price for oil is whatever you can get plus 10%.

ALI AHMED ATTIGA
Saudi Arabian delegate to OPEC
Quoted in *Observer* 1974

Value has been defined as the ability to command the price.

LOUIS DEMBITZ BRANDEIS 1856–1941
US Supreme Court judge
St Louis & Ohio Railroad v. US 1928

If the choice lies between the production or purchase of two

commodities, the value of one is measured by the sacrifice of going without the other.

H J DAVENPORT 1861–1931
US economist
'The Formula of Sacrifice' in *Journal of Political Economy*

If you would know the value of money, go and try to borrow some.

BENJAMIN FRANKLIN 1706–1790
US author, scientist, and statesman
The Way to Wealth

The value of a thing is the amount of laboring or work that its possession will save the possessor.

HENRY GEORGE 1839–1897
US economist
The Science of Political Economy

Ill ware is never cheap.

GEORGE HERBERT 1593–1633
English cleric and writer
Jacula Prudentum

The real issue is value, not price.

ROBERT T LINDGREN
Cross & Trecker Corp.
Harvard Business Review 1988

A man who knows the price of everything and the value of nothing.

OSCAR WILDE 1854–1900
Irish poet, dramatist, and wit
Definition of a cynic, *Lady Windermere's Fan*

PRIORITIES

The three most important things a man has are, briefly, his private parts, his money, and his religious opinions.

SAMUEL BUTLER 1835–1902
British author
Further Extracts from Notebooks

The essence of effective time and life management is to organize and execute around balanced priorities.

STEPHEN R COVEY
Founder of the Institute of Principle-Centred Leadership
The Seven Habits of Highly Effective People

Selectivity – the determination to choose what we will attempt to get done and what we won't – is the only way out of the panic that excessive demands on our time can create.

ANDREW S GROVE
CEO of Intel Corp.
One-to-One With Andy Grove

The trouble ... is that we constantly put second things first.

LYNDON BAINES JOHNSON 1908–1973
36th president of the USA
Quoted in Mackenzie, *The Time Trap*

Nothing reveals more of what a company really cares about than its stories and legends ... Listening to a company's stories is the surest route to determining its real priorities and who symbolizes them.

TOM PETERS AND NANCY AUSTIN
US international management consultant and bestselling business author; US management consultant and writer
A Passion for Excellence

PROBLEMS

There are two problems in my life. The political ones are insoluble and the economic ones are incomprehensible.

ALEC DOUGLAS-HOME
British prime minister
Attributed

We are always buying nostrums of some kind, those patent medicines sold with exaggerated claims, even in business, where we call them concepts, because we're always looking for simple formulas that will solve our complex problems.

HAROLD GENEEN
Business consultant and chairman of ITT
Managing

Try several solutions at once. Maybe none of them, alone, would solve the problem, but in combination they do the job.

RAY JOSEPHS
President of Ray Josephs Associates, Inc.
Leadership in Office

When we got into office, the thing that surprised me most was to find that things were just as bad as we'd been saying they were.

JOHN F KENNEDY 1917–1963
35th president of the USA
Speech, White House, 1961

There cannot be a crisis next week. My schedule is already full.

HENRY KISSINGER
US politician, diplomat and academic
New York Times Magazine 1969

Problems can become opportunities when the right people come together.

ROBERT REDFORD
US actor and film director
Harvard Business Review 1987

I need problems. A good problem makes me come alive.

TINY ROWLAND
Entrepreneur and CEO of Lonrho
Sunday Times 1990

No matter how complicated a problem is, it usually can be reduced to a simple, comprehensible form which is often the best solution.

AN WANG
CEO of Wang Laboratories
Nation's Business 1987

Most people would rush ahead and implement a solution before they know what the problem is.

Q T WILES
US management consultant
Inc. Magazine

PRODUCTIVITY

Most of the collective bargaining since the 1940s has resulted in wage settlements in excess of productivity increases.

COURTNEY C BROWN
US academic
Dun's Review 1979

Knowledge is the only instrument of production that is not subject to diminishing returns.

JOHN MAURICE CLARK
US academic
Journal of Political Economy 1927

To obtain the most from a man's energy it is necessary to increase the effect without increasing the fatigue.

CHARLES AUGUSTIN COULOMB 1736–1806
French scientist
Observations 1791

The productivity of work is not the responsibility of the worker but of the manager.

PETER F DRUCKER
US management expert
Management in Turbulent Times

Because we don't have as many people pounding out manufactured things as we once did, many fallaciously conclude our productivity has withered.

MALCOLM F FORBES 1919–1990
US publisher of *Forbes* magazine
Forbes 1988

The output of a manager is the output of the organizational units under his supervision or influence.

ANDREW S GROVE
CEO Intel Corp.
High Output Management

One way to increase productivity is to do whatever we are doing now, but *faster* ... There is a second way.

We can change the *nature* of the work we do, not how fast we do it.

ANDREW S GROVE
CEO Intel Corp.
High Output Management

Cost accounting is the number one enemy of productivity.

H THOMAS JOHNSON AND ROBERT S KAPLAN
US writers
Relevance Lost: The Rise and Fall of Management Accounting

Looking for differences between the more productive and less productive organizations, we found that the most striking difference is the number of people who are involved and feel responsibility for solving problems.

MICHAEL MCTAGUE
US management-training consultant
Personnel Journal 1986

It is significant that in Japan trade unions are among the most vocal advocates of long-term investment strategies that emphasize productivity and growth.

ROBERT B REICH
US academic
The Next American Frontier

Man does not live by GNP alone.

PAUL ANTHONY SAMUELSON
US economist
Economics
Pun on the original biblical proverb,
'Man cannot live by bread alone ...'

It is in changing the way people work that I think the answers to productivity are going to be found.

JOHN SCULLY
CEO of Apple Computer Co.
Fortune 1987

We can no longer plonk a machine in front of a guy and make him more productive. Those days are over.

PAUL TROTTER
Information-systems manager, Chemical Bank
PC Week 1987

The way to get higher productivity is to train better managers and have fewer of them.

WILLIAM WOODSIDE
US chairman of Primerica
Quoted in Tom Peters, *Thriving on Chaos*

PROFIT AND LOSS

Civilization and profits go hand in hand.

CALVIN COOLIDGE 1872–1933
30th president of the USA
Speech, New York City, 1920

For the first four years, no new enterprise produces profits. Even Mozart didn't start writing music until he was four.

PETER F DRUCKER
US management expert
Financial Times 1986

Take care to sell your horse before he dies. The art of life is passing losses on.

ROBERT FROST 1874–1963
US poet
The Ingenuities of Debt

It is more important to minimize risk than to maximize profit.

BERNARD S GLASSMAN
US builder and developer
Speech, Bethesda, Maryland, 1987

We should re-define the word 'profits' to mean only the surplus available for distribution to shareholders after having allowed for that amount of investment necessary for a reasonable rate of growth.

JAMES GOLDSMITH
British financier
Quoted in Geoffrey Wansell, *Sir James Goldsmith*

The worst crime against working people is a company which fails to operate at a profit.

SAMUEL GOMPERS 1850–1924
President of the American Federation of Labor
Attributed

When business is great, growth and profits hide a multitude of sins.

DAVID JONES
Managing director of Next plc
Marketing 1989

Without competition the pursuit of profit is immoral and mere exploitation.

KEITH JOSEPH 1918–1994
British secretary of state for industry
Speech, Oxford University Conservative Association, 1978

You don't need an MBA from Harvard to figure out how to lose money.

ROYAL LITTLE
US founder of Textron
Best of Business Quarterly 1987

The problem with the City is that it is only interested in the bottom line. But you can enjoy yourself and still pay the wages without doubling your profits every year.

DEBBIE MOORE
British founder of Pineapple Dance Company
Quoted in *Financial Weekly* 1989

You must deodorize profits and make people understand that profit is not something offensive, but as important to a company as breathing.

PETER PARKER
Chairman of British Rail
Sunday Telegraph 1976

It is not the aim of [Marks and Spencer] to make more money than is prudent.

LORD RAYNER
Director of Marks and Spencer plc
Quoted in *Observer* 1987

There is profit in other people's pleasure.

MARGARET THATCHER
British prime minister
Sunday Times 1986

Turnover is vanity, profit is sanity.

> Traditional saying, quoted by Tina Knight
> in Carol Dix, *Enterprising Women*

PROFIT SHARING

Share profits and watch them grow.

> **JAMES A BELASCO**
> US academic and management consultant
> *Teaching the Elephant to Dance*

It's easy to work hard when it's your own money at stake.

> **AUBREY CUTLAND**
> Miner and part-owner of
> Tower Colliery, South Wales
> *Sunday Times* 1995

The time will come when an individual will find that the annual pay packet comes in four lumps. The largest lump will be the pay for the job, reflecting one's standing in the organization ... This lump might be only 50% of the total take-home pay in a good year. The other lumps would be a share in the overall surplus of the group or corporation, a share in the value added by one's work unit ... and, finally, a personal bonus reflecting one's individual contribution.

> **CHARLES HANDY**
> Business executive and writer, and
> professor at the London Business School
> *The Empty Raincoat*

If the company does well it is right and proper that our people should share the rewards. After all it is they who have to bear the brunt of the personal effect on their lives, hopes and ambitions if things go badly.

> **JOHN HARVEY-JONES**
> Business writer and chairman of ICI
> *Making It Happen*

At Semco, profit sharing is democratic. We negotiated with our workers over the basic percentage to be distributed – about a quarter of our corporate profits, as it turned out – and they hold assemblies to decide how to split it.

> **RICARDO SEMLER**
> Brazilian CEO of Semco
> *Maverick*

Profit sharing doesn't create employee involvement; it requires it.

> **RICARDO SEMLER**
> Brazilian CEO of Semco
> *Maverick*

PROGRESS AND CHANGE
(*SEE ALSO* REORGANIZING AND RESTRUCTURING)

Like an ox-cart driver in monsoon season or the skipper of a grounded ship, one must sometimes go forward by going backward.

> **JOHN BARTH**
> US writer
> *New York Times* 1984

Organizations are like elephants – slow to change.

> **JAMES A BELASCO**
> US academic and management consultant
> *Teaching the Elephant to Dance*

Needing change doesn't make it happen.

> **JAMES A BELASCO**
> US academic and management consultant
> *Teaching the Elephant to Dance*

All progress is based upon a universal innate desire on the part of every organism to live beyond its income.

> **SAMUEL BUTLER** 1835–1902
> English author
> 'Life' in *Notebooks*

The urgent question of our time is whether we can make change our friend and not our enemy.

BILL CLINTON
42nd president of the USA
Inaugural address, 1993

Excellence results from dedication to daily progress. Making something a little bit better every day.

ROBERT HALL
US academic
Quoted in Tom Peters, *Thriving on Chaos*

Change, after all, is only another word for growth, another synonym for learning. We can all do it, and enjoy it, if we want to.

CHARLES HANDY
Business executive and writer, and professor at the London Business School
The Age of Unreason

A frog if put in cold water will not bestir itself if that water is heated up slowly and gradually and will in the end let itself be boiled alive, too comfortable with continuity to realize that continuous change at some point becomes discontinuous and demands a change in behaviour. If we want to avoid the fate of ... the boiling frog we must learn to look for and embrace discontinuous change.

CHARLES HANDY
Business executive and writer, and professor at the London Business School
The Age of Unreason

Discontinuous change requires discontinuous upside-down thinking to deal with it, even if both thinkers and thoughts appear absurd at first sight.

CHARLES HANDY
Business executive and writer, and professor at the London Business School
The Age of Unreason

Without change nothing is possible. Not to change is a sure sign of imminent extinction. Remember the dinosaurs! Whether change is comfortable or not, it is inevitable.

JOHN HARVEY-JONES
Business writer and chairman of ICI
Making It Happen

Successful managers in the nineties, as I have reiterated over and over again, will be those who have the flexibility to adapt their organizations and behaviour to the needs of their people rather than the reverse.

JOHN HARVEY-JONES
Business writer and chairman of ICI
Managing to Survive

The commonest complaints about change programmes are that the top and the bottom are OK but the process gets bogged down in the middle. It is always the middle people who are blamed and are believed to be preserving their own entrenched positions and cosy life. This view is the more unfathomable since practically all of us either are in the middle, or have been, or will be.

JOHN HARVEY-JONES
Business writer and chairman of ICI
Managing to Survive

Change or the prospect of change will frighten everybody.

JOHN HARVEY-JONES
Business writer and chairman of ICI
Making it Happen

It is hardly progress for a cannibal to use a knife and fork.

GEOFFREY HOWE
British chancellor of the Exchequer
Quoted in *Independent* 1989

Educated workers in rich countries do not like to be organized from the top ... It will be nonsense to sit in hierarchical offices trying to arrange what people in the offices below do with their imaginations.

NORMAN McCRAE
Associate editor of *The Economist*
The Economist 1976

Most organizations, left to their own devices, are going to atrophy, to get so institutional, so bureaucratic, that they get to the point where their original reason for existence has been lost, and they stagnate. So you have to change, and by that I mean dramatic change.

WILLIAM G McGOWAN
Chairman of MCI Communications Corp.
Inc. Magazine 1986

We are shifting from a managerial society to an entrepreneurial society.

JOHN NAISBITT
US chairman of Naisbitt Group
Megatrends

To be a good change agent, you must be able to anticipate developments in the outside world, assess their implications for your organization, create the sense of urgency and priority for changes that your vision requires in the light of these developments, promote experimentation, and empower people to make the necessary changes. You must also be able to build flexibility into your organization and operations and encourage prudent risk taking.

BURT NANUS
US business academic and writer
Visionary Leadership

Progress might have been all right once, but it's gone on too long.

OGDEN NASH 1902–1971
US writer
Quoted in *Reader's Digest* 1975

Companies have got to learn to eat change for breakfast.

TOM PETERS
US international management consultant
and bestselling business author
Manhattan Inc. 1990

The key to the future is the midsize company – big enough to spend on technology, small enough to change.

TOM PETERS
US international management consultant
and bestselling business author
Manhattan, Inc. 1990

They disobeyed a superior and revolutionized an industry.

MARK B ROMAN
US contributing editor of *Success*
On IBM Nobel prize-winning employees Alex
Müller and Georg Bednorz, quoted in *Success* 1988

Resistance to change is neither capricious not mysterious. It almost always arises from threats to traditional norms and ways of doing things.

PETER M SENGE
Business academic and director of the
organizational learning programme at MIT
*The Fifth Discipline: The Art and Practice of the
Learning Organization*

The reasonable man adapts himself to the world: the unreasonable one persists in trying to adapt the world to himself. Therefore all progress depends on the unreasonable man.

GEORGE BERNARD SHAW 1850–1859
Irish dramatist and critic
Man and Superman

PROMOTION

Promote people who reflect your vision. Promoting those people who use your vision empowers others to do the same.

JAMES A BELASCO
US academic and management consultant
Teaching the Elephant to Dance

We won't promote anyone until he has trained a capable replacement. Otherwise, the promotion would leave us too vulnerable.

ROBERT CAMPION
US chairman of Lear Siegler
Quoted in Charles Garfield, *Peak Performers*

To blame a promotion that fails on the promoted person, as is usually done, is no more rational than to blame a capital investment that has gone sour on the money that was put into it.

PETER F DRUCKER
US management expert
Management in Turbulent Times

Politics and business can be settled by influence, cooks and doctors can only be promoted on their skill.

PENELOPE FITZGERALD
British writer
Innocence

A bonus is the appropriate reward for a job well done. Advancement to a new job is not. In the aftermath of reengineering, the distinction between advancement and performance is firmly drawn. Advancement to another job within the organization is a function of ability, not performance. It is a change, not a reward.

MICHAEL HAMMER AND JAMES CHAMPY
US international management
consultants and business authors
Reengineering the Corporation

We believe in keeping the units small and recruiting the best people we can find, giving them as much responsibility as early as we can, moving them up rapidly, and keeping track of them.

IRWIN HOLTSMAN
US vice-president of Johnson & Johnson
Fortune 1987

Progress in the Foreign Service is either vaginal or rectal. You marry the bosses daughter or you crawl up his bottom.

NICHOLAS MONSARRAT 1910–1979
British novelist
Smith and Jones

The Peter Principle: In a Hierarchy Every Employee Tends to Rise to His Level of Incompetence.

LAURENCE J PETER 1910–1990
Canadian writer, educationalist, and
self-proclaimed 'researcher of
remedies for incompetence'
Chapter heading, *The Peter Principle*

I don't want workaholics working for me.

GEORGE SCHAEFER
CEO of Caterpillar Corp.
Business Week 1987

I never hesitated to promote someone I didn't like. The comfortable assistant – the nice guy you like to go on fishing trips with – is a great pitfall. Instead, I looked for those sharp, scratchy, harsh, almost unpleasant guys who see and tell you about things as they really are. If you can get enough of them around you, and have patience enough to hear them out, there is no limit to where you can go.

THOMAS J WATSON JR
US ambassador to the former Soviet
Union and CEO of IBM
Fortune 1977

PROPERTY

Property has its duties as well as its rights.

THOMAS DRUMMOND 1797–1840
English engineer
Letter to the Earl of Donoughmore, 1838

Some people talk of morality, and some of religion, but give me a little snug property.

MARIA EDGEWORTH 1767–1849
Irish novelist
The Absentee

If a man owns land, the land owns him. Now let him leave home if he dare.

RALPH WALDO EMERSON 1803–1882
US philosopher and poet
'Wealth' in *The Conduct of Life*

Property is not theft, but a good deal of theft becomes property.

R H TAWNEY 1880–1962
English economic historian
Religion and the Rise of Capitalism

PROSPERITY

Every man or woman should have the opportunity to prosper to the limit of their ability. It is extraordinary that many continue to debate whether the very idea of prosperity is a good thing. As long as we do, the conditions for prosperity will elude us.

RALPH HALPERN
Chairman of Burton Group
The Times 1987

If you don't want prosperity to falter, then Buy, Buy, Buy – on credit of course. In other words, the surest way of bringing on a rainy day is to prepare for it.

JOSEPH WOOD KRUTCH 1893–1970
US writer and teacher
Human Nature and the Human Condition

In today's competitive legal market, a firm needs a marketing strategy, perhaps not to survive but to prosper.

SONIA RAPPAPORT
US lawyer
Washington Lawyer 1987

Few of us can stand prosperity. Another man's, I mean.

MARK TWAIN 1835–1910
US writer
Pudd'nhead Wilson's New Calendar

To me, one of the most vivid proofs that there is a moral governance in the Universe is the fact that when men or governments work intelligently and far-sightedly for the good of others, they achieve their own prosperity too.

BARBARA WARD 1914–1981
British economist, writer, and president of the
Institute for Environment and Development
The Rich Nations and the Poor Nations

Prosperity is necessarily the first theme of a political campaign.

WOODROW WILSON 1856–1924
28th president of the USA
Speech, 1912

PUBLIC OFFICE
(SEE ALSO GOVERNMENT)

I will undoubtedly have to seek what is happily known as gainful employment, which I am glad to say does not describe holding public office.

DEAN ACHESON 1891–1971
US politician
On leaving the post of US secretary
of state, *The Times* 1952

How to educate broad-gauged professionals for the public service; how to keep professional specialists accountable to politically responsible generalists within the executive and legislative branches; these are at present and prospectively among the most important unresolved issues.

STEPHEN K BAILEY
President of the American Society of
Public Administration
Agenda for the Nation

We underpay all our public servants and we little deserve the honesty and integrity we get.

FRED CATHERWOOD
Northern Ireland Euro-MP
Speech, Institute of Chartered Accountants, 1974

A lot of top business people become totally frustrated when they move into a cabinet position or as head of a department. They're used to much more power in business ... In government, they must suddenly follow strict procedures and regulations. It's a difficult adjustment.

GERALD FORD
38th president of the USA
Harvard Business Review 1987

This high official, all allow,/ Is grossly overpaid./ There wasn't any Board; and now/ There isn't any trade.

A P HERBERT 1890–1971
British writer and politician
'President of the Board of Trade'

We believe many able people would not wish to enter Parliament if they not only had to take a substantial drop in income, but also run the risk of seeing their source of livelihood disappear altogether if they were to lose their seats.

LORD NOLAN
British law lord
Report from the Nolan Committee
Report on Standards in Public Life 1995

I thought that Britain would benefit from greater job mobility between the private and public sectors ... But I do know that many good people in the commercial world are put off by the tabloid intrusion into the private lives of those in public positions.

RUPERT PENNANT-REA
British economist and financier
Letter of resignation as deputy governor
of the Bank of England, prompted by the media
scandal surrounding the discovery of an alleged
extra-marital affair, 1995

The nine most terrifying words in the English language are, 'I'm from the government and I'm here to help'.

RONALD REAGAN
40th president of the USA
Said at a press conference on government
help for farmers, Chicago, 1986

I think one may fairly generalize that a government employee ... is seriously restricted in his freedom of speech with respect to any matter for which he has been assigned responsibility.

WILLIAM REHNQUIST
US Supreme Court chief justice
Quoted in Peters and Branch, *Blowing the Whistle*

The time has gone when a professional person would give up an excellent career to serve the public good.

ANNE WORTHINGTON
Photographer
Guardian 1995

PUBLIC RELATIONS
(*SEE ALSO* DIPLOMACY AND TACT)

Headlines make history.

EDWARD BERNAYS 1891–1995
Austrian-born US 'father of public relations'
In response to Czechoslovakian leader Tomás
Masaryk's objection, 'But that would be making
history for headlines', who had been advised to
declare Czechoslovakian independence on a
Sunday to ensure maximum international
attention. Quoted in obituary of Bernays,
Independent 1995.

The market is so saturated, it just isn't good enough to be a very good fund manager. You have to be a very good fund manager and tell people about it.

ROBIN BERRILL
Chairman of Lazard Unit Trust Managers
Sunday Times 1995

Some are born great, some achieve greatness, and some hire public relations officers.

DANIEL J BOORSTIN
US writer, academic, and librarian of Congress
The Image

PR cannot overcome things that shouldn't have been done.

HAROLD BURSON
US CEO of Burson-Marsteller public relations
USA Today 1993

There are a million definitions of public relations. I have found it to be the craft of arranging the truth so that people will like you.

ALAN HARRINGTON
US writer
Life in the Crystal Palace

Avoid slickness at all costs.

REESE SCHONFIELD
President of CNN television
Advice on PR, quoted in
Tom Peters, *Liberation Management*

The public be damned!

WILLIAM HENRY VANDERBILT 1821–1885
US financier and railway promoter
Reply when asked if the public
should be consulted about luxury trains,
New York Times 1918

PUBLIC SPEAKING

The best audience is intelligent, well-educated, and a little drunk.

ALBEN W BARKLEY 1877–1956
US vice-president
Quoted in an obituary, 1956

I do not object to people looking at their watches when I am speaking. But I strongly object when they start shaking them to make certain they are still going.

LORD BIRKETT 1883–1962
English judge
Observer 1960

I have heard speakers use the phrase, 'I can say without fear of contradiction ...' Anyone who says this in a modern democracy, or to the shareholders of a modern company, should see the doctor.

LORD CHANDOS 1893–1980
British banking and metals executive
Memoirs of Lord Chandos

One of the penalties of any top job is that you will do an immense amount of public speaking.

JOHN HARVEY-JONES
Business writer and chairman of ICI
Making It Happen

The greater the potential scandal, the more humorous and downbeat the speech should be.

SIMON HOGGART
British journalist
Guardian 1995

PUBLICITY
(*SEE ALSO* ADVERTISING AND PRODUCT PROMOTION; PUBLIC RELATIONS)

The effect of power and publicity on all men is the aggravation of self, a sort of tumor that ends by killing the victim's sympathies.

HENRY BROOKS ADAMS 1838–1910
US writer and historian
The Education of Henry Adams

There's no such thing as bad publicity except your own obituary.

BRENDAN BEHAN 1923–1964
Irish dramatist
Quoted in Dominic Behan, *My Brother Brendan*

The price of justice is eternal publicity.

ARNOLD BENNETT 1867–1931
English novelist
'Secret Trials' in *Things That Have Interested Me*

If you've done it, it ain't braggin'.

DIZZY DEAN
US baseball player
Attributed

A publicist without a passion cannot make a place for himself.

SHEMARYA LEVIN 1867–1935
Russian writer and polemicist
The Arena

You can't make a dime off publicity.

MICHAEL MILKEN
US junk-bond dealer
Sunday Telegraph 1989

The Annual Report was originally a dull, if respectable publication ... For the modern stockholder the Company must provide, and does provide, a brightly coloured, smartly illustrated brochure, printed on art paper and bound in imitation vellum ... The general effect is festive, innocent and gay, well suited to the more junior groups at kindergarten.

C NORTHCOTE PARKINSON
British historian, writer, and formulator
of Parkinson's law
In-Laws and Outlaws

Publicity, *publicity* PUBLICITY is the greatest moral factor and force in our public life.

JOSEPH PULITZER 1847–1911
US newspaper publisher and business executive
Speech to the editors of *New York World*, 1895

QUALITY

The [quality control] issue has more to do with people and motivation and less to do with capital and equipment than one would think. It involves a cultural change.

MICHAEL BEER
US academic
Washington Post 1987

If you're going to put your name on all your products, you should never produce a bad product. If you make a mistake, you'll hurt your whole company.

BRUNO BICH
US vice-president of sales and
marketing, Bic Pen Co.
Quoted in Alsop and Abrams,
The Wall Street Journal on Marketing

The quality of the workers who leave the factory door every evening is an even more important thing than the quality of the products which it delivers to the customers.

SAMUEL COURTAULD 1876–1947
British chairman of Courtaulds Ltd and
donor of the Courtauld Institute of Art
Ideals and Industry

The key to quality products and services is a quality person. And the key to our personal quality is character and competence and the emotional bank account we have with other people. Principle-centred people get quantity through quality, results through relationships.

STEPHEN R COVEY
Founder of the Institute of Principle-
Centred Leadership
Principle-Centered Leadership

Once you brand something, it ceases to be the possession of the person who produced it and becomes the property of the brand. If you emblazon a T-shirt with a new product that is about to be launched and on the first wash it shrinks, that affects the quality of the brand, not the shirt.

MARIAN ELLIOT
Chief executive of British Promotional
Merchandise Association
Marketing Week 1995

When a product is manufactured by workers who find their work meaningful, it will inevitably be a product of high quality.

PEHR GUSTAF GYLLENHAMMAR
CEO of Volvo
Quoted in Henry L Tosi and Stephen J Carroll,
Management

As great as computers are, they cannot tell you about the quality of your product. The profitability, yes, but not the quality. The human eye, the human experience, is the one thing that can make quality better – or poorer.

STANLEY MARCUS
Chairman emeritus of Neiman-Marcus
Quoted in Peters and Austin,
A Passion for Excellence

You can't go far unless the product stands out.

RICHARD NEEDHAM
British trade minister
Nottingham Evening Post 1995

There is hardly anything in the world that some man cannot make a little worse and sell a little cheaper.

JOHN RUSKIN 1819–1900
English art critic and social observer
The Seven Lamps of Architecture

REDUNDANCY AND RESIGNATION
(*SEE ALSO* HIRING AND FIRING)

'We're going to have to let you go'. So who's *making* you? And why are you talking about me as though I were a fish? Only the last word has any meaning. Go.

ANONYMOUS
Quoted in *Cosmopolitan* 1992

Anyone who says he isn't going to resign, four times, definitely will.

J K GALBRAITH
US diplomat, economist, and writer
Town and Country 1979

I cannot continue to work for a company which no longer cares about its clients or staff and is apparently so utterly ignorant of the advertising business and how much client relationships and agency morale matter.

DAVID KERSHAW
UK chief of Saatchi & Saatchi
Letter of resignation, 1995

In the language of football, 'resign' is a code word meaning 'he was given the choice of quitting, being fired, or having the fans blow up his house'.

GENE KLEIN
Owner of the San Diego Chargers
First Down and a Billion

When a company has a layoff, it's most often the management's fault.

KENNETH OLSEN
Founder and CEO of Digital Equipment Corp.
Speech, 1982

We are an indispensable team; *you* are overmanned; *they* are redundant.

ANTHONY SAMPSON
British writer and social commentator
Observer 1981

When plants faced hard times, their factory committees would take the initiative and lower wages or increase hours, saving money and protecting jobs. When layoffs were unavoidable, the committees got involved in the sensitive and unfortunate task of deciding who would go. Together we tried to be socially just, taking into consideration such factors as a workers' history with the company, loyalty, ability to find a new job, and family commitments ... Sometimes the committee members complained that in our effort to be equitable we dragged out the process ... and increased the pain. Perhaps that was an unavoidable price for corporate democracy.

RICARDO SEMLER
Brazilian CEO of Semco
On factory committees and redundancy, *Maverick*

The company is in the grip of people who do not understand the business and seem prepared to ignore the advice of those who do.

JEREMY SINCLAIR
Chief creative director at Saatchi & Saatchi
Letter of resignation, 1995

The son of a bitch isn't going to resign on me. I want him fired.

HARRY S TRUMAN 1884–1972
33rd president of the USA
On General MacArthur, attributed

REORGANIZING AND RESTRUCTURING

(*SEE ALSO* PROGRESS AND CHANGE)

Never reorganize except for a good business reason. But if you haven't reorganized in a while, that's a good business reason.

JOHN AKERS
CEO of IBM
Quoted in Waterman, *The Renewal Factor*

It is better to be the reorganizer than the reorganizee.

NORMAN R AUGUSTINE
CEO and president of Martin Marietta Corp.
Augustine's Laws

The restructuring going on in industries, companies, and countries is a way of dealing with global overcapacity.

JOSEPH L BOWER
US academic
Fortune 1987

The original guru passed down his arcane, but eternal, knowledge orally, to chosen disciples. The modern one sells his in airport bookstalls, so that every three years he has to reinvent the whole shtick, which explains why they are so keen on managing for change.

ANDREW BROWN AND PAUL VALLELY
British journalists
Independent 1995

Restructuring is rather like planting asparagus. You know you should have started three years ago.

CHARLES DOSZHER
CEO of Enichem International
International Management 1987

Companies do not go bankrupt the way they used to, and countries are not declared in default. We talk about restructuring instead. We are prolonging the pains. We are postponing deaths. We are preventing new dynamic structures being created when others die. I think this is detrimental. We cannot abolish death.

PEHR GUSTAF GYLLENHAMMAR
CEO of Volvo
Financial Times 1983

Downsizing and restructuring only mean doing less with less. Reengineering, by contrast, means doing *more* with less.

MICHAEL HAMMER AND JAMES CHAMPY
US international management
consultants and business authors
Reengineering the Corporation

Old rule: Business must choose between centralization and decentralization *Disruptive technology*: Telecommunications network *New rule*: Businesses can simultaneously reap the benefits of centralization and decentralization.

MICHAEL HAMMER AND JAMES CHAMPY
US international management
consultants and business authors
Reengineering the Corporation

Successful big corporations should devolve into becoming 'confederations of entrepreneurs'.

NORMAN MCCRAE
British associate editor of *The Economist*
The Economist 1976

The whittling away of middle management is further reinforcing the trend for companies to smash the hierarchical pyramid and adopt new people structures such as networks, intrapreneurs, and small teams.

JOHN NAISBETT AND PATRICIA ABURDENE
US business writers and social researchers
Re-inventing the Corporation

Sooner or later, the time will come when an organization needs redirection or perhaps a complete transformation, and then the first step should always be a new vision, a wake-up call to everyone involved with the organization that fundamental change is needed and is on the way.

BURT NANUS
US business academic and writer
Visionary Leadership

One of the vices or the virtue of decentralization is that people don't share ideas.

ANTHONY J F O'REILLY
US academic
New York Times 1988

After you've done a thing the same way for two years look it over carefully. After five years look at it with suspicion and after ten years throw it away and start all over again.

ALFRED EDWARD PERLMAN
US railway executive
New York Times 1958

Start restructuring when things are going well and not when the water is already up to your neck.

FRITZ LEUTWILER
Chairman of Brown Boveri & CIE
International Management 1987

Make sure you have a 'vice-president in charge of revolution', to engender ferment among your more conventional colleagues.

DAVID OGILVY
Advertising guru and founder
of Ogilvy and Mather
Ogilvy on Advertising

Revitalizing General Motors is like teaching an elephant to tap dance. You find the sensitive spots and start poking.

H ROSS PEROT
US presidential candidate and founder
of Electronic Data Systems
International Management 1987

The greatest danger in the wave of mergers, layoffs and restructuring of company men is the destruction of the continuity on which that quality depends.

ANTHONY SAMPSON
British writer and social commentator
On corporate excellence, *Company Man:
The Rise and Fall of Corporate Life*

The great achievement of Mr Sloan of General Motors was to structure this gigantic firm in such a manner that it became, in fact, a federation of fairly reasonably sized firms.

E F SCHUMACHER 1911–1977
German-born British economist
Small is Beautiful

Large organizations can't tolerate constant turmoil.

PHILIP SMITH
US chairman of General Foods
Fortune 1987

So much has been written about employees' resistance to change that we are sometimes tempted to forget that they can also react favorably.

NATHANIEL STEWART
Director of the Management Development Center
at the US Agency for International Development
Leadership in the Office

Mutiny is such an unpleasant word – think of it more as a management reshuffle.

ALISTAIR SWINERTON
British screen writer
Said by the character Long John Silver in
the children's television cartoon
The Adventures of Treasure Island, 1995

REPUTATION

What is so utterly repellent about the current wave of boardroom piracy is the proof it offers that Top People no longer give a damn about what their fellow citizens think of them. There was a time when mere exposure would have occasioned a change of behaviour. Now they carry on regardless, while accusing the rest of us of envy.

IAN AITKEN
British journalist
Guardian 1995

A tradesman's credit, and a maid's virtue, ought to be equally sacred from the tongues of men: and 'tis a very unhappy truth, that as times now go, they are neither of them regarded among us as they ought to be.

DANIEL DEFOE c. 1660–1731
British writer
The Complete English Tradesman

If you last you'll see your reputation die three times.

OSKAR KOKOSCHKA 1886–1980
Austrian Expressionist painter and writer
Said at the age of 80, quoted
in Ian Hamilton, *Robert Lowell*

I would to God thou and I knew where a commodity of good names were to be bought.

WILLIAM SHAKESPEARE 1564–1616
English dramatist and poet
Richard II

A good reputation is more valuable than money.

PUBLIUS SYRUS 1ST CENTURY BC
Roman writer
Maxims

Personal moral reliability was crucial to business success. The warm hassock in the numbered pew and the scrubbed doorstep to the weeded garden were the credit cards of yesterday.

PAUL THOMPSON
British writer
New Society 1987

There was worlds of reputation in it, but no money.

MARK TWAIN 1835–1910
US writer
A Connecticut Yankee in the Court of King Arthur

RESEARCH AND DEVELOPMENT (R&D)

If new product development is your competitive edge, then set such numeric expectations as total launch time for new products, product and process development milestones, key characteristics of new products in comparison with customer need and competitors' design, and customer satisfaction with new products.

JAMES A BELASCO
US academic and management consultant
Teaching the Elephant to Dance

Significant advances rarely come through to commercialization in less than five years – usually the range is 10 to 15 years.

THEODORE L CAIRNS
Director of central research at Du Pont
Speech, San Francisco, 1974

For me, the best CEOs come out of R&D. They're articulate, creative, inventive – but they're also rigorous.

LAUREL CUTLER
US vice chairman of FCB/Leber Katz Partners
Inc. Magazine 1987

The presence of a body of well-instructed men, who do not have to labour for their daily bread, is important to a degree which cannot be overestimated; as all high intellectual work is carried on by them, and on such work material progress of all kinds mainly depends.

CHARLES DARWIN 1809–1882
English naturalist and propounder of the
theory of evolution and natural selection
Descent of Man

Our largest challenge is to cut the time it takes to get technology out of the lab and into operations.

GORDON FORWARD
US president of Chaparral Steel
Washington Business Journal 1987

Our technological standing will continue to decline without the discoveries that come only from basic research.

PHILLIP A GRIFFITHS
US academic
High Technology 1987

It takes five years to develop a new car in this country. Heck, we won World War II in four years.

H ROSS PEROT
US presidential candidate and founder
of Electronic Data Systems
Interview, 1970, quoted in Tom Peters
Thriving on Chaos

I like to think of research as the distance we must travel between the problem and the answer. In my own field, I have seen this distance travelled many times against many obstacles – both natural and man-made – which at the time, seemed insurmountable.

DAVID SARNOFF 1891–1971
Founder of RCA Corporation
Wisdom of Sarnoff and the World of RCA

By treating everything as a research problem, we tend to devise elegant, inventive solutions without adequate attention to cost, manufacturability, and quality.

ROLAND SCHMITT
Chief scientist and vice-president
of General Electric Co.
Washington Business Journal 1987

We try to picture what the products will be and then say, what technology should we be working on today to help us get there?

JOHN SCULLY
CEO of Apple Computer Co.
Inc. Magazine 1988

RETIREMENT AND OLD AGE

There is no such thing as 'on the way out'. As long as you are still doing something interesting and good, you're in business because you're still breathing.

LOUIS ARMSTRONG 'SATCHMO' 1900–1971
US jazz trumpeter, bandleader, and singer
Quoted in Martin Manser, *Chambers Book of
Business Quotations*

To me, old age is always 15 years older than I am.

BERNARD BARUCH 1870–1965
US presidential advisor and investment broker
On reaching his 85th birthday, quoted
in *Observer* 1955

I prefer old age to the alternative.

MAURICE CHEVALIER 1888–1972
French singer and actor
Remark, 1962

The role of a retired person is no longer to possess one.

SIMONE DE BEAUVOIR 1908–1986
French writer
The Coming of Age

Growing old is a bad habit which a busy man has no time to form.

ANDRÉ GIDE 1869–1951
French writer
Quoted in *Independent* 1995

One of the strange things about growing older is the gradual realization that 'they' don't know, that the Treasury is *not* all-wise, that 'they' are on the whole just like you, muddling through, and not very interested in you anyway.

CHARLES HANDY
Business executive and writer, and professor at the London Business School
Age of Unreason

My second fixed idea is the uselessness of men above 60 years of age, and the incalculable benefit it would be in commercial, political and professional life if, as a matter of course, men stopped work at this age.

WILLIAM OSLER 1849–1919
Canadian physician
Speech, Baltimore, 1905

I would like to see a society in which retirement is regarded as a liberation, as an incentive to live actively, to do things which you have always wanted to, but never found the time.

LEN MURRAY
British general secretary of the TUC
Daily Telegraph 1978

I can't complain. Life's been good to me. I've had exciting times.

TINY ROWLAND
Entrepreneur and CEO of Lonrho
On his final retirement from Lonrho after failing to become its president, quoted in
BusinessAge 1995

I'm against retiring. The thing that keeps a man alive is having something to do. Sitting in a rocker never appealed to me. Golf or fishing isn't as much fun as working.

COL HARLAN SANDERS 1890–1980
US entrepreneur and founder of Kentucky Fried Chicken
Quoted in Rolf White, *Business Quotations*

All of us were ready to retire. Or better yet, become consultants.

RICARDO SEMLER
Brazilian CEO of Semco
Maverick

I'll never make the mistake of being 70 again.

CASEY STENGEL 1889–1975
US baseball player and manager
On being fired by the Yankees baseball team who justified its action as part of a pro-youth movement, quoted in Ira Berkow and Jim Kaplan
The Gospel According to Casey

I will need a lot of money to retire on, at least £5 million. Well, £10 million would be safer because it's a tough world.

MARK THATCHER
US-based British business executive and son of Margaret Thatcher
Sunday Times 1995

Statutory senility.

WALTER WRISTON
CEO of Citibank
Opinion on a mandatory retirement age,
New York Times 1993

RISK AND RISK AVOIDANCE

One of the primary, fundamental faults with American management is that over the years it has lost its zest for adventure, for taking risk, for doing something that no one has done before.

HAROLD GENEEN
Business consultant and chairman of ITT
Managing

The ultimate risk is not taking a risk.

JAMES GOLDSMITH
British financier
Quoted in *Independent* 1989

Sometimes it's risky not to take a risk – if you walk backward you never stub your toe.

HARVEY MACKAY
US writer
Quoted in *Home Office Computing* 1993

A boss's mere expression of an opinion can be interpreted as a decision – even a direct order – by a staff member caught in the clutches of risk avoidance.

R ALEC MACKENZIE
US management consultant and author
The Time Trap

No-risk managements run both no-win and no-fun businesses.

ALLEN NEUHARTH
US CEO of Gannett Company
Quoted in Daniel Kehrer, *Doing Business Boldly*

At first it was hard for us. But with a great deal of commiseration and consultation the shock of rulelessness began to subside, and our middle managers began to remove their armour plates. I like to tell them that a turtle may live for hundreds of years because it is well protected by its shell, but it only moves forward when it sticks out its head.

RICARDO SEMLER
Brazilian CEO of Semco
Maverick

The time you save in not making changes and taking risks can be used to perfect current practices. Your employees will be grateful to you for letting them know exactly where they stand – and will reward you by being unimaginative, uninspired and unhappy.

DONALD WHITHAM
Supervisory special agent at the FBI Academy
National Sheriff 1986

SALES EXECUTIVES
(*SEE ALSO* BUYING AND SELLING GOODS)

There is no such thing as 'soft sell' or 'hard sell.' There is only 'smart sell' and 'Stupid sell.'

CHARLES BROWER
US president of Batton, Barton,
Durstine & Osborn
Editor & Publisher

Work hard, keep quiet, let the customer talk himself into giving you the order. Silence is a very powerful selling tool.

PHILIP CUSHING
British managing director of Inchcape
Quoted in *BusinessAge* 1995

In Britain the salesperson has never enjoyed a high profile and consequently it is hard to recruit the best, especially at graduate level. In America, by contrast, they are cultural heroes. Here, sadly, our perception of the typical salesman is Arthur Daley.

ANDREW DICKINSON
British journalist
On the British opinion of salespeople, using the
example of the fictitious wheeler-dealer 'hero' of
the *Minder* television series, *Sunday Times* 1995

Knowing the man is the essence of salesmanship.

HAROLD GENEEN
Business consultant and chairman of ITT
Managing

Anyone who doesn't know what it means to have painful feet doesn't know what selling is.

ALFRED 'FREDDY' HEINEKEN
Chairman of Heineken Breweries
On his youthful experiences of selling when he
peddled his father's beer from bar to bar in Times
Square. Attributed remark quoted in Julia Vitullo-
Martin and J Robert Moskin,
The Executive's Book of Quotations

A salesman with bad breath is dear at any price.

ELBERT HUBBARD 1856–1915
US writer and printer
Notebook

You can't sell anything that you wouldn't buy yourself.

VICTOR KIAM
CEO of Remington
Going For It!

Sell solutions, not just products.

KLAUS M LEISINGER
Departmental director of Ciba-Geigy Ltd
New York Times 1988

Most salesmen try to take the horse to water and make him drink. Your job is to make the horse thirsty.

GABRIEL M SIEGEL
President of MediCab of New York, Inc.
Speech to the sales force, 1984

Elements of the classic salesman will always persist – instinct and knowing how to communicate with consumers. You can give somebody any amount of technology and information, but unless they can communicate they are not going to be particularly good marketers.

PROFESSOR MICHAEL THOMAS
British chairman of the Chartered
Institute of Marketing
Guardian 1995

SAVING AND ECONOMY
(*SEE ALSO* INCOME; PAY)

Mere parsimony is not economy ... Expense, and great expense, may be an essential part of true economy. Economy is a distributive virtue, and consists not in saving but selection. Parsimony requires no providence, no

sagacity, no powers of combination, no comparison, no judgement.

EDMUND BURKE 1729–1797
Irish statesman and political theorist
Letter to a Noble Lord

It is not economical to go to bed early to save the candles if the results are twins.

Chinese proverb

Saving is a very fine thing. Especially when your parents have done it for you.

WINSTON CHURCHILL 1874–1965
British statesman and prime minister
Attributed

Whenever you save five shillings, you put a man out of work for a day.

JOHN MAYNARD KEYNES 1883–1946
English economist
'Inflation and Deflation' in *Essays in Persuasion*

I would rather have my people laugh at my economies than weep for my extravagance.

OSCAR II 1829–1907
King of Sweden
Attributed

Unequal distribution of income is an excessively uneconomic method of getting the necessary saving done.

JOAN ROBINSON 1903–1983
British professor of economics
at Cambridge University
Essay on Marxian Economics

I was on a basic of £100,000 a year. You don't make many savings on that.

ERNEST SAUNDERS
CEO and chairman of Guinness plc
later found guilty of a share
supporting operation in the Guinness
takeover bid for Distillers
Quoted in *Observer* 1987

SECRETARIES AND PERSONAL ASSISTANTS

If you want to get something done, give it to a busy man so he can get his secretary to do it.

ANONYMOUS

A good secretary is worth killing for.

MARY ANN ALLISON AND ERIC ALLISON
Vice-president of CitiCorp; financial writer
Managing Up, Managing Down

A good secretary can save her boss more time in a year than a business jet plane can.

MALCOLM BALDRIDGE
British business executive
Quoted in Michéle Brown and Ann O'Connor,
Woman Talk

The secretary you hire this year will need a higher level of computer competency than a mid-level manager needed seven or eight years ago.

BUCK BLESSING
Founding partner of Blessing/White, Inc.
Training and Development Journal 1986

Secretaries will never go to Heaven. We spend half our time telling little white lies.

GWEN COWAN
British personal assistant to Peter Parker,
Chairman of British Rail
Business 1987

You can run the office without a boss, but you can't run an office without secretaries.

JANE FONDA
US actress, fitness expert, and political activist
Quoted in *Observer* 1982

Particularly for people a long way down the line, the chairman's secretary can be a very forbidding person, and if you want to pursue an open door policy you are not going to get very far if the secretary carries her – perhaps necessary – task of protection to extremes, and in a dictatorial or tactless way.

JOHN HARVEY-JONES
Business writer and chairman of ICI
Making It Happen

Practically every secretary is a typist, but not every typist is a secretary.

PHILIP W MATZGER
US computer analyst and management writer
Managing Programming People

Most secretaries rarely stay in any one job for more than three years. While employers refuse to invest in secretaries the grass is always likely to be greener elsewhere and while experience remains the only means of learning, the ambitious secretary will be the most mobile – if she decides to remain a secretary at all.

BILL SAUNDERS
British journalist
Guardian 1995

We don't have secretaries ... or personal assistants. We don't believe in cluttering up the payroll with ungratifying, dead-end jobs. Everyone at Semco, even top managers, fetches guests, stands over photocopiers, sends faxes, types letters, and dials the phone ... At Semco we have stripped away the unnecessary perks and privileges that feed the ego but hurt the balance sheet.

RICARDO SEMLER
Brazilian CEO of Semco
Maverick

As managers have more to do but fewer people to delegate to, the need for secretaries to take on more managerial responsibilities is increasing and even taken for granted. However, the formal training that would improve the secretary's ability to meet these requirements only ever seems to be directed at the managers themselves.

GINI TATE
British managing director of Tate Appointments
Guardian 1995

SELF-EMPLOYMENT

Being in your own business is working 80 hours a week so that you can avoid working 40 hours a week for someone else.

RAMONA ARNETT
President of Ramona Enterprises Inc.
Speech, Boston, 1973

The first rule has to be that you do something you really love – you can't make it otherwise.

DAVID BIRCH
US economist
US News & World Report 1987

Perfect freedom is reserved for the man who lives by his own work, and in that work does what he wants to do.

ROBIN GEORGE COLLINGWOOD 1889–1943
English philosopher
Speculum Mentis

I enjoy not having to work for somebody else. An outside investor would give me a lot of stress.

PATRICIA L DE MARVIL
CEO of Securigard, Inc.
Hispanic Business 1987

Work is never seen by women as a totally separate picture. They integrate their working lives with the rest of their lives. That must explain ultimately why so many want to run their own businesses, because only in

that way do they feel more in touch with their whole lives.

CAROL DIX
British writer
Enterprising Women

An ego is just imagination. And if a man doesn't have imagination he'll be working for someone else for the rest of his life.

JIMMY HOFFA 1913–1975
US president of the Teamsters' Union
Esquire

The worst way to treat the contractor is to give him or her nothing to do.

HELEN JOHNSTONE
British journalist
On contracted IT staff, *Evening Standard* 1995

The man who goes alone can start today; but he who travels with another must wait till that other is ready.

HENRY DAVID THOREAU 1817–1862
US naturalist and writer
Walden

SOCIAL RESPONSIBILITIES OF BUSINESS
(SEE ALSO ETHICS)

There's nothing wrong with serving your own ends as long as you serve society at the same time.

WARREN AVIS
US entrepreneur and founder of Avis
Daily Telegraph 1986

Freedom [in society] is the by-product of economic surplus.

ANEURIN ('NYE') BEVAN 1897–1960
British Labour politician
Quoted in Michael Foot, *Aneurin Bevan*

The people who know where the levers of power are have a duty to help those who don't and those who can't help themselves.

GODFREY BRADMAN
British chairman and joint chief
executive of Rosehaugh plc
Sunday Correspondent Magazine 1989

It's important if you're successful that you set an example for the people who work for you in the way you conduct your life. You know, jumping on a train rather than jumping in a limousine, or going second class rather than first class. Little things are quite important.

RICHARD BRANSON
Entrepreneur and founder of Virgin Group
Inc. Magazine 1987

Conducting your business in a socially responsible way is good business. It means that you can attract better employees and that customers will know what you stand for and like you for it.

M ANTHONY BURNS
US CEO of Ryder Systems
New York Times 1988

Business leaders today can't shrink from their obligation to set a moral example.

WILLARD C BUTCHER
Chairman of Chase Manhattan Corp.
Speech, New Orleans, 1987

To boycott products of child and bonded labour is not the answer. While we must not condone the use of forced labour, we should acknowledge that families who send their children to work voluntarily do so out of necessity. It is crucial, however, that children are fairly paid, properly protected, trained and encouraged to continue their education.

MIKE DRURY
British spokesman at The Fairtrade Foundation
Letter to *Sunday Times* 1995

The challenge ... is to find a socially responsible niche where you can effectively give back to the community in which you operate and in which you have prospered.

EARL G GRAVES
US publisher and editor of Black Enterprise
New York Times 1988

It may well be that corporations should drop all ideas about their supposed 'social responsibilities,' or at least confine their good works to community-chest drives, gifts to universities and playing fields for the [junior baseball] Little League. Once companies begin to assume more grandiose and controversial obligations, they will inevitably be judged by standards they are ill-equipped to meet.

ANDREW HACKER
US academic
New York Times 1963

The men who create productivity, opportunity, employment, wealth and wages for a community are public benefactors and should be recognized as such.

WILLIAM RANDOLPH HEARST 1863–1951
US newspaper magnate and congressman
Editorial, 1918

Managers have an awareness that they are the direct representatives of the employees.

TAKASHI ISHIHARA
President of Nissan Motor Co.
Cherry Blossoms and Robotics

In our general disdain for the sources of wealth creation we remain unique among modern nations. Until that cultural ignorance ... is replaced by recognition of industry's paramount importance [to society], Britain can never completely close the competitive gap.

ANDREW LORENZ
British business columnist
Sunday Times 1995

I believe strongly in the social function of business ... It is industry which creates our social patterns, it determines the whole form of our society, whether it is education or the design of cities.

PETER PARKER
Chairman of British Rail
Quoted in Cary L Cooper and Peter Hingley, *The Change Makers*

I want to work for a company that contributes to and is part of the community. I want something not just to invest in. I want something to believe in.

ANITA RODDICK
British entrepreneur and founder of The Body Shop
Daily Telegraph 1987

We demand that big business give people a square deal: in return we insist that when anyone engaged in big business honestly endeavours to do right, he shall himself be given a square deal.

THEODORE ROOSEVELT 1858–1919
26th president of the USA
Autobiography

A successful business which looks after its employees and shareholders also has a responsibility to the wider community and is proud of acting accordingly.

LORD SIEFF
Honorary president of Marks and Spencer plc
Management the Marks and Spencer Way

Business only contributes fully to society if it is efficient, profitable and socially responsible.

LORD SIEFF
Honorary president of Marks and Spencer plc
Attributed

The experience of the Second World War, which taught many of us that democracy could not prevail against tyranny unless it were armed with the tools of superior industrial might, had salutary lessons for us.

LORD SIEFF
Honorary president of Marks and Spencer plc
Management the Marks and Spencer Way

I personally believe that capitalism, as it is now, won't survive unless it becomes more socially responsible.

JIM SLATER
British founder of Slater Walker Securities
Financial Times 1973

Few of Britain's biggest and best businesses would not claim to be part of their communities. It is not a fashion, but a long-term recipe for success.

TERRY THOMAS
British managing director of Co-operative Bank
Guardian 1995

For years I thought what was good for our country was good for General Motors and vice versa. The difference did not exist. Our company is too big. It goes with the welfare of the country. Our contribution to the nation is quite considerable.

CHARLES E WILSON 1890–1961
US engineer and business executive
Testimony to the Senate Armed Services
Committee on his proposed nomination as
secretary of defence, 1953

Business underlies everything in our national life, including our spiritual life. Witness the fact that in the Lord's Prayer the first petition is for daily bread. No one can worship God or love his neighbour on an empty stomach.

WOODROW WILSON 1856–1924
28th president of the USA
Speech, New York, 1912

STATISTICS

Any figure that looks interesting is probably wrong.

ANONYMOUS

One to mislead the public, another to mislead the Cabinet, and the third to mislead itself.

H H ASQUITH 1852–1928
British prime minister
Claiming that the War Office kept three different
sets of figures, quoted in Alastair Horne,
The Price of Glory

Statistics are no substitute for judgement.

HENRY CLAY 1777–1852
US statesman
Quoted in Tryon Edwards, *The New
Dictionary of Thoughts*

The professional's grasp of the numbers is a measure of the control he has over the events that the figures represent.

HAROLD GENEEN
Business consultant and chairman of ITT
Managing

Probability is the very guide of life.

THOMAS HOBBES 1588–1679
British philosopher
Leviathan

Statistics are like alienists – they will testify for either side.

FIORELLO LA GUARDIA 1882–1947
Mayor of New York and Republican politician
Attributed

He uses statistics as a drunken man uses lamp-posts – for support rather than illumination.

ANDREW LANG 1844–1912
Scottish scholar and writer
Attributed

If you torture the data long enough, they will confess.

MIT T-shirt slogan

People, including managers, do not live by pie charts alone – or by bar graphs or three inch statistical appendices to 300 page reports. People live, reason, and are moved by symbols and stories.

TOM PETERS
US international management consultant
and bestselling business author
Thriving on Chaos

There are two kinds of statistics, the kind you look up and the kind you make up.

REX STOUT 1886–1975
US detective-fiction writer
Death of a Doxy

There are three kinds of lies: lies, damned lies, and statistics.

MARK TWAIN 1835–1910
US writer
Autobiography

STOCKS AND SHARES

The holding of shares ... confers not only economic rights but a wider social responsibility. If capitalism is the only system around, it is all the more important to keep it on the leash.

ANONYMOUS
Guardian 1995

There is no such thing as an innocent purchaser of stocks.

LOUIS DEMBITZ BRANDEIS 1856–1941
US Supreme Court justice
Testimony, Senate Committee
on Interstate Commerce, 1911

Buy stocks like you buy your groceries, not like you buy your perfume.

WARREN BUFFET
US owner of ABC network
Quoted in *Fortune* 1992

The privatization programme has created up to 10 million private shareholders, but that gave no consideration to ownership and governance rather than the investment aspects. The government should have given more thought to ownership. People went into the shareholding game and gradually woke up to the fact that it is different from putting money into a building society.

DONALD BUTCHER
Chairman of UK Shareholders Association
Guardian 1995

Financial memory from one period of sophisticated stupidity to another is about 10 to 15 years ... any new generation getting rich has a vested interest in euphoria.

J K GALBRAITH
US diplomat, economist, and writer
The Times 1987

Like the surfer who is always looking for the perfect wave, there's a continuing quest for the perfect hedge.

JOHN PHELAN
Chairman of the New York Stock Exchange
Financial Post 1988

Management have been allowed to act like owners. But it is the stockholders who own companies, not managements and the stockholders are just beginning to realize it.

T BOONE PICKENS
US chairman of Mesa Petroleum
Company and corporate raider
Sunday Times Magazine 1985

Chief executives, who themselves own few shares of their companies, have no more feeling for the average stockholder than they do for baboons in Africa.

T BOONE PICKENS
US chairman of Mesa Petroleum
Company and corporate raider
Harvard Business Review 1986

I have long believed there is a close inverse correlation between top executives' golf handicaps and their companies' share-price performance. The rule of thumb is: don't buy shares in companies whose chairmen can play consistently below their handicap. They are either playing too much golf or they cheat.

JEFF RANDALL
British business journalist
Sunday Times 1995

Sell the shares when the chairman or chief executive becomes president of the CBI.

MARK WEINBERG
Chairman of Allied Dunbar Assurance
The Times 1987

STOCKBROKERS AND STOCKBROKING
(*SEE ALSO* THE CITY; STOCK MARKETS

It's often said that after a while [brokers] cease to be frightened of money, but it is equally true that you lose all respect for it.

Anonymous comment on the enormous debts
often run up by brokers, *Independent* 1995

Recently I was talking to one of Japan's best foreign-exchange dealers, and I asked him to name the factors he considered in buying and selling. He said, 'Many factors, sometimes very short term, and some medium, and some long term'. I became very interested when he said he considered the long term and asked him what he meant by that time frame. He paused a few seconds and replied with genuine seriousness. 'Probably ten minutes'. That is the way the market is moving these days.

TOYOO GYOHTEN
Japanese vice-minister in the Ministry of Finance
Changing Fortunes, co-written with Paul Volcker.
The paragraph was quoted as the epigraph in
Tom Peters, *Liberation Management*

A very good speculator gets the market right about 60% of the time, no more. He aims to make three times the profits on those successes than the losses he will accrue 40% of the time. The trader who survives is the one who respects the market. You must never allow your ego to make you think you can beat the market. The market is always right.

DEREK IBSEN
British broker for Daiwa Bank
Independent 1995

You are only as good as your last trade ... If you make money, the banks don't care who you are. They don't care if you're green and hairy. A woman who doesn't make money is out as fast as any man.

SAMANTHA SPIERS
British futures and options trader
with Monument Derivatives
Cosmopolitan 1995

Buyers are graded not only on their successes, but also on their failures. Too many hits means the buyer isn't taking enough chances.

LES WEXNER
US entrepreneur and founder of The Limited
Forbes 1987

A broker is a man who takes your fortune and runs it into a shoestring.

ALEXANDER WOOLLCOTT 1887–1943
US theatre critic and literary figure
Quoted in S H Adams, *Alexander Woollcott*

STOCK MARKETS
(SEE ALSO THE CITY; STOCKBROKERS AND STOCKBROKING)

Of all the mysteries of the stock exchange there is none so impenetrable as why there should be a buyer for everyone who seeks to sell.

J K GALBRAITH
US diplomat, economist, and writer
The Great Crash, 1929

I buy when other people are selling.

J PAUL GETTY 1892–1976
US millionaire oil executive
Quoted in Robert Lenzner, *The Great Getty*

If I see something I like, I buy it, then I try to sell it.

LORD GRADE
Film and television magnate
Sun 1987

If the share price of a company with a great product is dropping, go back and look at the product. If it's still good, hold on.

PETER LYNCH
US manager of Fidelity Magellan Fund
Fortune 1991

Gentlemen prefer bonds.

ANDREW MELLON 1855–1937
US financier
All About Money

In the 'soft' world, where the human imagination is all (and 90% of stock market value), even a huge corporation (with a billion-dollar price tag) can literally turn to 'nothing' almost overnight. How much would Microsoft be worth if something happened to founder Bill Gates? Several *billion* dollars less than yesterday.

TOM PETERS
US international management consultant
and bestselling business author
Liberation Management

Nobody who has been on a falling elevator and survived ever again approaches such a conveyance without a fundamentally reduced degree of confidence.

ROBERT RENO
US investment analyst and financial writer
On the aftereffects of the Oct 1987 stock market
'meltdown', quoted in *Time* 1987

There are two times in a man's life when he should not speculate: when he can't afford it, and when he can.

MARK TWAIN 1835–1910
US writer
Following the Equator

STRIKES
(*SEE ALSO* INDUSTRIAL RELATIONS;
NEGOTIATIONS)

A strike has to reach a climax before it gets better, just like a boil.

JOH BJELKE-PETERSEN
Australian politician
Quoted in *Sydney Morning Herald* 1985

I cannot tolerate strikes. What would my workers say if I go on strike and say I'm not going to sign any more cheques today?

ALAN BOND
Australian entrepreneur
Financial Times 1981

Not a penny off the pay: not a minute on the day.

A J COOK 1885–1931
British miners' leader
Slogan of resistance adopted by the miners during
the strike of 1926, after a royal commission (the
Samuel Report) had recommended a cut in wages

There is no right to strike against the public safety by anybody, anywhere, any time.

CALVIN COOLIDGE 1872–1933
30th president of the USA
Telegram to Samuel Gompers, president of the
American Federation of Labor, 1919

The trouble with employers is that they like ballots as long as you lose them.

JIMMY KNAPP
Scottish general secretary of the NUR
Independent 1989

The main thing that distinguishes democracies from dictatorships is the right to go on strike.

LEN MURRAY
British general secretary of the TUC
Quoted in *Observer* 1983

There is no virtue in being on strike. The virtue lies in winning.

JIMMY REID
British trade unionist
Quoted in *Observer* 1985

SUCCESS
(*SEE ALSO* AMBITION; FAILURE;
'GOING FOR IT')

When you look at any great business enterprise, you'll find that it's *people* who make it excel. Outstanding businesses are composed of outstanding people. If you have any doubts about that, witness the long list of failures that resulted from acquisitions in the 1970s, when acquiring companies replaced existing managements with their own executives.

MARY KAY ASH
US entrepreneur and founder
of Mary Kay Cosmetics
Mary Kay on People Management

Those who are blessed with the *most talent* don't necessarily outperform everyone else. It's the people with *follow-through* who excel.

MARY KAY ASH
US entrepreneur and founder
of Mary Kay Cosmetics
Mary Kay on People Management

One's religion is whatever he is most interested in, and yours is Success.

JAMES M BARRIE 1860–1937
Scottish playwright and novelist
The Twelve-Pound Look

The toughest thing about success is that you've got to keep on being a success.

IRVING BERLIN 1888–1988
Russian-born US songwriter
Theatre Arts 1958

Always make yourself essential, that's been my golden rule.

JOH BJELKE-PETERSEN
Australian politician
Quoted in *Sydney Morning Herald* 1986

When you struggle hard and lose money, you're a hero. When you start making money you become a capitalist swine.

TERENCE CONRAN
British designer, entrepreneur and
founder of Habitat
Quoted in Jeffrey Robinson, *The Risk Takers*

To be successful you have to be lucky, or a little mad, or very talented, or to find yourself in a rapid-growth field.

EDWARD DE BONO
Maltese-born British writer, medical doctor,
and author of the concept of lateral thinking
Tactics: The Art and Science of Success

Ignore all the statistics that tell you that 95% of all new businesses fail in the first eight years. Not only are these 'statistics' riddled with widely wrong assumptions and false failure rates, but they don't apply to you. Dwelling on the statistics is like staying up to study divorce rates on your wedding night.

PAUL DICKSON
Writer
International Management 1986

If A is a success in life, then A equals x plus y plus z. Work is x; y is play; and z is keeping your mouth shut.

ALBERT EINSTEIN 1879–1955
Physicist and formulator of the theories of relativity
Observer 1950

Victory usually goes to those green enough to underestimate the monumental hurdles they are facing.

RICHARD FEYNMAN 1918–1988
US physicist
Also attributed to Eric Hoffer, US philosopher

It's fine to celebrate success but it is more important to heed the lessons of failure.

BILL GATES
Founder of Microsoft
Guardian 1995

Business is often about killing your favourite children to allow others to succeed.

JOHN HARVEY-JONES
Business writer and chairman of ICI
From the *Troubleshooter* television series, 1990

He was a self-made man who owed his lack of success to nobody.

JOSEPH HELLER
US writer
Catch-22

If a guy has a really good success pattern, I'll go along with him if he says he can go to the moon on Scotch tape.

RAYMOND HERZOG
US CEO of 3M
Quoted in Deal and Kennedy, *Corporate Cultures*

Most success comes from ignoring the obvious.

TREVOR HOLDSWORTH
Chairman of National Power
Quoted in Berry Ritchie and Walter Goldsmith,
The New Elite

The key to success for Sony, and to everything in business, science, and technology for that matter, is never to follow the others.

MASARU IBUKA
Co-founder and chairman of Sony
Fortune 1992

I cannot bear successful people who are miserable.

ELTON JOHN
British singer-songwriter
Quoted in *Sydney Morning Herald* 1986

In business, if you are persistent you normally arrive. It's the old tortoise and hare story.

NOEL LISTER
Co-founder MFI Furniture Group
Quoted in William Kay, *Tycoons*

Success is that old ABC – ability, brakes and courage.

CHARLES LUCKMAN
US architect
New York Mirror 1955

It is important for everyone to believe, whether they succeed or not, that success is linked with some kind of logic and beholden to some notion of legitimacy ... To put it another way, it is psychologically intolerable, having risen to the heights, to be badgered by doubt that you do not really deserve it.

ALISTAIR MANT
British writer
The Rise and Fall of the British Manager

None of us has gotten where we are solely by pulling ourselves up from our own bootstraps. We got here because somebody – a parent, a teacher, an Ivy League crony or a few nuns – bent down and helped us pick up our boots.

THURGOOD MARSHALL
US Supreme Court justice
Newsweek 1991

I don't think women are embarrassed to talk about money. I just don't think they measure achievement and success in personal financial terms. The pleasure is in the success of the business rather than the financial reward.

SOPHIE MIRMAN
Co-founder of The Sock Shop
The Times 1987

Success depends on three things: who says it, what he says, how he says it; and of these three things, what he says is the least important.

JOHN MORLEY 1838–1923
British writer and statesman
Recollections

You don't get any marks for trying; you must actually succeed. I'm not interested in any sophisticated reasons for failure.

ALLEN SHEPPARD
CEO of Grand Metropolitan
Business 1990

If you do it right 51% of the time you will end up a hero.

ALFRED P SLOAN 1875–1966
US president and chairman of General Motors
Quoted in Deal & Kennedy, *Corporate Cultures*

It's the truth, our ratings are higher whenever there's a disaster. But I would far rather have lower ratings and lower profits and live in a prosperous, happy, kind and loving world.

TED TURNER
US founder of CNN
Interview, *Independent* 1995

TAKEOVERS AND MERGERS

In the 1960s and the 1970s you put it together; in the 1980s you tear it apart; then in the 1990s you put it all together again.

RAND ARASKOG
Chairman of ITT
Quoted in *Financial Times* 1990

It is better to take over and build upon an existing business than to start a new one.

HAROLD GENEEN
Business consultant and chairman of ITT
Managing

Takeovers are for the public good, but that's not why I do it. I do it to make money.

JAMES GOLDSMITH
British financier
Sunday Times 1985

In such battles [involved in takeovers], the stakes are high, the pressures intense and the rewards of success potentially corrupting. The danger is that when men are hell-bent on victory and greed is in the saddle, all normal commercial propriety and respect of the law are cast aside in the rush, and the individual voice of conscience cannot be heard.

MR JUSTICE HENRY
English judge
On the convictions for theft and fraud of the
'Guinness Four' – former chairman Ernest
Saunders, investors Gerald Ronson and Jack
Lyons, and stockbroker Tony Parnes – at the end
of the Guinness-Distillers takeover trial, quoted in
The Times 1990

You don't understand. In America, anyone can sell anything he wants, at any time. You're going to have to get that straight. That is just American capitalism.

THOMAS KEMPNER
Member of the board of *New York* magazine
Riposte to Byron Dobell's accusation 'You don't'

have the right to sell people', referring to the proposed sale of *New York* to Rupert Murdoch.
Quoted in William Shawcross, *Murdoch*

This is not a hostile bid. It is unilaterally friendly.

PETER MULLER
US CEO of Adia Personnel Services
On his company's bid for Hesair plc, quoted in
Financial Weekly 1989

I went out and got my clients, this little jerk just buys them.

DAVID OGILVY
Advertising guru and founder
of Ogilvy and Mather
On the takeover of Ogilvy and Mather by Martin
Sorrell's WPP Group, quoted in
Financial Times 1989

These Armani-outfitted, BMW-driving know-it-alls broke corporations into pieces in the name of short-term profits, and broke the hearts of those whose dreams the corporations embodied.

RICARDO SEMLER
Brazilian CEO of Semco
Maverick

Of course the days when directors took a man on because he went to such and such a public school or his father knew one of their fathers are over in most businesses and the ones where they are not over are those we have an eye on.

JIM SLATER
British founder of Slater Walker Securities
and corporate raider
Financial Times 1970

TAXATION AND TAX AVOIDANCE

He's spending a year dead for tax reasons.

DOUGLAS ADAMS
British writer
The Restaurant at the End of the Universe

The only way to get your windows cleaned these days is to give the man cash and not ask if he is reporting it to the revenue.

LAWRENCE AIREY
British chairman of the board at Inland Revenue
On the black economy, said to the House of
Commons Public Accounts Committee, 1981

It is better to tax 25% of something rather than 60% of nothing.

JOH BJELKE-PETERSEN
Australian politician
Quoted in *Sydney Morning Herald* 1985

An economy breathes through its tax loopholes.

BARRY BRACEWELL-MILNES
British writer
Daily Telegraph 1979

To tax and to please, no more than to love and to be wise, is not given to men.

EDMUND BURKE 1729–1797
Irish statesman and political theorist
'On American Taxation', one of Burke's
famous speeches on the American question,
House of Commons, 1774

Read my lips – no new taxes.

GEORGE BUSH
41st president of the USA
Promise made during his presidential
campaign, 1988

There is no such thing as a good tax.

WINSTON CHURCHILL 1874–1965
British statesman and prime minister
quoted in *Observer* 1937

I have not yet found the money tree from which I can pick £10 notes. Until that day, if I spend, I tax. If I don't spend, I don't tax.

KENNETH CLARKE
British chancellor of the Exchequer
Speech, Mansion House, London, 1995

No man in this country is under the smallest obligation, moral or other, so to arrange his legal relations of his business or to his property as to enable the Inland Revenue to put the largest possible shovel into his stores.

LORD CLYDE 1863–1944
Lord justice-general of Scotland
Ayreshire Pullman Motor Services and D M Ritchie v.
The Commissioners of Inland Revenue 1929

The Inland Revenue is not slow – and quite rightly – to take every advantage which is open to it under the taxing statutes for the purpose of depleting the taxpayer's pocket.

LORD CLYDE 1863–1944
Lord justice-general of Scotland
Ayreshire Pullman Motor Services and D M Ritchie v.
The Commissioners of Inland Revenue 1929

The avoidance of tax may be lawful, but it is not yet a virtue.

LORD DENNING
English Master of the Rolls
On Weston's Settlements, 1969

There are few greater stimuli to human ingenuity than the prospect of avoiding fiscal liability. Experience shows that under this stimulus human ingenuity outreaches Parliamentary prescience.

LORD DIPLOCK 1907–1985
English judge
Commissioners of Customs and Excise v.
Top Ten Promotions Ltd 1969

If you give Congress a dollar of unnecessary taxes, they'll spend about 1.75 dollars and that's inflationary. Inflation is unAmerican: therefore tax avoidance is patriotic.

WILLIAM DONOGHUE
US newsletter publisher
Fortune 1988

The hardest thing in the world to understand is income tax.

ALBERT EINSTEIN 1879–1955
Physicist and formulator of the theories of relativity
Attributed

But in this world nothing can be said to be certain, except death and taxes.

BENJAMIN FRANKLIN 1706–1790
US author, scientist, and statesman
Letter to Jean Baptiste Le Roy, 1789

Nobody should run away with the idea that you can sustain social tranquillity by handing out tax cuts to the rich.

J K GALBRAITH
US diplomat, economist, and writer
Daily Mirror 1981

I never said that 'I would squeeze the rich until the pips squeak' though I did quote Tony Crosland using this phrase of Lloyd George's in reference to property speculators, not to the rich in general.

DENNIS HEALEY
British chancellor of the Exchequer
The Time of My Life

We don't pay tax. Only little people pay taxes.

LEONA HELMSLEY
US hotelier
Said during her trial for tax evasion,
quoted in *Sunday Times* 1989

Getting out of Hell is a bit like successfully defrauding the Revenue; many people will tell you they know someone who's managed it, but the name somehow eludes them. In practice, it's never happened.

TOM HOLT
British writer
Faust Among Equals

The avoidance of taxes is the only pursuit that still carries any reward.

JOHN MAYNARD KEYNES 1883–1946
English economist
Attributed

You don't make the poor rich by making the rich poor.

NIGEL LAWSON
British chancellor of the Exchequer
On economics, quoting economist Professor B
Bauer, *Financial Times* 1987

Any one may so arrange his affairs that his taxes shall be as low as possible; he is not bound to choose that pattern which will best pay the Treasury; there is not even a patriotic duty to increase one's taxes.

LEARNED HAND 1872–1961
US judge
Helvering v. Gregory 1934

If it isn't hurting, it isn't working.

JOHN MAJOR
British prime minister
On fiscal policy, said on his first
day as chancellor of the Exchequer, 1989

Death and taxes and childbirth! There's never any convenient time for any of them.

MARGARET MITCHELL 1900–1949
US novelist
Gone with the Wind

The federal government of the United States of America takes away between a fifth and a quarter of all our money every year. This is eight times the Islamic zakat, the almsgiving required of believers by the Koran; it is double the tithe of the medieval church and twice the royal tribute that the prophet Samuel warned the Israelites against when they wanted him to anoint a ruler.

P J O'ROURKE
US writer
Parliament of Whores

They [Inland Revenue] often decide to start taxing things they had not sought to tax before. You and I would call it moving the goalposts, the Revenue calls it applying the tax law as it was always understood to apply.

MAURICE PARRY-WINGFIELD
British accountant
On the Inland Revenue in Britain,
quoted in *BusinessAge* 1995

All money nowadays seems to be produced with a natural homing instinct for the Treasury.

PRINCE PHILIP
Duke of Edinburgh
Quoted in *Observer* 1963

Taxes, after all, are the dues that we pay for the privileges of membership in an organized society.

FRANKLIN D ROOSEVELT 1882–1945
32nd president of the USA
Speech, Worcester, Massachusetts, 1936 (In 1904 Oliver Wendell Holmes had said, 'Taxes are what we pay for civilized society')

TECHNOLOGY

(*SEE ALSO* COMPUTERS AND COMPUTING; INFORMATION TECHNOLOGY; MACHINERY; TELECOMMUNICATIONS)

During my eighty-seven years I have witnessed a whole succession of technological revolutions. But none of them has done away with the need for character in the individual or the ability to think.

BERNARD BARUCH 1870–1965
US presidential adviser and investment broker
My Own Story

One of the only ways to compete is with technology.

JOHN H BEAKES
US co-founder of RWD Technologies
Washington Post 1988

Silicon Valley is like an individual running around in front of a steamroller. You can outrun the steamroller on any given day. But if you ever sit down you get squashed.

BOB BOSCHERT
US high-tech entrepreneur
Quoted in Craig R Hickman and Michael A Silva,
Creating Excellence

Any sufficiently advanced technology is indistinguishable from magic.

ARTHUR C CLARK
British science-fiction writer
Profiles of the Future

In many instances, a properly motivated person can outperform a robot. That high level of performance, however, could never, and likely should never, be sustained by a person day in and day out.

TERRY FEULNER AND BRIAN H KLEINER
US academic; section head of Hughes Aircraft Co.
Personnel Journal 1986

If you're not part of the steamroller, you're part of the road.

RICH FRANK
Studio president of Walt Disney
On the technological advances in Hollywood, *Wall Street Journal* 1993

It has always fascinated me that management fashions seem to spread across the world with the speed of light, whereas transferring technology appears to be an extraordinarily difficult task to achieve.

JOHN HARVEY-JONES
Business writer and chairman of ICI
Managing to Survive

Over the past years I have met and talked with many of the world's leading information technology companies. I have yet to find one who would claim to be using, in their own companies, as much as 60% of the technology available today.

JOHN HARVEY-JONES
Business writer and chairman of ICI
Managing to Survive

For tribal man space was the uncontrollable mystery. For technological man it is time that occupies the same role.

MARSHALL McLUHAN 1911–1980
Canadian communications theorist
The Mechanical Bride

The new electronic interdependence recreates the world in the image of a global village.

MARSHALL McLUHAN 1911–1980
Canadian communications theorist
Gutenberg Galaxy

If you ask me whether this technological process makes us any happier, I'd have to answer 'probably not'. The whole trend of technology is towards a fragmented community, with fewer and fewer shared experiences. I think this is bound to make for a much more disjointed society. Scientific progress could offer so much, but I'm not sure it will.

JEREMY PAXMAN
British journalist and television presenter
Guardian 1995

There are three roads to ruin: women, gambling and technology. The most pleasant is with women, the quickest is with gambling, but the surest is with technology.

GEORGES POMPIDOU 1911–1974
French president
Quoted in Singapore's *Straits Times* 1987

I don't think that literature, good literature, has anything to fear from technology. The very opposite. The more technology, the more people will be interested in what the human mind can produce *without* the help of electronics.

ISAAC BASHEVIS SINGER 1904–1991
Polish-born US writer
Interview, *Writers at Work* 5th series, 1981

TELECOMMUNICATIONS
(*SEE ALSO* COMMUNICATION;
TECHNOLOGY)

We surf in the mysterious twilight zone between my keyboard and your screen, and it is not at all like listening to the Beach Boys.

PETER ASPDEN
British journalist
Financial Times 1995

Advocates love to push the benefits of direct communication [by E-mail]. Managers send and receive messages on a one-to-one basis. Now that secretaries don't fix their sloppy writing, the whole world wonders how they passed English ...

DAVID J BUERGER
US academic
Infoworld 1988

Telecommunications enables companies to move information rather than people.

**ERIC K CLEMENS AND
F WARREN McFARLAN**
US academics
Harvard Business Review 1986

It is ironic, but true, that in this age of electronic communications, personal interaction is becoming more important than ever.

REGIS McKENNA
US marketing consultant and writer
The Regis Touch

Teleconferencing is so rational, it will never succeed.

JOHN NAISBITT
US chairman of Naisbitt Group
Megatrends

People act and respond more openly in a 'phone meeting than they would in memos or one-on-one meetings with their boss.

RON OWENS
US vice-president of Houghton Mifflin Company
On holding telephone conferences,
Administrative Management 1987

TELEWORKING
(SEE ALSO TECHNOLOGY)

Teleworkers have to come up with the goods. It's the only way anyone can tell they are working.

ANONYMOUS interviewee's comment on teleworking, *Independent* 1995

It is perfectly possible, today, to run much of our business from home. Meetings can be organized by tele-conference instead of travelling, it is possible to communicate instantly by electronic mail, to avoid filing paper altogether ... But we don't. We adapt slowly and take up the advantages at our own pace.

JOHN HARVEY-JONES
Business writer and chairman of ICI
Making It Happen

I have found the problems of networking from home much greater than I expected, while the very thing which I had most cherished and hoped to defend, my home life, has suffered.

JOHN HARVEY-JONES
Business writer and chairman of ICI
Managing to Survive

The opportunities offered by telecommunications through telephone, fax and modem for real remunerative productive work in the home are inestimable. Teleworking is one of the few products of the Information Age that really bring technology back to human proportions.

CAROLINE MACKENZIE
British editor
Society of Freelance Editors and Proofreaders Newsletter 1995

When you control the level and pace of your work, you are more productive ... There's virtually no absenteeism with homeworkers – feeling too rough to haul yourself into work doesn't always prevent you staggering to the PC in the next room.

ROS MILES
British publishing editor
Cosmopolitan 1995

It's against corporate culture not to have people on site. Executives want to own their employees.

MARGRETH OLSON
US director of the Center for Research on Information Systems
Working Woman 1988

Freed from most of the constraints of paperwork, I started working more at home, with an answering machine, a personal computer, and, later, a fax. I encouraged others to work at home too. 'I need to be here', some would protest. But once they tried it and found out how much more efficient they were without all the distractions, they became Work at Home evangelists, too.

RICARDO SEMLER
Brazilian CEO of Semco
Maverick

THEFT AND PIRACY
(SEE ALSO CRIME AND CORRUPTION; FRAUD; HONESTY)

We've fabricated a society of wolves and coyotes. Why does anybody think that we are better than we were in robber baron days?

LOUIS AUCHINLOSS
US novelist and lawyer
Honorable Men

Opportunity makes a thief.

FRANCIS BACON 1561–1626
English politician, philosopher, and essayist
Letter to the Earl of Essex, 1598

If you treat your employees right,
they won't steal from you.

PHILIP CROSBY
Founder of Philip Crosby Associates, Inc.
Inc. Magazine 1988

It's much safer to steal from your
employer than the tax man.

DICK FRANCIS
British writer
Risk

For de little stealin' dey gits you in
jail soon or late. For de big stealin'
dey makes you Emperor and puts
you in de Hall o' Fame when you
croaks.

EUGENE O'NEILL 1888–1953
US dramatist
Emperor Jones

What we are talking about is
thievery, short and simple. The theft
of property that belongs to someone
else, and that is sold at a profit by
the thieves. Copyright abuse ... is one
of the cosmic issues facing us around
the world.

JACK VALENTI
Chairman of the Motion Picture
Association of America.
Speech on copyright piracy, Peking, 1995

THEORY VERSUS PRACTICE
(*SEE ALSO* EDUCATION AND TRAINING)

Theories are always very thin and
insubstantial; experience only is
tangible.

HOSEA BALLOU 1771–1852
US cleric
Universalist Expositor

True wisdom is plenty of experience,
observation and reflection. False
wisdom is plenty of ignorance,
arrogance and impudence.

**JOSH BILLINGS (HENRY
WHEELER SHAW)** 1818–1885
US writer and auctioneer
Josh Billings: His Book

Put the policy manual back on the
shelf when common sense points to a
better way.

THOMAS BONOMA
US academic
Harvard Business Review 1986

Wisdom is not to be obtained from
text-books, but must be coined out of
human experience.

MORRIS RAPHAEL COHEN 1880–1947
US philosopher and educationalist
A Dreamer's Journey

The only relevant test of the validity
of a hypothesis is comparison of
prediction with experience.

MILTON FRIEDMAN
US economist
Essays in Positive Economics

You cannot run a business, or
anything else, on a theory.

HAROLD GENEEN
Business consultant and chairman of ITT
Managing

Too many people rely too heavily
upon theories and rigid formulas
because they are looking for an easy,
structured approach to business
decisions.

HAROLD GENEEN
Business consultant and chairman of ITT
Managing

People prefer theory to practice
because it involves them in no more
real responsibility than a game of
checkers, while it permits them to
feel they're doing something serious
and important.

LEO STEIN 1872–1947
US writer and editor
Journey into the Self

TIME
(SEE ALSO LEISURE)

There's never enough time to do it right, but there's always time to do it over.

JACK BERGMAN
Vice-president of Jordache Enterprises, Inc.
Speech, New York, 1987

How does a project get to be a year behind schedule? One day at a time.

FRED BROOKS
US chief designer of System 360, IBM
Quoted in Tom Peters, *Thriving on Chaos*

There is a maxim, 'Never put off till tomorrow what you can do today.' It is a maxim for sluggards. A better reading of it is, 'Never do today what you can as well do tomorrow' because something may occur to make you regret your premature action.

AARON BURR 1756–1836
US senator
Quoted in Parton, *Life of Aaron Burr*

When I invited one executive to involve all his people and take six months to write a corporate mission statement, he said, 'You don't understand us, Stephen. We will whip this baby out this week-end.' I see people trying to do it all over a weekend – trying to rebuild their marriage on a weekend, trying to rebuild an alienated relationship with their son on a weekend, trying to change a company culture on a weekend. But some things just can't be done on a weekend.

STEPHEN R COVEY
Founder of the Institute of Principle-
Centred Leadership
Leaders: The Strategies for Taking Charge

The supply of time is totally inelastic. Time is totally perishable and cannot be stored. Time is totally irreplaceable ... there is no substitute for time.

PETER F DRUCKER
US management expert
The Effective Manager

Those who make the worst use of their time are the first to complain of its brevity.

JEAN DE LA BRUYÈRE 1645–1696
French writer
Characters

Time flies. [*Tempus fugit*]

PUBLIUS OVID 43 BC–C. AD 17
Roman poet
Fasti

Work expands so as to fill the time available for its completion.

C NORTHCOTE PARKINSON
British historian, writer, and formulator
of Parkinson's law
Parkinson's Law and Other Studies in Administration

Half our life is spent trying to find something to do with the time we have rushed through life trying to save.

WILL ROGERS 1879–1935
US comedian and actor
The Autobiography of Will Rogers

If you do things by the job, you are perpetually driven; the hours are scourges. If you work by the hour, you gently sail on a stream of Time, which is always bearing you on to the heaven of Pay, whether you make any effort or not.

CHARLES DUDLEY WARNER 1929–1903
US editor and writer
My Summer in a Garden

I've been working 15 or 16 hours a day trying to shorten working hours.

TOSHIO YAMAGUCHI
Japanese Labour minister
Management

TOP EXECUTIVES

(*SEE ALSO* BOSSES; CHAIRMEN, CHAIRWOMEN, AND CEOs; NON-EXECUTIVE DIRECTORS)

I find it rather easy to portray a businessman. Being bland, rather cruel and incompetent comes naturally to me.

JOHN CLEESE
British actor, comedian, and producer of training videos
Newsweek 1987

New executives usually bring in other new people, and if enough of this goes on, no one knows how the business runs. Things almost always slow down when there's a new executive on the job. The learning curve can last up to a year.

RICHARD GOULD
US organizational psychologist
Sacked: Why Good People Get Fired and how to Avoid It

The executive must choose between using his power to strengthen the organization and using his power to strengthen his personal power base.

BRUCE HENDERSON
CEO of Boston Consulting Group
Henderson on Corporate Strategy

Three characteristics of top executives are slow speech, impressive appearance and a complete lack of a sense of humour.

JOHNSON O'CONNOR
US entrepreneur and founder of Human Engineering Laboratory
Quoted in Vance Packard, *The Pyramid Climbers*

The best executive is the one who has sense enough to pick good men to do what he wants done, and self-restraint enough to keep from meddling with them while they do it.

THEODORE ROOSEVELT 1858–1919
26th president of the USA
Quoted in Martin Manser, *Chambers Book of Business Quotes*

Executives spend too much time analysing and too little time acting.

PHILIP SMITH
US chairman of General Foods
Fortune 1987

An overburdened, stretched executive is the best executive, because he or she doesn't have time to meddle, to deal in trivia, to bother people.

JOHN WELCH 1935
US chairman of General Electric
Quoted in *Financial Times* 1989

TRADE

(*SEE ALSO* BUYING AND SELLING GOODS)

It is the privilege of a trader in a free country, in all matters not contrary to the law, to regulate his own mode of carrying it on according to his own discretion and choice.

LORD ALDERSON 1787–1857
English judge
Hilton v. Eckersley 1855

It makes no difference whether the United States exports potato chips or silicon chips.

MICHAEL BOSKIN
US chairman of the Council of Economic Advisers
Wall Street Journal 1992

Being a trade minister is the nearest thing you can get to being war minister in peacetime. It is not for nothing that world trade is expressed daily in adversarial terms of rivalry and defeats.

ALAN CLARK
British politician
Quoted in *Sydney Morning Herald* 1986

Often English Christians forget that their whole society, with all its hopes of progress, rested on the trade they despised.

VERY REVD DAVID EDWARDS
British provost of Southwark Cathedral
On the Church's doctrinal ambivalence
towards private enterprise and the affluent
society, *The Times* 1990

Forget the cant about consumer choice. The real motivations behind 'freeing up' Sunday trading came from a big business community prepared to flout the law in order to get what it wanted. And it has worked.

LARRY ELLIOT
British journalist
Guardian 1995

No nation was ever ruined by trade.

BENJAMIN FRANKLIN 1706–1790
US author, scientist, and statesman
'Thoughts on Commercial Subjects'

People don't seem to understand that trade is like war.

JOHN HARVEY-JONES
Business writer and chairman of ICI
Quoted in David Lomax, *The Money Makers*

The propensity to truck, barter and exchange one thing for another ... is common to all men, and is to be found in no other race of animals.

ADAM SMITH 1723–1790
Scottish economist
Wealth of Nations

UNEMPLOYMENT
(SEE ALSO EMPLOYMENT; WORK)

You can't fail to see the scar of unemployment and how poverty actually disfigures people. It is one of the greatest evils of all. To deprive people of opportunity is a sin.

GORDON BROWN
British shadow chancellor of the Exchequer
Guardian 1995

Nobody is unemployable.

JULIEN FAUBERT
British proprietor of Intelink Career Services
Guardian 1995

What hope can you build into a person's life if there is no chance of work?

FRANK FIELD
British politician
Making Welfare Work

The calm acceptance of more than three million out of work just isn't good enough.

CAMPBELL FRASER
Scottish president of the
Confederation of British Industry
Speech at the Confederation of British Industry
annual conference, 1983

To pay millions of people for doing nothing, however badly you pay them, is extremely inflationary.

KEN GILL
British joint general secretary of the MSFU
On unemployment benefit, *Morning Star* 1985

If firms are to take decisions to expand their capacity they must be confident that increased demand for their products will justify it. We are ... in a 'Catch-22' situation – the authorities are reining back demand for fear of capacity limitations leading to inflation, but firms are afraid to expand their capacity because demand prospects do not justify it. This is the critical dilemma that must be resolved if we are to secure any long-term reduction in unemployment.

JOHN GRIEVE SMITH
Senior bursar of Robinson College, Cambridge
Guardian 1995

I always say to executives that they ought to go and see *King Lear*, because they'll be out there too one day, wandering on the heath without a company car.

CHARLES HANDY
Business executive and writer, and
professor at the London Business School
The Times 1989

A corporation prefers to offer a job to a man who already has one, or doesn't immediately need one. The company accepts you if you are already accepted. To obtain entry into paradise, in terms of employment, you should be in a full state of grace.

ALAN HARRINGTON
US advertising executive and manager
Life in the Crystal Palace

There are few jobs in which the penalty for error is to be eaten by a 500 lb Siberian tiger. But the statistical chances of survival, in what were once cushy white-collar billets, are becoming almost as bad as those of the keepers in Aspinall's zoos.

BORIS JOHNSON
British journalist
Spectator 1994

Busiless At leisure; without business; unemployed.

**SAMUEL JOHNSON '
DR JOHNSON'** 1709–1784
English man of letters and lexicographer
Dictionary of the English Language

I used to like to go to work but they shut it down/ I've got a right to go to work but there's no work here to be found.

MARK KNOPFLER/DIRE STRAITS
British rock musician
From the song 'Telegraph Road'

I cannot understand why there is anything good in laying off people. If management takes the risk and responsibility of hiring personnel, then it is the management's ongoing responsibility to keep them employed ... When a recession comes, why should the employee have to suffer for the management decision to hire him?

AKIO MORITA
Co-founder of Sony
Made in Japan

When you're out of work, people always tell you to start a business based on what you enjoy. But I don't want a life made up of just my hobbies.

PAM PARTRIDGE
British insurance employee
Cosmopolitan 1995

In a Deeside town eight thousand went down/ On a February day in the driving rain/ As the picket lines fell and the industry died.

**MIKE PETERS AND EDDIE
MACDONALD/THE ALARM**
Welsh rock musicians
From the song 'Deeside', which took its
inspiration from the closure of the
Shotton Steel Works, Deeside, Clwyd

I don't think people are free if they are unemployed.

PETER SHORE
British politician
Quoted in *Observer* 1983

He [Tebbit's unemployed father] didn't riot. He got on his bike and looked for work.

NORMAN TEBBIT
British secretary of state for employment
On unemployment, Conservative Party conference,
1981. At a time of recession and high
unemployment, Tebbit's remarks incensed the
general public who quickly dubbed his speech
'On Your Bike'

I would feel desperate if I had been without a good regular income for 20 weeks.

MARGARET THATCHER
British prime minister
Quoted in *Observer* 1984

It's a recession when your neighbour loses his job; its a depression when you lose yours.

HARRY S TRUMAN 1884–1972
33rd president of the USA
Quoted in *Observer* 1958

It is 'only' unemployment, but it could destroy our societies just as surely as totalitarianism destroyed Europe in the thirties.

MARTIN WOOLACOTT
British journalist
Guardian 1995

VISION
(*SEE ALSO* FORECASTING AND PLANNING; FUTURE)

Vision is needed at all levels in an organization. The supervisor of the mailroom needs a vision for that mailroom. The manager of data processing needs a vision for the DP department. The accounts payable clerk needs a vision for his/her job. Vision – throughout the organization – focuses and inspires effort.

JAMES A BELASCO
US academic and management consultant
Teaching the Elephant to Dance

Use your vision in doing things differently. That's the best way to empower others to use it. The injunction is clear – set the personal example!

JAMES A BELASCO
US academic and management consultant
Teaching the Elephant to Dance

The majority of people expect the chief executive to have a personal vision of where the company should be going. I believe, on the contrary, that in deciding where you would like to be, as opposed to where you are probably going to end up, you need a great deal of discussion and a great deal of development of new thinking and new processes.

JOHN HARVEY-JONES
Business writer and chairman of ICI
On the role of directors, *Making It Happen*

The very essence of leadership is that you have to have a vision. It's got to be a vision you articulate clearly and forcefully on every occasion. You can't blow an uncertain trumpet.

FATHER THEODORE HESBURGH
US president of Notre Dame University
Time 1987

Capital isn't scarce; vision is.

MICHAEL MILKEN
US junk-bond dealer
The Nation 1991

Vision is where tomorrow begins, for it expresses what you and others who share the vision will be working hard to create. Since most people don't take the time to think systematically about the future, those who do – and who base their strategies and actions on their visions – have inordinate power to shape the future.

BURT NANUS
US business academic and writer
Visionary Leadership

A strategy is only as good as the vision that guides it.

BURT NANUS
US business academic and writer
Visionary Leadership

Where there is a genuine vision (as opposed to the all-too-familiar 'vision statement'), people excel and learn, not because they are told to, but because they want to.

PETER M SENGE
Business academic and director of the organizational learning programme at MIT
The Fifth Discipline: The Art and Practice of the Learning Organization

WEALTH

(*SEE ALSO* ASSETS; MONEY; PROSPERITY)

Once you are past your first million pounds it doesn't make much difference. We're amused by it, it just seems slightly ridiculous.

RICHARD BRANSON
Entrepreneur and founder of Virgin Group
Daily Mirror 1972

Most of the richest people are people you've never heard of.

ROBERT STEPHEN COHEN
US lawyer
Sunday Times 1995

Wealth is not without its advantages and the case to the contrary, although it has often been made, has never proved widely persuasive.

J K GALBRAITH
US diplomat, economist, and writer
The Affluent Society

Wealth, in even the most improbable cases, manages to convey the aspect of intelligence.

J K GALBRAITH
US diplomat, economist, and writer
Sydney Morning Herald 1982

If you can actually count your money, then you are not really a rich man.

J PAUL GETTY 1892–1976
US millionare oil executive
Quoted in *Observer* 1957

There is no great secret to fortune making. All you have to do is buy cheap and sell dear, act with thrift and shrewdness and be persistent.

HETTY GREEN 'THE WITCH OF WALL STREET' 1834–1916
US speculator and investor
Quoted in Robert Sharp, *The Lore and Legends of Wall Street*

I do think this country does suffer from a wealth creation problem; we do not think it is really quite nice to be wealthy and there is something positively distasteful about a person or organization which is good at making money.

RALPH HALPERN
Chairman of Burton Group
Guardian 1984

Affluence means influence.

JACK LONDON 1876–1916
US writer
Attributed

I want to see wealth cascading down the generations. We don't see each generation starting out anew with the past cut off and the future ignored ... we must go much further in encouraging every family to save and to own; to extend every family's ability to pass something on to their children; to build up something of their own, for their own.

JOHN MAJOR
British prime minister
Speech at the Conservative Party conference, 1991

I get so tired listening to one million dollars here, one million dollars there. It's so petty.

IMELDA MARCOS
Philippine politician-wife
of president Ferdinand Marcos
Financial Weekly 1990

After a certain point money is meaningless. It ceases to be the goal. The game is what counts.

ARISTOTLE ONASSIS 1900–1975
Greek shipping tycoon
Quoted in *Esquire* 1969

Making money is rather like being a blonde. It is more fun but not vital.

MARY QUANT
British fashion designer and entrepreneur
Quoted in *Observer* 1986

Nobody ever feels rich.

ESTHER RANTZEN
British television presenter
Quoted in *Observer* 1983

The only things that create wealth in the world are things like fishing and farming and mining and taking resources and creating something.

DENIS ROOKE
Chairman of British Gas
Financial Times 1984

Money is the most important thing in the world. It represents health, strength, generosity, and beauty as conspicuously and undeniably as the want of it represents illness, weakness, disgrace, meanness, and ugliness.

GEORGE BERNARD SHAW 1856–1950
Irish dramatist and critic
Major Barbara

It's just as easy to be happy with a lot of money as a little.

MARVIN TRAUB
CEO of Bloomingdale's
7 Days 1989

Nobody who has wealth to distribute ever omits himself.

LEON TROTSKY 1879–1940
Russian communist revolutionary
Quoted in *Observer* 1937

No man should keep more than £100,000. That's enough for any man. The rest should go to charity.

ISAAC WOLFSON 1897–1991
British philanthropist and
chairman of Great Universal Stores
Quoted in Stephen Aris, *The Jews in Business*

WORK
(*SEE ALSO* **EMPLOYMENT; UNEMPLOYMENT**)

Human labour is an *end* but not a *means*.

CLAUDE-FRÉDÉRIC BASTIAT 1801–1850
French economist
Sophismes èconomiques

You can't think and hit the ball at the same time.

YOGI BERRA
US baseball player and coach
Attributed

I wouldn't say I was an ideal person, but I'm certainly not a mad workaholic. I'm extremely distrustful of people who work a 90 hour week.

NIGEL BROAKES
Chairman of Trafalgar House
Financial Times 1988

I found I could add nearly two hours to my working day by going to bed for an hour after luncheon.

WINSTON CHURCHILL 1874–1965
British statesman and prime minister
My Early Life

The worker is the slave of capitalist society, the female worker is the slave of that slave.

JAMES CONNOLLY 1870–1916
Irish labour leader
Re-conquest of Ireland

Work is much more fun than fun.

NOEL COWARD 1899–1973
British actor and writer
Quoted in *Observer* 1963

One of the best ways of avoiding necessary and even urgent tasks is to seem to be busily employed on things that are already done.

J K GALBRAITH
US diplomat, economist, and writer
The Affluent Society

We are not born to work, we are born to enjoy life. Work is only part of it.

JOE GORMLEY
British president of the NUM
Speech at the Labour Party annual
conference, 1979

America holds work in such deep and abiding respect that children are introduced to it at the earliest possible opportunity and nothing is too menial, even for the children of the wealthy.

LINDA GRANT
British journalist
Guardian 1995

It is the little changes which can in fact make the biggest differences to our lives, even if these go unnoticed at the time, and ... it is the changes in the way our *work* is organized which will make the biggest differences to the way we all will *live*.

CHARLES HANDY
Business executive and writer, and professor at the London Business School
The Age of Unreason

As long as people do their jobs well, I see no reason why they shouldn't have as much fun as they possibly can.

ANDY JACOBS
US co-founder of Jacob's Bros. Bagels
Brown Alumni Monthly 1988

For many wage earners *work is perceived as a form of punishment* which is the price to be paid for various kinds of satisfactions away from the job.

D MCGREGOR
British writer
The Human Side of Enterprise

Before I was a genius I was a drudge.

IGNACE PADEREWSKI 1860–1941
Polish pianist and statesman
Remark to reporters, 1936

Work is accomplished by those employees who have not yet reached their level of incompetence.

LAURENCE J PETER 1910–1990
Canadian writer, educationalist, and researcher of remedies for incompetence
Peter Principle

The increase of the 'black' economy shows that people do not, once they

are freed of their companies, their unions and, to a certain extent, their Government, shirk the idea of work.

PRINCE CHARLES
Prince of Wales
Quoted in *Observer* 1981

Work is of two kinds: first, altering the position of matter at or near the earth's surface relatively to other matter; second telling other people to do so. The first kind is unpleasant and ill paid, the second is pleasant and highly paid.

BERTRAND RUSSELL 1872–1970
English philosopher and mathematician
In Praise of Idleness

Far and away the best prize that life offers is the chance to work hard at work worth doing.

THEODORE ROOSEVELT 1858–1919
26th president of the USA
Labor Day speech, Syracuse, New York, 1903

The test of a vocation is the love of the drudgery it involves.

LOGAN PEARSALL SMITH 1865–1946
US-born British writer
Afterthoughts

There are always going to be brainier or better-connected people than you, but you can always work really hard.

JANET STREET-PORTER
British television executive
Cosmopolitan 1995

At Amstrad the staff start early and finish late. Nobody takes lunches – they may get a sandwich slung on their desk – there's no small talk. It's all action and the atmosphere is amazing, and the *esprit de corps* is terrific. Working hard is fun.

ALAN SUGAR
Entrepreneur and founder of Amstrad plc
Lecture given at the City University
Business School, 1987

If work was so good, the rich would have hogged it for themselves.

> **MARK TWAIN** 1835–1910
> US writer
> Quoted in *Independent* 1994 (also attributed to union leader Lane Kirkland)

WORKER PARTICIPATION
(*SEE ALSO* PROFIT SHARING)

At present, firms are typically accountable to their shareholders, who are the firm's voters. But it is the workers, not the shareholders, who are subject to the authority of the firm. Ethically, therefore, it is the workers, not the shareholders, who should be the firm's voters.

> **ROBIN ARCHER**
> British academic
> *Guardian* 1995

I'm not going to have the monkeys running the zoo.

> **FRANK BORMAN**
> US astronaut and CEO of Eastern Airlines
> On worker participation, *Washington Monthly* 1986

The employer puts his money into ... business and the workman his life. The one has as much right as the other to regulate that business.

> **CLARENCE DARROW** 1857–1938
> US lawyer and reformer
> Interview, 1909

Most workers know that they are not the cause of the country's malaise. They do not own it. They do not control it. They never chartered the disastrous courses, nor blueprinted any of the derelict plans of yesteryear.

> **KEN GILL**
> General secretary of AUEW
> *The Times* 1974

Every annual report by every chairman all over the world ends up by paying a tribute to 'our people – our greatest resource'. Yet boards of directors hardly ever take time out to look at the totality of the environment in which 'our greatest resource' works.

> **JOHN HARVEY-JONES**
> Business writer and chairman of ICI
> *Managing to Survive*

Management's ability to get the best from people increases when it chooses to share its power.

> **TONY KIZILOS AND ROGER P HEINISCH**
> Employees of Systems and Research Center of Aerospace and Defense, Honeywell Corp.
> *Harvard Business Review* 1986

Almost all businessmen think their employees are involved in the firm and are its greatest asset. Almost all employees think they are given too little attention and respect, and cannot say what they really think.

> **RICARDO SEMLER**
> Brazilian CEO of Semco
> *Maverick*

We simply do not believe our employees have an interest in coming in late, leaving early, and doing as little as possible for as much money as their union can wheedle out of us. After all, these same people raise children, join the PTA, elect mayors, governors, senators, and presidents. They are adults. At Semco, we treat them like adults. We trust them. We don't make our employees ask permission to go to the bathroom, or have security guards search them as they leave for the day. We get out of their way and let them do their jobs.

> **RICARDO SEMLER**
> Brazilian CEO of Semco
> *Maverick*

I saw top management sitting at a table with me and listening to what we had to say and willing to do something about it. I saw this was a place where the employees could grow and the company could grow.

JOÃO SOARES
Brazilian employee at Semco
On Semco's introduction of factory committees,
quoted in Ricardo Semler, *Maverick*

FINAL STATEMENT

He who owns the most when he dies, wins.

IVAN BOESKY
US financier
Slogan on T-shirt worn by Boesky, reported in *The Times* 1986. He was later found guilty of insider trading and sentenced to three years in jail.

Here lies a man who knew how to enlist into his service people better than himself.

ANDREW CARNEGIE 1835–1919
Industrialist and philanthropist
Epitaph

The man who dies rich, dies disgraced.

ANDREW CARNEGIE 1835–1919
Industrialist and philanthropist
'The Administration of Wealth' in *The Gospel of Wealth and Other Timely Essays*

Know what I want them to put on my tombstone? Do not disturb.

TED TURNER
US founder of CNN
Evening Standard 1988

Abrams, Creighton 24
Aburdene, Patricia 142
Acheson, Dean 17, 63, 136
Ackoff, Russell L 84
Acton, Lord 125
Adams, Anthony 84
Adams, Charles 4
Adams, Douglas 158
Adams, Henry Brooks 55, 62, 138
Adams, Walter 90
Adler, Fred 59, 71
Adler, Larry 59
Aesop 57
Airey, Lawrence 159
Aitken, Ian 143
Aitken, Jonathan 115
Akers, John 141
Alarm, The 5, 168
Alderson, Lord 166
Allen, Brandt 29
Allen, Fred 31, 120
Allen, Robert 61
Allen, Woody 111
Allison, Eric 27, 41, 84, 97, 148
Allison, Mary Ann 27, 41, 84, 97, 148
Amabile, Teresa 72
Andoh, Tatsuhiko 49
Andrus, Cecil 97
Appel, Bernard 74
Appleyard, Bryan 64
Aragon, Louis 87
Araskog, Rand 158
Arbuthnot, John 93
Archer, Mary 1
Archer, Robin 173
Argyris, Chris 99
Aristotle 35, 39, 52, 124
Armstrong, Louis 'Satchmo' 111, 144
Arnett, Ramona E F 52, 72, 149
Arnold, John 76
Arrow, Kenneth J 84
Ascherson, Neil 44, 51, 61, 68
Ash, Mary Kay 14, 24, 26, 36, 55, 58, 78, 99, 120, 155–56, 156
Ash, Roy 51
Ashcroft, John 99, 119, 120
Ashley, Laura 37
Aspden, Peter 162
Asquith, H H 152
Athos, Anthony G 70
Atkinson, Brooks 17
Attiga, Ali Ahmed 128
Attlee, Clement 40
Auchinloss, Louis 163
Auden, W H 14, 57–8
Augustine, Norman R 78, 141
Austin, Nancy 129
Avis, Warren 149
Ayckbourn, Alan 44

Babbit, Bruce 44
Bach, Johnny 66

Bacon, Francis 62, 74, 125, 163
Bagehot, Walter 10, 11, 125
Bailey, Stephen K 136
Bakatin, Vadim 20
Baker, James 106
Baldridge, Malcolm 148
Baldwin, James 111, 124
Baldwin, Stanley 80–1
Balfour, Arthur 108
Ballou, Hosea 164
Bamford, Joe 28
Banham, John 24
Barada, Paul W 89
Barchetti, Katherine 37
Bardwick, Judith M 8, 9, 40
Baring, Maurice 64
Barkley, Alben W 138
Barnum, Phineas T 19
Barrie, James M 105, 156
Barth, John 132
Bartolme, Fernando 15
Baruch, Bernard 84, 126, 144, 161
Basinger, Kim 33
Bastiat, Claude-Frédéric 171
Bauman, Al 14
Bayley, Bjorn 17
Beakes, John H 161
Beauvoir, Simone de 19, 145
Beaverbrook, Lord 19
Beckman, Bob 91
Beecher, Henry Ward 39, 124, 126
Beer, Michael 139
Beerbohm, Max 58
Behan, Brendan 138
Belasco, James A 9, 21, 21–2, 72, 89, 109, 132, 134, 143, 169
Bell, Emily 102
Bell, Tim 4
Belloc, Hilaire 111
Benington, Lucy 50
Bennett, Arnold 138
Bennis, Warren G 5, 9, 24, 36, 76, 95, 98, 117
Bentley, John 1
Bergman, Jack 165
Berlin, Irving 156
Bermar, Amy 99
Bernays, Edward 137
Bernstein, Albert J 104
Berra, Yogi 171
Berrill, Robin 137
Bersoff, Ed 70
Betjeman, John 92
Bevan, Aneurin ('Nye') 29, 55, 118, 149
Bible 14, 64, 124
Bich, Bruno 139
Bierce, Ambrose 1, 34, 64
Biggar, James M 119
Bignell, Lynn Tendler 72
Billings, Josh (Henry Wheeler Shaw) 109, 164
Birch, David 149
Birkett, Lord 138
Bjelke-Petersen, Joh 155, 156, 159

Black, Conrad 68
Blair, Tony 51, 123
Blake, William 40
Blanchard, Kenneth H 9, 26, 99
Blessing, Buck 148
Blighe, Frank 91
Bloch, Arthur 106
Block, A Harvey 16
Blythman, Jo 122–23
Bock, Lud 76
Boesky, Ivan 19, 174
Bohr, Neils 63
Bond, Alan 12, 155
Bono, Edward de 156
Bonoma, Thomas 164
Boorstin, Daniel J 85, 105, 137
Borman, Frank 12, 173
Boschert, Bob 161
Boseley, Sarah 53
Boskin, Michael 166
Bowe, Colette 26
Bower, Joseph L 141
Bracewell-Milnes, Barry 159
Bradley, Omar Nelson 55
Bradman, Godfrey 1, 149–50
Braiker, Harriet 106
Bramante, Fred Jr 73
Brandeis, Louis Dembitz 9, 34, 53, 69, 71, 118,
    128, 152
Branson, Richard 7, 12, 25, 44, 46, 51, 58, 62,
    77, 150, 170
Branson, Robert M 126
Brasher, Chris 49
Brazell, Thomas 'Wayne' 9
Brecht, Bertolt 11, 88
Bretherton, Russell 106–7
Brewster, Kingman 92
Bridgewater, Emma 82–83, 102
Broakes, Nigel 171
Brock, James 90
Brooks, Fred 165
Broun, Heywood 64
Brower, Charles 146
Brown, Andrew 68, 141
Brown, Courtney C 130
Brown, Gordon 167
Browne-Wilkinson, Nicholas 93
Browning, Guy 9, 15, 77, 115
Bruderle, Rainer 123
Bryan, Charles E 81
Bryant, Paul 'Bear' 78
Buchan, James 11, 35
Buckman, Dr Laurence 16
Buerger, David J 162
Buffet, Warren 153
Buffett, Walter 88, 99
Bullock, Donald 40
Burger, Alvin 55
Burke, Edmund 63, 147, 159
Burnett, Leo 4
Burns, M Anthony 150
Burr, Aaron 165
Burroughs, William S 69
Burson, Harold 138

Burton, John C 1
Burton, Paul 53
Bush, George 159
Bushnell, Nolan 51
Butcher, Donald 153
Butcher, Willard C 44, 150
Butler, Samuel 124, 128, 132
Buzzell, Robert 47

Cadbury, Adrian 40, 55
Cairncross, Alec 59
Cairns, Theodore L 143–44
Caldwell, Philip 42
Callaghan, James 40, 95, 126
Calloway, D Wayne 47, 100, 118
Camden, William 7
Campbell, Colin 43
Campion, Robert 134
Capek, Karel 99
Capote, Truman 58
Carayol, Rene 47
Cardenas, Ruben 12
Carling, Will 73
Carlucci, Frank C 16
Carnegie, Andrew 34, 174
Carnegie, Dale 7, 120
Carnegie, Rod 123
Carrigan, Patricia M 120
Carroll, Maureen 95
Carruthers, Peter 79
Carter, Jimmy 117
Casa, Giovani della 7
Cathcart, Brian 94
Catherine II 'The Great' 79
Catherwood, Fred 136
Cecil, Lyn 89
Céline, Louis-Ferdinand 124
Challenger, James E 89
Chambers, Paul 47
Champy, James 9, 17, 26, 30, 99, 135, 141
Chandler, Raymond 1
Chandos, Lord 138
Chanel, Coco 50
Chapman, John Jay 7
Charles, Prince 100, 172
Chase, Alexander 124
Chesterfield, Lord 21
Chesterton, G K 48, 58, 71
Chevalier, Maurice 144
Churchill, Winston 24, 57, 87, 147, 159, 171
Cicero, Marcus Tullius 5, 7, 93, 95
Clark, Alan 166
Clark, Arthur C 161
Clark, John Maurice 130
Clarke, Kenneth 43, 159
Clay, Henry 61, 152
Cleese, John 166
Clemens, Eric K 162
Cleveland, Grover 94
Clinton, Bill 133
Clough, Arthur Hugh 27
Clyde, Lord 159
Cobbett, William 124
Cockburn, Claud 35

Cocks, Barnett 23
Cocteau, Jean 98
Cohen, John 'Jack' 102
Cohen, Morris Raphael 164
Cohen, Robert Stephen 170
Cohn, Harry 126
Collingwood, Robin George 149
Collins, Joan 66
Colton, Charles Caleb 33
Confucius 48, 63, 91
Connolly, Cyril 21
Connolly, James 171
Conran, Shirley 48
Conran, Terence 51, 156
Cook, A J 155
Cook, Paul 2
Cooke, Alistair 35
Coolidge, Calvin 131, 155
Cooper, Cary L 126
Corby, Brian 50
Coren, Alan 88–9
Cork, Kenneth 22, 60, 81
Corker, Susan 73
Coulomb, Charles Augustin 130
Courtauld, Samuel 139
Cousins, Frank 83
Covey, Stephen R 1, 8, 9, 41–2, 62, 86, 128, 139, 165
Cowan, Gwen 148
Coward, Noel 171
Crichton, Michael 85
Cronbach, Lee J 73
Crook, Jayne 14
Crosby, Philip 164
Cumberledge, Baroness 108
Cushing, Philip 146
Cuthbert, Steve 37
Cutland, Aubrey 132
Cutler, Laurel 8, 63, 102, 144

Daniels, Bob 126
Darrow, Clarence 81, 173
Darwin, Charles 144
Davenport, H J 128
Davidson, Andrew 69
Davidson, Jeffrey P 50
Davies, George 127
Davies, Howard 10
Davis, Keith 16
Day, Clarence 47
Day, Graham 37, 73
Dayan, Moshe 62
Deal, Terence E 83
Dean, Dizzy 138
Dearden, John 9
de Bono, Edward 156
Defoe, Daniel 143
Dejan, Sudjic 102
Della Femina, Jerry 4
de Marvil, Patricia L 149
Deming, W Edwards 34
Demosthenes 60
Denning, Lord 159
de Quincey, Thomas 103

Descartes, René 26
Dickey, Alan 17
Dickinson, Andrew 146
Dickson, Paul 156
Diplock, Lord 94, 159
Dire Straits 168
Disney, Walt 8, 87
Disraeli, Benjamin 36, 39, 43, 114
Dix, Carol 149
Dixon, Phil 49
Djilas, Milovan 124
Dole, Bob 55
Donaldson, John 94
Donner, Michael 92
Donoghue, William 159
Donovan, Patrick 6
Doszher, Charles 141
Douglas, Norman 4
Douglas-Home, Alec 129
Doyle, Arthur Conan 84
Drake, John D 89
Dressler, Fritz R S 63
Drucker, Peter F 29, 34, 47, 53, 88, 91, 100, 130, 131, 135, 165
Drummond, John 55
Drummond, Thomas 135
Drury, Mike 150
Duncan, Alan 124
Duncan, G A 123
Dunne, Jim 127
Durant, Ariel 63
Durant, Will 63
Dyer, William G 8, 24, 79, 88
Dylan, Bob 111

Earhart, Amelia 58
Eby, Sheila M 30
Eden, Anthony 34
Edge, The 124–25
Edgeworth, Maria 135
Edison, Thomas Alva 90, 127
Edwardes, Michael 1, 100
Edwards, Mark 4
Edwards, Very Revd David 167
Egan, John 37
Eigen, Lewis D 30
Einhorn, Hillel J 59
Einstein, Albert 47, 63, 156, 159
Eisner, Michael 70
Eliot, George (Mary Ann Evans) 10
Elliot, Larry 167
Elliot, Marian 139
Ellis, Tim III 53
Elton, Ben 69
Emerson, Ralph Waldo 35, 68, 94, 111, 124, 136
Enfield, Harry 45
Engels, Friedrich 53
Erhard, Ludwig 29
Esber, Edward M 30
Esrey, William T 66
Estrin, Melvyn 102
Evans, David 'The Edge' 124–25

Evans, Marcus 98
Evert, Chris 66

Fairchild, John 125
Fairley, Jo 69
Fantoni, Barry 2
Farquhar, George 68
Faubert, Julien 167
Feather, Vic 81
Feiffer, Jules 125
Feldman, Marty 105
Feulner, Terry 161
Feynman, Richard 156
Fick, Oliver A 40
Field, Frank 50, 167
Fieldes, Christopher 23
Fields, Rubye 53
Fields, W C 53
Fink, William 30
Firnstahl, Timothy 42
Fisher, Irving 45
Fisher, Paul 77, 100
Fitzgerald, Edward 22
Fitzgerald, F Scott 26, 31
Fitzgerald, Niall 95
Fitzgerald, Penelope 135
Flaubert, Gustave 14
Fleming, Ian 64
Flores, Frank 42
Flynn, Errol 39, 80
Follett, Barbara 125
Follett, Mary Parker 10
Fonda, Jane 148
Foot, Isaac 126
Forbes, Malcolm F 130
Ford, Gerald 137
Ford, Henry 37, 83, 111, 120
Ford, Henry II 73
Forward, Gordon 109, 144
Foster, Roger 109
Foulston, Nicola 12–13
Fowles, Jib 59
France, Anatole 97, 125
Francis, Dick 164
Frank, Rich 161
Frankfurter, Felix 94
Franklin, Benjamin 128, 160, 167
Fraser, Campbell 167
Freedley, Edwin T 2
Friedman, Milton 20, 67, 83, 112, 119, 164
Fromm, Erich 58, 86
Frost, Robert 15, 131
Fuller, Thomas 38, 103

Galbraith, J K 33, 45, 58, 59, 60, 107, 123, 126, 140, 153, 154, 160, 170, 171
Gandhi, Mahatma 19, 20, 75, 94
Gapper, Steve 86
Garfield, Charles 1
Gash, Jonathan 61
Gates, Bill 70, 156
Geldard, Robin 123
Gellerman, Saul W 6, 55
Geneen, Harold 2, 3, 6, 10, 13, 19, 22, 40, 59,

66, 79, 95, 95–6, 100, 103, 107, 109, 115, 117, 119, 121, 129, 145, 146, 152, 158, 164
George, Eddie 11, 45
George, Henry 20, 119, 128
Gershwin, Ira 34
Gerstenhaber, Moshe 47
Gerstner, Lou 92
Getty, J Paul 10, 74, 121, 154, 170
Geus, Arie de 27
Gibbon, Edward 35
Gibson, Fiona 89
Gide, André 145
Gilbert, Steven 59
Gilbert, W S 89
Gill, Ken 167, 173
Gillen, Terry 117
Gilman, Charlotte Perkins 53
Glancey, Jonathan 2
Glassman, Bernard S 131
Goethe, Johann Wolfgang von 97
Gohel, Jayvantsinnji 61
Goizueta, Roberto 110
Goldsmith, Harvey 11
Goldsmith, James 21, 69, 88, 112, 117, 131, 146, 158
Goldsmith, Walter 81
Goldwyn, Samuel 34, 40
Gomme, Alison 15
Gompers, Samuel 131
Goodison, Nicholas 17
Gore, William L 96
Gormley, Joe 81, 114, 171
Goss, Priscilla 121
Gotti, John 15
Gould, Larry 107
Gould, Richard 100, 166
Grabowsky, Axel L 127
Grace, Peter 79
Grade, Lord 8, 154
Gramling, Nadine 42
Grant, Albert A 15
Grant, Alistair 7
Grant, James 39
Grant, Linda 53–4, 171–72
Grant, Phillip C 14
Grant, Ulysses S 58
Graves, Earl G 150
Graves, Robert 111
Gray, John 50, 54
Grayson, Paula 89
Green, Estill I 16
Green, Hetty 'The Witch of Wall Street' 170
Greenspan, Dr Alan 83
Greer, Germaine 54
Gresham, Thomas 111
Griffiths, Phillip A 144
Griggs, Richard E 59
Grossart, Angus 9
Grossmith, George 74
Grossmith, Weedon 74
Grove, Andrew S 84–5, 107, 129, 130
Guerra, Robert 127
Gulliver, James 42, 111
Gummer, John Selwyn 65

Gyllenhammar, Pehr Gustaf 139, 141
Gyngell, Bruce 71
Gyohten, Toyoo 153–54

Hacker, Andrew 150
Hailsham, Lord 7, 94
Half, Robert 90, 110
Hall, Robert 133
Halpern, Ralph 71, 80, 136, 170
Hamlyn, Paul 104
Hammer, Michael 9, 17, 26, 30, 99, 135, 141
Hammerskjöld, Dag 121
Hampton, Christopher 105
Hand, Learned 92, 160
Handy, Charles 29, 30, 38, 47, 50, 51, 63, 68, 93, 110, 121, 132, 133, 145, 168, 172
Hanson, Lord 6, 43, 70
Harkness, Richard 23
Harrington, Alan 138, 168
Hartzell, Betty 81
Harvey, Eric 86
Harvey-Jones, John 6, 13, 24, 36, 39, 49, 55, 71, 73, 76, 83, 86, 90, 96, 100, 112, 115, 116, 121, 132, 133, 138, 148, 156, 161, 163, 167, 169, 173
Hattersley, Roy 103
Hawkins, Trip 79
Hayes, James L 17, 51, 56, 100
Healey, Dennis 160
Hearn, Barry 66
Hearst, William Randolph 58, 150
Heath, Christopher 65
Heath, Edward 20
Hegg, George 76
Heineken, Alfred 'Freddy' 146
Heinisch, Roger P 173
Heisenberg, Werner Carl 32
Heller, Joseph 26, 113, 156
Heller, Robert 3, 101, 107
Helmsley, Leona 160
Henderson, Bruce 56, 79, 91, 96, 127, 166
Hendry, Linda 70
Henry, Mr Justice 158
Henry, O 61
Herbert, A P 67, 94, 137
Herbert, George 14, 15, 79, 94, 128
Herodotus 64
Hersey, Paul 26
Herzberg, Frederick 119
Herzog, Raymond 156–57
Hesburgh, Father Theodore 169
Heseltine, Michael 110
Hicks, John 45
Hipple, Eric von 88
Hobbes, Thomas 152
Hobhouse, Henry 61
Hobson, Dominic 124
Hoffa, Jimmy 149
Hogarth, Robin M 59
Hoggart, Simon 138
Holdsworth, Trevor 83, 157
Holmes, Oliver Wendell Jr 34
Holmes, Oliver Wendell Sr 72, 91
Holmes à Court, Robert 19, 114
Holt, Tom 4, 98, 160

Holtsman, Irwin 135
Holtz, Herman 32
Hook, Harold S 117
Hoover, Herbert 45
Hopper, Grace Murray 16, 43, 76, 86, 96
Hore-Belisha, Lord 114
Hornby, Simon 123
Horton, Thomas R 2
Hoskyns, John 17, 96
Howe, Edgar Watson 56
Howe, Geoffrey 23, 45, 133
Howell, James 35
Hubbard, Elbert 26, 99, 147
Hubbard, Frank McKinney ('Kin') 7, 77
Hughes, Howard H 40
Hume, David 45
Hussein, Jaffar 11
Hutchinson, Tim Hely 104
Hutton, Thomas J 114
Hutton, Will 123
Huxley, Aldous 4, 54, 85
Huxley, Julian 22

Iacocca, Lee 15, 101, 127
Ibsen, Derek 154
Ibuka, Masaru 157
Icahn, Carl C 13, 22
Ilich, John 114
Illich, Ivan 33
Ingrams, Richard 94
Ishihara, Takashi 150

Jackson, Holbrook 121
Jackson, Kevin Goldstein 91
Jacobs, Andy 172
Jacobs, Jane 45
Jam, The 21
James, P D 66
Jaquith, David 60
Jay, Anthony 23, 67, 86–7
Jefferson, Thomas 39, 56
Jenkins, Roy 67
Jerome, Jerome K 76, 97
Jerrold, Douglas 64
Jevons, William Stanley 45
Johansson, Henry J 110
John, Elton 157
Johnson, Boris 168
Johnson, H Thomas 130
Johnson, Lyndon Baines 126, 129
Johnson, Samuel 'Dr Johnson' 25, 62, 75, 76, 168
Johnstone, Helen 149
Jonas, Gary F 10
Jones, David 131
Jones, Patricia 66
Jordan, Michael 12
Joseph, Keith 131
Josephs, Ray 129
Juvenal 19

Kaagan, Stephen S 7
Kabaidze, Vladimir 17
Kadis, Betty 20

Kahaner, Larry 66
Kantor, Rosabeth Moss 10
Kaplan, Robert S 130
Karatsu, Hajima 83
Kay, Alan 64
Kay, John 27, 88
Kearton, Lord 104, 121
Keating, Paul 45
Keegan, Victor 51
Keith, Lord 105
Kelly, Donald P 28
Kelly, Joe 10
Kemp, Mike 89
Kempner, Thomas 158
Kennedt, Allen A 83
Kennedy, Florynce R 118
Kennedy, John F 30, 48, 51, 54, 114, 125, 129
Kennedy, Joseph P 66, 111, 114
Keogh, Donald 6
Kerkorian, Kirk 46
Kerr, Jean 127
Kershaw, David 140
Kettering, Charles F 49
Kettle, Martin 56
Keynes, John Maynard 11, 21, 46, 110, 111,
   123–24, 147, 160
Khasoogi, Adnan 104
Kiam, Victor 1, 25, 40, 114, 116, 147
Kimoto, Tak 37
King, Christine 66
King, Don 116
Kipling, Rudyard 72
Kirkland, Lane 16
Kissinger, Henry 129
Kizilos, Tony 173
Klein, Gene 140
Kleiner, Brian H 161
Knapp, Jimmy 155
Knight, Ann 34–5
Knight, Charles 3
Knopfler, Mark 168
Knowles, Barry 30
Kohn, Alfie 28
Kokoschka, Oskar 143
Kolb, Harry D 107
Kopczynski, Edward 107
Krafve, Richard E 42
Krannert, Herman 75
Kroc, Ray 28, 65
Krutch, Joseph Wood 136
Kyd, Charles W 30

La Bruyère, Jean de 125, 165
La Guardia, Fiorello 152
Laird, Gavin 105
Laker, Freddie 18
Lamb, Charles 12
Lang, Andrew 152
Lansky, Meyer 103
La Rochefoucauld, François 27
Larson, Erik 60
Lauer, Howard C 79
Laurent, André} 15
Lawless, John 24

Lawrie, Ian 123
Lawson, Nigel 67, 105–6, 160
Lawson, Peter 30
Leach, Penelope 54
Leacock, Stephen 4, 98
Leaman, Adrian 115–16
Lecoeur, Gerard 92
Leeke, Jim 56
Lehmann, Rosamond 116
Lehr, Lewis 36–7
Leisinger, Klaus M 147
Leith-Ross, Frederick 83
Lenin, Vladimir Illych 2
Leutwiler, Fritz 142
Leverhulme, Lord 4
Levi, Primo 20, 32, 37
Levin, Bernard 39
Levin, Shemarya 139
Levine, Joseph E 4
Levitt, Ted 52, 117
Lewis, Roy 121
Lincoln, Neil 30
Lindgren, Robert T 128
Lindley, Geoff 43
Lindley, Lord 81
Linnecar, Robin 47
Lippmann, Walter 96
Lister, Noel 157
Little, Royal 90, 116, 131
Livingstone, Ken 91
Lloyd George, David 57, 65, 72
Loewy, Raymond 42
Lombardi, Vince 66, 73, 96, 127
London, Jack 170
Long, Jonelle 96
Long, Roland 84
Lorber, Robert 9, 99
Lorenz, Andrew 150–51
Louis, Joe 111
Lowe, Frank 5
Luce, R Duncan 85
Luckman, Charles 157
Lynch, Peter 154
Lynn, Jonathan 23, 67, 86–7

McAdams, Jerry 14
McCarthy, Mary 18, 33, 41
McCormack, Mark 38, 44, 48, 62, 70, 77
McCrae, Norman 133–34, 142
Macdonald, Eddie 5, 168
McFarlan, F Warren 162
McGowan, William G 28, 42, 134
McGregor, D 172
McGregor, Ian 127
McGregor, Lord 5
MacGuire, Rosemary 49
Machiavelli, Niccolo{grave} 57, 108
Mackay, Harvey 146
McKay, Joe J 24
McKay, Peter 11
McKenna, Regis 162
Mackenzie, Caroline 163
Mackenzie, R Alec 25, 48, 107, 146
McKinney, Craig 98

McLaughlin, Mignon 104
McLuhan, Marshal 5, 25, 106, 161, 162
Macmillan, Harold 15, 32, 80, 113
McMurry, Robert N 121–22
McNealy, Scott 28
MacNeice, Louis 65
McRae, Hamish 13, 15, 98, 115
McTague, Michael 130
Madden, John 32
Mager, Robert F 121
Maimonides, Moses 127
Maitland, Sara 75
Major, John 6, 160, 170
Mancroft, Lord 112
Manley, Marisa 42
Manley, Michael 103
Mant, Alistair 157
Marcos, Imelda 170
Marcus, Stanley 38, 140
Margolis, Jonathan 106
Margulies, Stuart 73
Mark, Robert 94
Markham, Margie 10
Marquand, David 103
Marquis, Don 76
Marrow, Alfred J 107
Marsh, Lord 25
Marshall, Alfred 80
Marshall, Colin 86
Marshall, John 34
Marshall, Thurgood 157
Martin, Justin 24
Marvil, Patricia L de 149
Mason, John 60
Matsushita, Konosuke 38
Matzger, Philip W 148
Maugham, W Somerset 29, 57, 112
Maverick, Maury 92
Maxton, James 104
Maxwell, Robert 104, 114
Mayhew, Ken 47
Mellon, Andrew William 39, 154
Mencken, H L 93
Meston, Lord 12
Metcalf, Joseph 18
Metzger, Philip W 14
Meyers, Gerald C 101
Middleton, Peter 46
Miles, Ros 15, 90, 163
Milken, Michael 139, 169
Mill, John Stuart 83
Miller, Harvey 12, 79
Miller, James C 37
Miller, Lawrence 7
Miller, Peter 62
Milligan, Spike 62–3
Mills, C Wright 122
Mills, Leif 23
Milne, A A 96
Ming, Celso 43
Mintzberg, Henry 85, 127
Mirman, Sophie 157
Mishcon, Lord 12
Mitchell, Margaret 160

Monsarrat, Nicholas 135
Montgomery, Robert L 48
Moore, Debbie 131
Moore, Suzanne 61
Morgan, John Pierpont 94
Morgan, Peter 48
Morgan, Rowland 113
Morita, Akio 50, 79, 81, 102, 110, 168
Morley, John 157
Morton, Alastair 109
Moser, Claus 48
Motley, John Lothrop 33
Muller, Herbert J 2
Muller, Peter 158
Murchison, Clint W 112
Murdoch, Rupert 52, 112
Murphy, Mike 108
Murray, Len 145, 155
Murray, Philip 81
Myners, Paul 7

Nader, Ralph 34, 56
Naisbett, John 142
Naisbitt, John 30, 134, 162
Naito, Masatoshi 33
Nanus, Burt 24, 36, 76, 95, 96, 117, 134, 142,
  169
Nash, Ogden 26, 134
Needham, Richard 140
Neuharth, Allen 76, 146
Newman, Kenneth 61
Nierenberg, Gerard 114
Nixon, Richard 96
Nolan, Lord 35–6, 137
Nordstrom Corp. 87
Norris, Steven 26
Noyce, Robert 90
Nunan, James C 114

Oakenshott, Matthew 91
O'Connor, Johnson 166
O'Dell, Carla 85
Ogilvy, David 5, 33, 73, 108, 119, 142, 158
Ohmae, Kenichi 29
Olsen, Kenneth 140
Olson, Margreth 163
Olsten, William 102
Onassis, Aristotle 29, 170
Oncken, William Jr 101
O'Neill, Eugene 164
Opel, John R 87
O'Reilly, Anthony J F 142
Oren, John 87
O'Rourke, P J 160
Orwell, George 93, 97, 106
Osborn, E B 127–28
Oscar II 147
Osler, William 145
O'Sullivan, Jack 56
O'Toole, James 54
O'Toole, Patricia 73
Ouseley, Herman 54
Ovid, Publius 165
Owens, Ron 162

Packer, Kerry 28
Paderewski, Ignace 172
Parella, Joseph R 78
Parker, Dorothy 119
Parker, Peter 113, 131, 151
Parkinson, C Northcote 31, 35, 41, 73, 108, 113, 117, 139, 165
Parry-Wingfield, Maurice 160
Partridge, Pam 168
Pascale, Richard T 70
Pasten, Mark 98
Patton, George 6, 98
Pauling, Linus 77
Paxman, Jeremy 162
Pedley, Frank 95
Peers, John 1, 18
Peloquin, Jerome 122
Penn, William 97
Pennant-Rea, Rupert 137
Pepys, Samuel 112
Percy, Charles 42
Perlman, Alfred Edward 142
Perot, H Ross 58, 119, 142, 144
Perrow, Charles 18
Peter, Laurence J 23, 27, 54, 135, 172
Peters, Mike 5, 168
Peters, Tom 18, 25, 38, 42–3, 58, 74, 77, 86, 101, 108, 112, 116, 117, 118, 129, 134, 152, 154–55
Peterson, Don 28
Phelan, John 153
Philip, Prince 70, 97, 161
Phillips, G Edward 2
Pickens, T Boone 153
Pilger, John 43
Pilkington, Edward 72
Pinchot, Gifford III 77, 88
Pindar 68
Pinero, Arthur Wing 2
Pink Floyd 80
Plato 76
Pöhl, Carl Otto 84
Pollard, William 48
Pollock, Frederick 76
Pompidou, Georges 162
Poppa, Ryal R 12
Porritt, Jonathan 70
Porter, Michael 28
Pratchett, Terry 16, 93, 117, 119
Price, Fiona 78
Priestly, J B 5
Prince Charles 100, 172
Prince Philip 70, 97, 161
Prior, Matthew 57
Proxmire, William 11
Pulitzer, Joseph 139
Puzo, Mario 36, 112

Quadracci, Henry V 62–63, 117–18
Quant, Mary 170
Quincey, Thomas de 103
Quintilian, Marcus Fabius (Quintilianus) 9
Quinton, John 124

Randall, Jeff 153
Rantzen, Esther 171
Rappaport, Sonia 48, 136
Ratajczak, George 35
Rathenau, Walther 6
Ravitch, Diane 51
Rayner, Lord 131
Reagan, Ronald 61, 68, 110, 137
Rechtin, Eberhardt 41
Redford, Robert 129
Reed, Kingsley 31
Rees, Herbert 18
Rehnquist, William 137
Reich, Robert 57, 130
Reid, Jimmy 155
Reid, Tony 102
Reinecke, John A 2
Reno, Robert 155
Revson, Charles 28
Ricci, Ruggiero 32
Rice, Robert 36
Richardson, Roy 124
Rickover, Hyman 18, 77
Roach, Stephen S 31
Robbins, Irvine 77
Robens, Lord 38, 97
Roberts, John 75
Robinson, Joan 43, 147
Rockefeller, John D 63, 122
Roddick, Anita 6, 21, 52, 56, 68–9, 102, 104, 151
Rogers, Will 32, 165
Rollwagen, John 87
Roman, Mark B 134
Rooke, Denis 171
Roosevelt, Franklin D 69, 82, 161
Roosevelt, Theodore 57, 63, 64, 151, 166, 172
Rosch, Leah 27
Rose, Billy 92
Rosener, Judy B 54
Rosewall, Bridget 90
Rowe, Geneva 128
Rowland, Tiny 21, 115, 129, 145
Rozen, Sydney Craft 104
Rubicam, Raymond 5
Rubin, Richard S 31
Runes, Dagobert D 44
Runyon, Damon 44, 64
Ruskin, John 61, 79, 140
Russell, Bertrand 72, 172
Russell, Peter 85

Saatchi, Maurice 66
Sahlin, Mona 119
Saki 61, 80
Samuelson, Paul Anthony 130
Sampson, Anthony 140, 142
San Concordio, Bartolommeo de 59
Sanders, Col Harlan 145
Santayana, George 78
Sarnoff, David 28, 144
Saunders, Bill 148
Saunders, Diane 56
Saunders, Ernest 105, 147
Scanlon, Hugh 82

Schaefer, George 135
Schaller, Lyle E 7, 20, 88
Schatz, Kenneth 101
Schatz, Linda 101
Schiavon, Walter 82
Schiller, Johann von 27
Schlesinger, James R 16, 18
Schmitt, Roland 144
Schmookler, Jacob 90–1
Schoell, William F 2
Schoenberg, Robert J 9
Schonfield, Reese 138
Schreyer, William A 122
Schroeder, Patricia 109
Schulman, Bernard 101
Schumacher, E F 46, 69, 70, 99, 142
Scott, Charles 2, 67
Scott, C P 106
Scott, Howard 34
Scott, Peter L 70
Scully, John 22, 130, 144
Sebastian, Dom 65
Seear, Beatrice 22
Séguéla, Jacques 5
Seibert, Donald 16
Selfridge, H Gordon 38
Seligman, Daniel 36
Semler, Ricardo 2–3, 15, 17, 18, 25, 31, 49, 70–1,
    72, 74, 78, 82, 85, 87, 88, 101, 118, 122, 132,
    140, 145, 146, 148, 158, 163, 173
Semple, Bob 31
Seneca, Lucius Annaeus 39
Senge, Peter M 27, 71, 113, 134, 169
Seymour, Jim 31
Shad, John 32
Shakespeare, William 40, 143
Shanahan, Eileen 108
Sharples, Christopher 11
Shaw, George Bernard 27, 36, 68, 112, 116, 120,
    134, 171
Shea, Michael 41, 97
Sheckley, Robert 18, 31
Sheen, J Fulton 93
Sheer, Thomas L 36
Sheppard, Allen 157
Shmitt, Roland 60
Shore, Peter 168
Shorris, Earl 118
Sickert, Walter 109
Sieff, Lord 50, 52, 56, 65, 82, 102–3, 122, 151
Siegel, Gabriel M 147
Siegel, Robert L 118
Siegel, William J 60, 87
Silguy, Yves-Thibault de 44
Sinclair, Jeremy 5, 141
Singer, Isaac Bashevis 162
Slater, Jim 23, 151, 158
Slater, Philip 79
Sloan, Alfred P 10, 157
Smith, Adam 20, 64, 167
Smith, David 46
Smith, F E 65
Smith, Giles 33
Smith, John Grieve 167

Smith, Logan Pearsall 67, 80, 172
Smith, Margie 29
Smith, Philip 142, 166
Smith, Richard 114
Smith, Robert H 60
Smith, Sydney 65, 125
Smurfit, Dr Michael 52
Soares, João 174
Solomon, Marlene 118
Spencer, Herbert 54
Spiers, Samantha 154
Springer, Louis 87
Stagner, Ross 41
Statman, Meir 92
Stein, Cyril 97
Stein, Gertrude 67
Stein, Leo 164
Stengel, Casey 27, 59, 101, 145
Steven, Stewart 105
Stevenson, Adlai 4, 126
Stevenson, Robert Louis 20, 75
Stewart, Nathaniel 143
Stewart, Rosemary 121
Stokes, Lord 23, 49
Stone, Dan G 109
Stone, Oliver 69
Stout, Rex 152
Strassmann, Paul 10
Street-Porter, Janet 172
Stuart, Keith 113
Sugar, Alan 38, 52, 103, 172
Sutcliffe, Thomas 5
Swaffer, Hannen 106
Swain, Robert L 128
Swanson, Huntington 41
Swayne, Noah Hayes 55
Swinerton, Alistair 143
Swope, Herbert B 59
Sykes, Trevor 3, 20
Syrus, Publius 60, 143

Taber, Carol A 42
Tabuchi, Yoshihisa 88
Takeuchi, Hirotaka 103
Tapie, Bernard 82
Tarrant, John 80
Tate, Gini 148–49
Tawney, R H 57, 136
Tebbit, Norman 168
Templeman, Lord 93
Thatcher, Margaret 6, 46, 62, 65, 84, 93, 113,
    131, 168
Thatcher, Mark 145
Thomas, Professor Michael 147
Thomas, Terry 151
Thompson, Adam 109
Thompson, Paul 143
Thomson, Lord 44
Thoreau, Henry David 49, 149
Thorp, Deborah 109
Thurber, James 72
Thurlow, Lord 34
Thurow, Lester C 60
Tigrett, Isaac 65

Toffler, Alvin 19
Tomasko, Robert M 85, 118
Tomlin, Lily 67
Townsend, Robert 3, 4, 8, 13, 39, 41, 75, 108, 122
Trahey, Jane 32
Traub, Marvin 171
Tree, Herbert Beerbohm 23
Tricker, R Ian 3
Trollope, Anthony 19, 120
Trotsky, Leon 82, 171
Trotter, Maurice S 41, 80
Trotter, Paul 130
Truman, Harry S 49, 74, 141, 169
Trump, Donald 39
Tucker, Sophie 112
Turner, Ted 67, 97, 157, 174
Tute, Warren 14
Twain, Mark 8, 36, 57, 62, 76, 97, 106, 120, 136, 143, 152, 155, 173

U2 124–25
Ulpian, Domitius 55
UNISON Spokesperson 113
Uzzell, W E 116

Vaizey, Lord 48
Valenti, Jack 164
Vallely, Bernadette 103
Vallely, Paul 68, 141
Vanderbilt, Cornelius 29, 126
Vanderbilt, William Henry 138
Vanderschmidt, Fred 101
Vaz, Patricia 114–15
Veblen, Thorstein 33, 57
Veeck, Bill 74
Vice, David 128
Vincent, Sally 106
Virgil 14
Voltaire, François Marie 82
Vorderman, Carol 92

Wadsworth, Guy M 50
Wahlstrüm, Björn 80
Walker, Walter 19
Walters, Alan 35
Walters, Vernon 63
Walton, Sam 3
Wang, An 129
Ward, Artemus 22
Ward, Barbara 136
Ward, Benjamin 1
Warner, Charles Dudley 165
Washington, George 8
Waterman, Robert H 85, 118, 119
Waters, Roger 80
Watkinson, Lord 82
Watson, Thomas J 31
Watson, Thomas J Jr 25, 98, 135
Watts, Patti 55
Waugh, Auberon 82
Weaver, Earl 102
Webb, James L 109
Webb, Sidney 46

Weiler, A H 67
Weinberg, Mark 88, 153
Weinstock, Lord 68
Welch, John 28, 166
Weller, Paul 21
Wellington, Arthur Mellen 99
Wells, H G 105
Wermter, Father Oskar 125
West, David 38
West, Rebecca 125
West, Roy A 44
Wexner, Les 154
Wheeling, Gordon W 74
Whistler, James McNeill 37, 67, 120
White, E B 26
White, Roderic 5
Whitehorn, Katherine 3, 13, 78, 116
Whitham, Donald 146
Whitman, Marina V N 60
Whyte, Walter H 74
Wiener, Norbert 99
Wiesenfeld, Paul R 27
Wildavsky, Aaron 17
Wilde, Oscar 6, 40, 63, 110, 125, 128
Wilder, Thornton 75, 90
Wiles, Q T 129
Wilkins, Richard 65
Williams, L D 78
Williams, Tenessee 37
Willis, Norman 48
Wilson, Brian 113
Wilson, Charles E 151
Wilson, Harold 68, 84, 120
Wilson, Woodrow 136, 151
Wodehouse, P G 95
Wolfe, Humbert 106
Wolfson, Isaac 171
Wood, Peter 69
Wood, Robert E 42, 87, 122
Woodside, William 131
Woolacott, Martin 169
Wooldridge, Adrian 48
Woollcott, Alexander 154
Woolsey, Robert 41
Worthington, Anne 137
Wright, Frank Lloyd 33, 105
Wright, Henry Beric 75
Wright, Vicky 102
Wriston, Walter 62, 145

Yamaguchi, Tomotsu 71
Yamaguchi, Toshio 165
Yamani, Sheik Ahmed 39, 46
Young, Judith 103
Young, Lord 28, 52

Zakon, Alan 21
Zaleznik, Abraham 52
Zand, Dale E 8
Zanuck, Darryl F 8
Zappa, Frank 19
Zenger, John H 97
Zimmerman, Richard A 22